MICROSOFT® Excel 2000

Advanced Course

Mastering and Using

H. Albert Napier
Philip J. Judd

VISIT US ON THE INTERNET
www.swep.com

South-Western Educational Publishing
an International Thomson Publishing company I(T)P®
www.thomson.com

Cincinnati • Albany, NY • Belmont, CA • Bonn • Boston • Detroit • Johannesburg • London • Madrid
Melbourne • Mexico City • New York • Paris • Singapore • Tokyo • Toronto • Washington

ISBN: 0-538-42807-4

1 2 3 4 5 6 7 XX 03 02 01 00

Managing Editor: Carol Volz
Project Manager/Editor: Cheryl L. Beck
Marketing Manager: Larry Qualls
Consulting Editor: Robin Romer, Pale Moon Productions
Production Services: GEX Publishing Services
Graphic Designer: Brenda Grannan, Grannan Graphics
Fee Writer: Benjamin Rand

I(T)P®
International Thomson Publishing

South-Western Educational Publishing is a division of International Thomson Publishing, Inc. The ITP logo is a registered trademark herein used under license by South-Western Educational Publishing.

Mastering and Using

Microsoft® Excel 2000 Advanced Course for Windows®

Journey into the Future . . .

Our NEW Napier & Judd series™, *Mastering and Using Microsoft Excel 2000 Advanced Course,* is designed for the advanced user who wants to go beyond the basic and intermediate level of the application software. This expertly written text along with its companion text, *Mastering and Using Microsoft Excel 2000 Intermediate Course,* provides all the instruction necessary to become a Microsoft Expert user of Excel.

Mastering and Using Microsoft Excel 2000 Advanced Course

- Student Text (perfect bound, soft cover) 0-538-42810-4
- Student Text/data CD-ROM Package 0-538-42807-4
- Activities Workbook (perfect bound, soft cover) 0-538-42624-1
- Electronic Instructor Package(Manual and CD-ROM) 0-538-42614-4
- Testing Package 0-538-42673-X

A new feature is the Electronic Instructor, a CD-ROM which includes lesson plans, SCAN correlations, scheduling charts, presentations slides, and much more! Books complementary to this book include the following:

Mastering and Using Microsoft Excel 2000 Comprehensive

- Student Text (perfect bound, soft cover) 0-538-42613-6
- Student Text/data CD-ROM Package 0-538-42615-2
- Activities Workbook (perfect bound, soft cover) 0-538-42624-1
- Electronic Instructor Package(Manual and CD-ROM) 0-538-42614-4
- Testing Package 0-538-42673-X

Mastering and Using Microsoft Excel 2000 Beginning Course

- Student Text (perfect bound, soft cover) 0-538-42808-2
- Student Text/data CD-ROM Package 0-538-42805-8
- Activities Workbook (perfect bound, soft cover) 0-538-42624-1
- Electronic Instructor Package(Manual and CD-ROM) 0-538-42614-4
- Testing Package 0-538-42673-X

Mastering and Using Microsoft Excel 2000 Intermediate Course

- Student Text (perfect bound, soft cover) 0-538-42809-0
- Student Text/data CD-ROM Package 0-538-42806-6
- Activities Workbook (perfect bound, soft cover) 0-538-42624-1
- Electronic Instructor Package(Manual and CD-ROM) 0-538-42614-4
- Testing Package 0-538-42673-X

South-Western Educational Publishing

For more information about these South-Western products and others:
Join us On the Internet at www.swep.com

What's New in Excel 2000

Office

- Different Office 2000 suites
- Personalized menus and toolbars
- Multi-language support
- Web-based analysis tools
- Improved Office Assistant
- Online collaboration with NetMeeting and Web discussions from inside Office applications
- E-mail from inside Office applications
- Collect and Paste and Office Clipboard toolbar
- New Open and Save As dialog box features
- Saving directly to Web server
- New Clip Gallery format and new clips

Excel

- See-through selection shading
- Euro currency symbol added to number formats
- Four-digit date formats
- List AutoFill automatically extends formatting of lists to new items
- PivotChart reports created from PivotTable reports
- Display units can be modified on charts
- Open and save HTML documents natively
- Create interactive PivotTables for the Web
- Create PivotTable reports directly on the worksheet
- Indented PivotTable report format
- PivotTable AutoFormat
- Row and column fields list arrow to hide or display items
- Create PivotTable reports using information stored in OLAP data cubes
- Create OLAP data cubes based on queries from other databases
- Digital signing of macros to ensure virus-free status
- Insert pictures directly from a scanner

Napier & Judd

In their over 48 years of combined experience, Al Napier and Phil Judd have developed a tested, realistic approach to mastering and using application software. As both academics and corporate trainers, Al and Phil have the unique ability to help students by teaching them the skills necessary to compete in today's complex business world.

H. Albert Napier, Ph.D. is the Director of the Center on the Management of Information Technology and Professor in the Jones Graduate School of Administration at Rice University. In addition, Al is a principal of Napier & Judd, Inc., a consulting company and corporate trainer in Houston, Texas, that has trained more than 90,000 people in computer applications.

Philip J. Judd is a former instructor in the Management Department and the Director of the Research and Instructional Computing Service at the University of Houston. Phil now dedicates himself to corporate training and consulting as a principal of Napier & Judd, Inc.

Philip J. Judd

H. Albert Napier, Ph.D.

Preface

At South-Western Educational Publishing, we believe that technology will change the way people teach and learn. Today there are millions of people using personal computers in their everyday lives—both as tools at work and for recreational activities. As a result, the personal computer has revolutionized the ways in which people interact with each other. The Napier and Judd series combines the following distinguishing features to allow people to do amazing things with their personal computers.

Distinguishing Features

All the textbooks in the *Mastering and Using* series share several key pedagogical features:

Case Project Approach. In their more than twenty years of business and corporate training and teaching experience, Napier and Judd have found that learners are more enthusiastic about learning a software application if they can see its real-world relevance. The textbook provides bountiful business-based profiles, exercises, and projects. It also emphasizes the skills most in demand by employers.

Comprehensive and Easy to Use. There is thorough coverage of new features. The narrative is clear and concise. Each unit or chapter thoroughly explains the concepts that underlie the skills and procedures. We explain not just the *how*, but the *why*.

Step-by-Step Instructions and Screen Illustrations. All examples in this text include step-by-step instructions that explain how to complete the specific task. Full-color screen illustrations are used extensively to provide the learner with a realistic picture of the software application feature.

Extensive Tips and Tricks. The author has placed informational boxes in the margin of the text. These boxes of information provide the learner with the following helpful tips:

- Quick Tip. Extra information provides shortcuts on how to perform common business-related functions.
- Caution Tip. This additional information explains how a mistake occurs and provides tips on how to avoid making similar mistakes in the future.
- Menu Tip. Additional explanation on how to use menu commands to perform application tasks.
- Mouse Tip. Further instructions on how to use the mouse to perform application tasks.
- Internet Tip. This information incorporates the power of the Internet to help learners use the Internet as they progress through the text.
- Design Tip. Hints for better presentation designs (found in only the PowerPoint book).

End-of-Chapter Materials. Each book in the *Mastering and Using* series places a heavy emphasis on providing learners with the opportunity to practice and reinforce the skills they are learning through extensive exercises. Each chapter has a summary, commands review, concepts review, skills review, and case projects so that the learner can master the material by doing. For more information on each of the end-of-chapter elements see page viii of the How to Use this Book section in this preface.

Appendixes. *Mastering and Using* series contains three appendixes to further help the learner prepare to be successful in the classroom or in the workplace. Appendix A teaches the learner to work with Windows 98. Appendix B teaches the learner how to use Windows Explorer; Appendix C illustrates how to format letters; how to insert a mailing notation; how to format envelopes (referencing the U.S. Postal Service documents); how to format interoffice memorandums; and how to key a formal outline. It also lists popular style guides and describes proofreader's marks.

Microsoft Office User Specialist (MOUS) Certification. The logo on the cover of this book indicates that these materials are officially certified by Microsoft Corporation. This certification is part of the MOUS program, which validates your skills as a knowledgeable user of Microsoft applications. Upon completing the lessons in the book, you will be prepared to take a test that could qualify you as either a core or expert user. To be certified, you will need to take an exam from a third-party testing company called an Authorization Certification Testing Center. Call **1-800-933-4493** to find the location of the testing center nearest you. Tests are conducted at different dates throughout the calendar year. To learn more about the entire line of training materials suitable for Microsoft Office certification, contact your South-Western Representative or call **1-800-824-5179**. Also visit our Web site at *www.swep.com.* To learn more about the MOUS program, you can visit Microsoft's Web site at *www.microsoft.com/train_cert/cert/.*

SCANS. In 1992, the U.S. Department of Labor and Education formed the Secretary's Commission on Achieving Necessary Skills, or SCANS, to study the kinds of competencies and skills that workers must have to succeed in today's marketplace. The results of the study were published in a document entitled *What Work Requires of Schools: A SCANS Report for America 2000.* The in-chapter and end-of-chapter exercises in this book are designed to meet the criteria outlined in the SCANS report and thus help prepare learners to be successful in today's workplace.

Instructional Support

All books in the *Mastering and Using* series are supplemented with the following items:

Instructor's Resource Package. This printed instructor's manual contains lesson plans with teaching materials and preparation suggestions, along with tips for implementing instruction and assessment ideas; a suggested syllabus for scheduling semester, block, and quarter classes; and SCANS workplace know how. The printed manual is packaged with an Electronic Instructor CD-ROM. The Electronic Instructor CD-ROM contains all the materials found in the printed manual as well as:

- Student lesson plans
- Data files
- Solutions files
- Test questions
- Transparencies
- PowerPoint presentations
- Portfolio assessment/worksheets
- Learning styles strategies
- Career worksheets
- Tech prep strategies

Testing Tools Package. Testing Tools is a powerful testing and assessment package that enables instructors to create and print tests from test banks designed specifically for South-Western Educational Publishing titles. In addition, instructors with access to a networked computer lab (LAN) or the Internet can administer, grade, and track tests online. Learners can also take online practice tests.

Course. Course is a template-based platform to deliver a Web-based syllabus. It allows instructors to create their own completely customized online syllabus, including lesson descriptions, dates, assignments, grades, and lesson links to other resources on the Web. To access this Web tool, an instructor must be a South-Western customer and contact sales support at 1-800-824-5179 for an access code. After the instructor has set up the online syllabus, students can access the Course.

Learner Support

Activity Workbooks. The workbook includes additional end-of-chapter exercises over and above those provided in the main text.

Data CD-ROM. To use this book, the learner must have the data CD-ROM (also referred to as the Data Disk). Data Files needed to complete exercises in the text are contained on this CD-ROM. These files can be copied to a hard drive or posted to a network drive.

How to Use This Book

Excel 2000

Quick Start for Excel

LEARNING OBJECTIVES

- Explore the Excel components
- Locate and open an existing workbook
- Navigate a worksheet
- Enter text, dates, and numbers
- Select cells
- Edit cell content
- Clear contents and formatting of cells
- Use Undo and Redo
- Enter formulas and functions
- Save workbooks
- Close workbooks and Exit Excel

Chapter Overview

In this chapter, you learn about the components of the Excel workbook window. You open an existing workbook, create a new workbook, enter and revise data, and save your work. You also learn about Excel's "workhorses"–formulas and functions.

Case profile

Amy Lee runs a rapidly growing candy business called Sweet Tooth. Today, her confections are sold to retail outlets in many states. Because Sweet Tooth is growing so rapidly, the company has hired you to computerize the company records. In this chapter, you use Excel to track how many items were sold at each location.

chapter one

Learning Objectives — A quick reference of the major topics learned in the chapter

Chapter Overview — A concise summary of what will be learned in the chapter

Case profile — Realistic scenarios that show the real world application of the material being covered

Full color screen illustrations provide a realistic picture to the user

Caution Tip — This additional information explains how a mistake occurs and provides tips on how to avoid making similar mistakes in the future

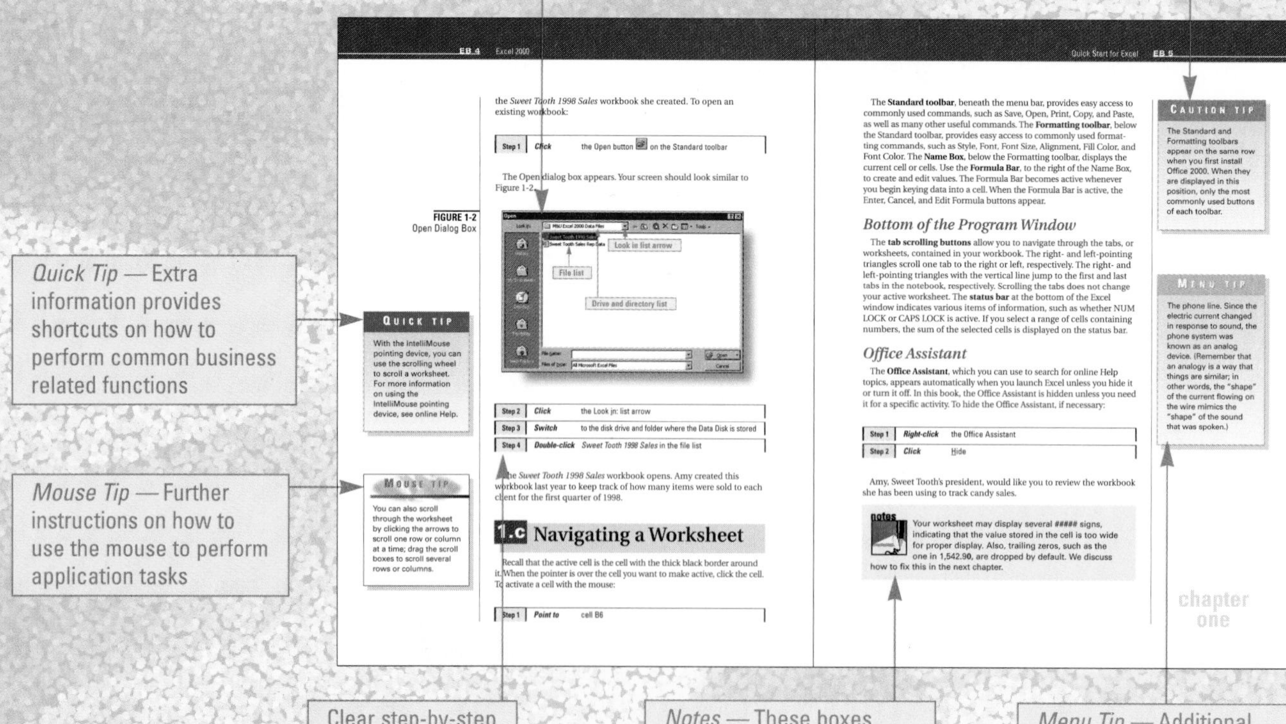

EB 4 Excel 2000

the *Sweet Tooth 1998 Sales* workbook she created. To open an existing workbook:

Step 1	Click	the Open button on the Standard toolbar

The Open dialog box appears. Your screen should look similar to Figure 1-2.

FIGURE 1-2 Open Dialog Box

QUICK TIP

With the IntelliMouse pointing device, you can use the scrolling wheel to scroll a worksheet. For more information on using the IntelliMouse pointing device, see online Help.

Step 2	Click	the Look in: list arrow
Step 3	Switch	to the disk drive and folder where the Data Disk is stored
Step 4	Double-click	*Sweet Tooth 1998 Sales* in the file list

The *Sweet Tooth 1998 Sales* workbook opens. Amy created this workbook last year to keep track of how many items were sold to each client for the first quarter of 1998.

MOUSE TIP

You can also scroll through the worksheet by clicking the arrows to scroll one row or column at a time; drag the scroll boxes to scroll several rows or columns.

1.c Navigating a Worksheet

Recall that the active cell is the cell with the thick black border around it. When the pointer is over the cell you want to make active, click the cell. To activate a cell with the mouse:

Step 1	Point to	cell B6

Quick Start for Excel EB 5

The **Standard toolbar**, beneath the menu bar, provides easy access to commonly used commands, such as Save, Open, Print, Copy, and Paste, as well as many other useful commands. The **Formatting toolbar**, below the Standard toolbar, provides easy access to commonly used formatting commands, such as Style, Font, Font Size, Alignment, Fill Color, and Font Color. The **Name Box**, below the Formatting toolbar, displays the current cell or cells. Use the **Formula Bar**, to the right of the Name Box, to create and edit values. The Formula Bar becomes active whenever you begin keying data into a cell. When the Formula Bar is active, the Enter, Cancel, and Edit Formula buttons appear.

Bottom of the Program Window

The **tab scrolling buttons** allow you to navigate through the tabs, or worksheets, contained in your workbook. The right- and left-pointing triangles scroll one tab to the right or left, respectively. The right- and left-pointing triangles with the vertical line jump to the first and last tabs in the notebook, respectively. Scrolling the tabs does not change your active worksheet. The **status bar** at the bottom of the Excel window indicates various items of information, such as whether NUM LOCK or CAPS LOCK is active. If you select a range of cells containing numbers, the sum of the selected cells is displayed on the status bar.

Office Assistant

The **Office Assistant**, which you can use to search for online Help topics, appears automatically when you launch Excel unless you hide it or turn it off. In this book, the Office Assistant is hidden unless you need it for a specific activity. To hide the Office Assistant, if necessary:

Step 1	Right-click	the Office Assistant
Step 2	Click	Hide

Amy, Sweet Tooth's president, would like you to review the workbook she has been using to track candy sales.

notes

Your worksheet may display several ##### signs, indicating that the value stored in the cell is too wide for proper display. Also, trailing zeros, such as the one in 1,542.90, are dropped by default. We discuss how to fix this in the next chapter.

CAUTION TIP

The Standard and Formatting toolbars appear on the same row when you first install Office 2000. When they are displayed in this position, only the most commonly used buttons of each toolbar.

MENU TIP

The phone line. Since the electric current changed in response to sound, the phone system was known as an analog device. (Remember that an analogy is a way that things are similar; in other words, the "shape" of the current flowing on the wire mimics the "shape" of the sound that was spoken.)

chapter one

Quick Tip — Extra information provides shortcuts on how to perform common business related functions

Mouse Tip — Further instructions on how to use the mouse to perform application tasks

Clear step-by-step directions explain how to complete the specific task

Notes — These boxes provide necessary information to assist you in completing the exercises

Menu Tip — Additional explanation on how to use menu commands to perform application tasks

End-of-Chapter Material

Concepts Review — Multiple choice and true or false questions help assess how well the reader has learned the chapter material

Summary — Reviews key topics discussed in the chapter

Commands Review — Provides a quick reference and reinforcement tool on multiple methods for performing actions discussed in the chapter

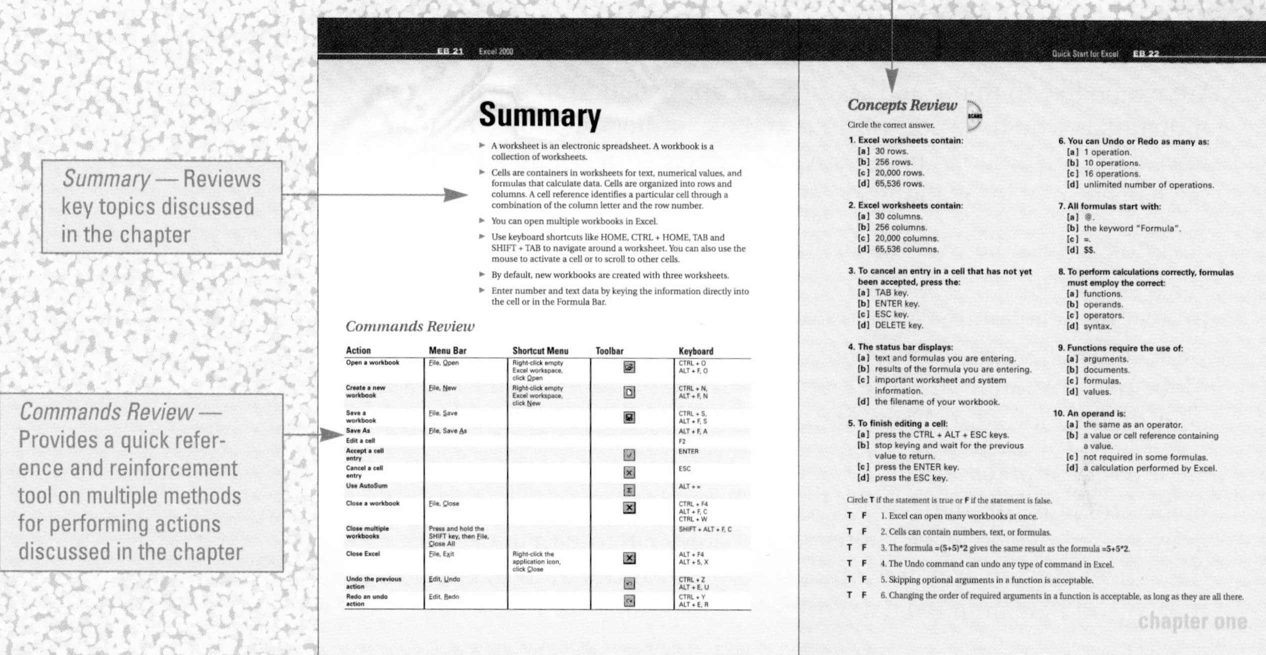

EB 21 Excel 2000

Summary

- A worksheet is an electronic spreadsheet. A workbook is a collection of worksheets.
- Cells are containers in worksheets for text, numerical values, and formulas that calculate data. Cells are organized into rows and columns. A cell reference identifies a particular cell through a combination of the column letter and the row number.
- You can open multiple workbooks in Excel.
- Use keyboard shortcuts like HOME, CTRL + HOME, TAB and SHIFT + TAB to navigate around a worksheet. You can also use the mouse to activate a cell or to scroll to other cells.
- By default, new workbooks are created with three worksheets.
- Enter number and text data by keying the information directly into the cell or in the Formula Bar.

Commands Review

Action	Menu Bar	Shortcut Menu	Toolbar	Keyboard
Open a workbook	File, Open	Right-click empty Excel workspace, click Open		CTRL + O ALT + F, O
Create a new workbook	File, New	Right-click empty Excel workspace, click New		CTRL + N, ALT + F, N
Save a workbook	File, Save			CTRL + S, ALT + F, S
Save As	File, Save As			ALT + F, A
Edit a cell				F2
Accept a cell entry				ENTER
Cancel a cell entry				ESC
Use AutoSum				ALT + =
Close a workbook	File, Close			CTRL + F4 ALT + F, C CTRL + W
Close multiple workbooks	Press and hold the SHIFT key, then File, Close All			SHIFT + ALT + F, C
Close Excel	File, Exit	Right-click the application icon, click Close		ALT + F4 ALT + 5, X
Undo the previous action	Edit, Undo			CTRL + Z ALT + E, U
Redo an undo action	Edit, Redo			CTRL + Y ALT + E, R

Quick Start for Excel EB 22

Concepts Review

Circle the correct answer.

1. Excel worksheets contain:
 [a] 30 rows.
 [b] 256 rows.
 [c] 20,000 rows.
 [d] 65,536 rows.
2. Excel worksheets contain:
 [a] 30 columns.
 [b] 256 columns.
 [c] 20,000 columns.
 [d] 65,536 columns.
3. To cancel an entry in a cell that has not yet been accepted, press the:
 [a] TAB key.
 [b] ENTER key.
 [c] ESC key.
 [d] DELETE key.
4. The status bar displays:
 [a] text and formulas you are entering.
 [b] results of the formula you are entering.
 [c] important worksheet and system information.
 [d] the filename of your workbook.
5. To finish editing a cell:
 [a] press the CTRL + ALT + ESC keys.
 [b] stop keying and wait for the previous value to return.
 [c] press the ENTER key.
 [d] press the ESC key.
6. You can Undo or Redo as many as:
 [a] 1 operation.
 [b] 10 operations.
 [c] 16 operations.
 [d] unlimited number of operations.
7. All formulas start with:
 [a] @.
 [b] the keyword "Formula".
 [c] =.
 [d] $$.
8. To perform calculations correctly, formulas must employ the correct:
 [a] functions.
 [b] operands.
 [c] operators.
 [d] syntax.
9. Functions require the use of:
 [a] arguments.
 [b] documents.
 [c] formulas.
 [d] values.
10. An operand is:
 [a] the same as an operator.
 [b] a value or cell reference containing a value.
 [c] not required in some formulas.
 [d] a calculation performed by Excel.

Circle **T** if the statement is true or **F** if the statement is false.

T F 1. Excel can open many workbooks at once.
T F 2. Cells can contain numbers, text, or formulas.
T F 3. The formula =(5+5)*2 gives the same result as the formula =5+5*2.
T F 4. The Undo command can undo any type of command in Excel.
T F 5. Skipping optional arguments in a function is acceptable.
T F 6. Changing the order of required arguments in a function is acceptable, as long as they are all there.

chapter one

Skills Review — Hands-on exercises provide the ability to practice the skills just learned in the chapter

Case Projects — Asks the reader to synthesize the material they learned in the chapter and complete an office assignment

Internet Case Projects — Allow the reader to practice using the World Wide Web

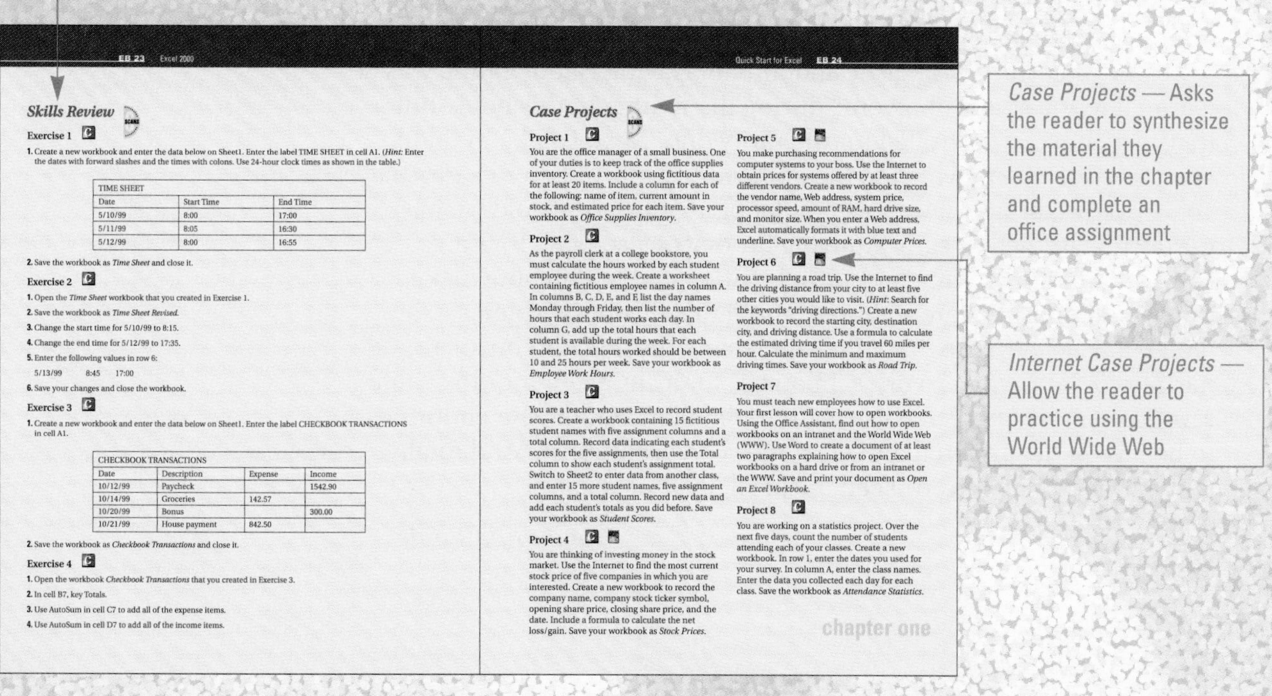

EB 23 Excel 2000

Skills Review

Exercise 1

1. Create a new workbook and enter the data below on Sheet1. Enter the label TIME SHEET in cell A1. (*Hint:* Enter the dates with forward slashes and the times with colons. Use 24-hour clock times as shown in the table.)

TIME SHEET		
Date	Start Time	End Time
5/10/99	8:00	17:00
5/11/99	8:05	16:30
5/12/99	8:00	16:55

2. Save the workbook as *Time Sheet* and close it.

Exercise 2

1. Open the *Time Sheet* workbook that you created in Exercise 1.
2. Save the workbook as *Time Sheet Revised.*
3. Change the start time for 5/10/99 to 8:15.
4. Change the end time for 5/12/99 to 17:35.
5. Enter the following values in row 6:
 5/13/99 8:45 17:00
6. Save your changes and close the workbook.

Exercise 3

1. Create a new workbook and enter the data below on Sheet1. Enter the label CHECKBOOK TRANSACTIONS in cell A1.

CHECKBOOK TRANSACTIONS			
Date	Description	Expense	Income
10/12/99	Paycheck		1542.90
10/14/99	Groceries	142.57	
10/20/99	Bonus		300.00
10/21/99	House payment	842.50	

2. Save the workbook as *Checkbook Transactions* and close it.

Exercise 4

1. Open the workbook *Checkbook Transactions* that you created in Exercise 3.
2. In cell B7, key Totals.
3. Use AutoSum in cell C7 to add all of the expense items.
4. Use AutoSum in cell D7 to add all of the income items.

Quick Start for Excel EB 24

Case Projects

Project 1

You are the office manager of a small business. One of your duties is to keep track of the office supplies inventory. Create a workbook using fictitious data for at least 20 items. Include a column for each of the following: name of item, current amount in stock, and estimated price for each item. Save your workbook as *Office Supplies Inventory*.

Project 2

As the payroll clerk at a college bookstore, you must calculate the hours worked by each student employee during the week. Create a worksheet containing fictitious employee names in column A. In columns B, C, D, E, and F list the day names Monday through Friday, then list the number of hours that each student works each day. In column G, add up the total hours that each student is available during the week. For each student, the total hours worked should be between 10 and 25 hours per week. Save your workbook as *Employee Work Hours*.

Project 3

You are a teacher who uses Excel to record student scores. Create a workbook containing 15 fictitious student names with five assignment columns and a total column. Record data indicating each student's scores for the five assignments, then use the Total column to show each student's assignment total. Switch to Sheet2 to enter data from another class, and enter 15 more student names, five assignment columns, and a total column. Record new data and add each student's totals as you did before. Save your workbook as *Student Scores*.

Project 4

You are thinking of investing money in the stock market. Use the Internet to find the most current stock price of five companies in which you are interested. Create a new workbook to record the company name, company stock ticker symbol, opening share price, closing share price, and the date. Include a formula to calculate the net loss/gain. Save your workbook as *Stock Prices*.

Project 5

You make purchasing recommendations for computer systems to your boss. Use the Internet to obtain prices for systems offered by at least three different vendors. Create a new workbook to record the vendor name, Web address, system price, processor speed, amount of RAM, hard drive size, and monitor size. When you enter a Web address, Excel automatically formats it with blue text and underline. Save your workbook as *Computer Prices*.

Project 6

You are planning a road trip. Use the Internet to find the driving distance from your city to at least five other cities you would like to visit. (*Hint:* Search for the keywords "driving directions.") Create a new workbook to record the starting city, destination city, and driving distance. Use a formula to calculate the estimated driving time if you travel 60 miles per hour. Calculate the minimum and maximum driving times. Save your workbook as *Road Trip*.

Project 7

You must teach new employees how to use Excel. Your first lesson will cover how to open workbooks. Using the Office Assistant, find out how to open workbooks on an intranet and the World Wide Web (WWW). Use Word to create a document of at least two paragraphs explaining how to open Excel workbooks on a hard drive or from an intranet or the WWW. Save and print your document as *Open an Excel Workbook*.

Project 8

You are working on a statistics project. Over the next five days, count the number of students attending each of your classes. Create a new workbook. In row 1, enter the dates you used for your survey. In column A, enter the class names. Enter the data you collected each day for each class. Save the workbook as *Attendance Statistics*.

chapter one

Acknowledgments

We would like to thank and express our appreciation to the many fine individuals who have contributed to the completion of this book. We have been fortunate to have a reviewer whose constructive comments have been so helpful: Kathy Koppy.

No book is possible without the motivation and support of an editorial staff. Therefore, we wish to acknowledge with great appreciation the project team at South-Western Educational Publishing: Cheryl Beck, project manager; Mike Broussard, art and designer coordinator; Angela McDonald, production coordinator; Kathy Hampton, manufacturing coordinator, and Carol Volz, managing editor.

We are very appreciative of the personnel at Napier & Judd, Inc., who helped prepare this book. We acknowledge, with great appreciation, the assistance provided by Ollie Rivers and Nancy Onarheim in preparing the Office unit and Appendixes for this book. We gratefully acknowledge the work of Benjamin Rand in writing the Excel unit for this series.

H. Albert Napier
Philip J. Judd

Thoreau wrote, "Most men live lives of quiet desperation." He obviously didn't have an editor and deadlines when he was writing, because there was nothing "quiet" about the desperation. First and foremost, my biggest debt of gratitude is owed to my wife, Erika, and my two wonderful boys, Casey and Jordan. Having Daddy home was elevated to the status of "Event" during the writing of this book, but they were never less thrilled for the rarity of it. Next, I'd like to thank everyone at ITP for giving me the opportunity to work on this project. To Kitty, my editor, can we meet on Jeopardy next, or would we have to stay up late/get up early studying for that? I also need to thank Mike and Karl for getting me started writing and helping me make the connections that are so important in this business. Thanks a lot (you know how to take that). I have to thank my dad and business partner for letting me go on "sabbatical" for a couple of months while I worked on this project. I also want to thank my mom who continues to believe in her children and what they can accomplish. And finally, to my friends who haven't seen me at all, I got next game.

Benjamin Rand

Contents

EXCEL UNIT

Microsoft Office 2000

Getting Started with Microsoft Office 2000

Chapter Overview

Microsoft Office 2000 provides the ability to enter, record, analyze, display, and present any type of business information. In this chapter you learn about the capabilities of Microsoft Office 2000, including its computer hardware and software requirements and elements common to all its applications. You also learn how to open and close those applications and get help.

Learning Objectives

- Describe Microsoft Office 2000
- Determine hardware and software requirements
- Identify common Office elements
- Start Office applications
- Get help in Office applications
- Close Office applications

chapter one

1.a What Is Microsoft Office 2000?

Microsoft Office 2000 is a software suite (or package) that contains a combination of software applications you use to create text documents, analyze numbers, create presentations, manage large files of data, create Web pages, and create professional-looking marketing materials. Table 1-1 lists four editions of the Office 2000 suite and the software applications included in each.

CAUTION TIP

This book assumes that you have little or no knowledge of Microsoft Office 2000, but that you have worked with personal computers and are familiar with Microsoft Windows 98 or Windows 95 operating systems.

Applications	Premium	Professional	Standard	Small Business
Word	X	X	X	X
Excel	X	X	X	X
PowerPoint	X	X	X	
Access	X	X		
Outlook	X	X	X	X
Publisher	X	X		X
FrontPage	X			

TABLE 1-1
Office 2000 Editions

The **Word 2000** software application provides you with word processing capabilities. **Word processing** is the preparation and production of text documents such as letters, memorandums, and reports. **Excel 2000** is software you use to analyze numbers with worksheets (sometimes called spreadsheets) and charts, as well as perform other tasks such as sorting data. A **worksheet** is a grid of columns and rows in which you enter labels and data. A **chart** is a visual or graphic representation of worksheet data. With Excel, you can create financial budgets, reports, and a variety of other forms.

PowerPoint 2000 software is used to create **presentations,** a collection of slides. A **slide** is the presentation output (actual 35mm slides, transparencies, computer screens, or printed pages) that contains text, charts, graphics, audio, and video. You can use PowerPoint slides to create a slide show on a computer attached to a projector, to broadcast a presentation over the Internet or company intranet, and to create handout materials for a presentation.

Access 2000 provides database management capabilities, enabling you to store and retrieve a large amount of data. A **database** is a collection of related information. A phone book or an address book are common examples of databases you use every day. Other databases include a price list, school registration information, or an inventory. You can query (or search) an Access database to answer specific questions about the stored data. For example, you can determine which customers in a particular state had sales in excess of a particular value during the month of June.

QUICK TIP

Microsoft Office 2000 is often called Office and the individual applications are called Word, Excel, PowerPoint, Access, Outlook, Publisher, and so on.

Outlook 2000 is a **personal information manager** that enables you to send and receive e-mail, as well as maintain a calendar, contacts list, journal, electronic notes, and an electronic "to do" list. **Publisher 2000** is desktop publishing software used to create publications, such as professional-looking marketing materials, newsletters, or brochures. Publisher wizards provide step-by-step instructions for creating a publication from an existing design; you also can design your own publication. The **FrontPage 2000** application is used to create and manage Web sites. **PhotoDraw 2000** is business graphics software that allows users to add custom graphics to marketing materials and Web pages.

A major advantage of using an Office suite is the ability to share data between applications. For example, you can include a portion of an Excel worksheet or chart in a Word document, use an outline created in a Word document as the starting point for a PowerPoint presentation, import an Excel worksheet into Access, merge names and addresses from an Outlook Address Book with a Word letter, or import a picture from PhotoDraw into a newsletter created in Publisher.

MENU TIP

Publisher tutorials are a series of hyperlinked windows providing a brief introduction to a specific topic. Each window contains a series of hyperlink buttons at the bottom of the window you use to advance to the next tutorial page or return to the main tutorial menu. To review the online tutorials, open Publisher, click the Help menu, and then click Publisher Tutorials.

1.b Hardware and Software Requirements

You must install Office 2000 applications in Windows 95, Windows 98, or Windows NT Workstation 4.0 with Service Pack 3.0 installed. The applications will not run in the Windows 3.x or the Windows NT Workstation 3.5 environments.

Microsoft recommends that you install Office on a computer that has a Pentium processor, at least 32 MB of RAM, a CD-ROM drive, Super VGA, 256-color video, Microsoft Mouse, Microsoft IntelliMouse, or another pointing device, and at least a 28,800-baud modem. To access certain features you should have a multimedia computer, e-mail software, and a Web browser. For detailed information on installing Office, see the documentation that comes with the software.

QUICK TIP

If you store your files and documents on diskette, make sure you have the proper type of diskette for your computer. A disk storage box is a good way to store and protect diskettes you are not using.

1.c Identifying Common Office Elements

Office applications share many common elements, making it easier for you to work efficiently in any application. A **window** is a rectangular area on your screen in which you view a software application, such as Excel. All the Office application windows have a similar look and arrangement of shortcuts, menus, and toolbars. In addition, they share many features, such as a common dictionary to use for spell checking your work and identical menu commands, toolbar buttons, shortcut menus, and keyboard shortcuts that enable you to perform tasks such as copying data from one location to another. Figure 1-1 shows the common elements in the Office application windows.

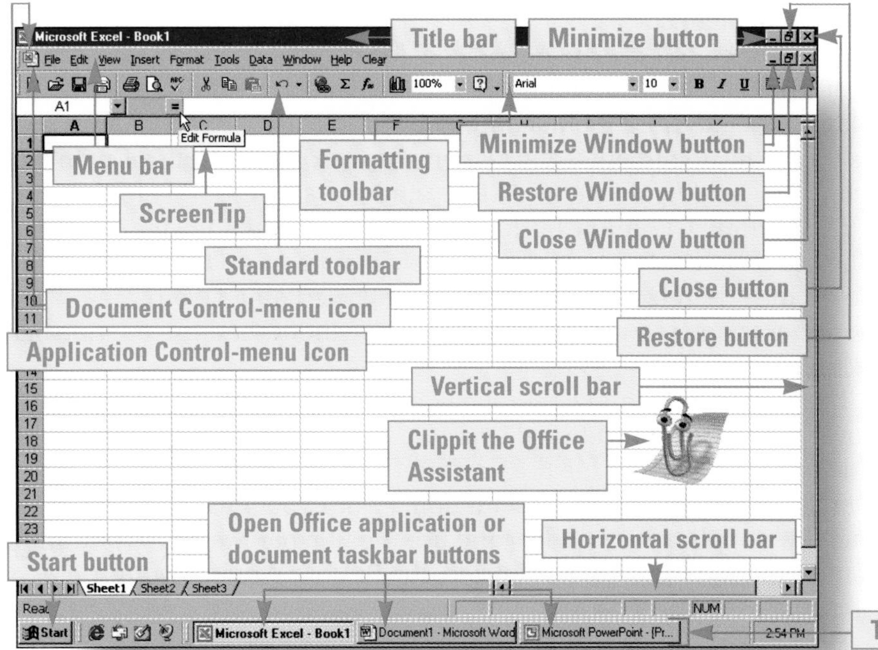

FIGURE 1-1
Common Elements in Office Application Windows

Title Bar

The application **title bar** at the top of the window includes the application Control-menu icon, the application name, the filename of the active document, and the Minimize, Restore (or Maximize), and Close buttons.

The **application Control-menu** icon, located in the left corner of the title bar, displays the Control menu. The Control menu commands manage the application window, and typically include commands such as: Restore, Move, Size, Minimize, Maximize, and Close. Commands that are currently available appear in a darker color. You can view the Control menu by clicking the Control-menu icon or by holding down the ALT key and then pressing the SPACEBAR key.

The **Minimize** button, near the right corner of the title bar reduces the application window to a taskbar button. The **Maximize** button, to the right of the Minimize button, enlarges the application window to fill the entire screen viewing area above the taskbar. If the window is already maximized, the Restore button appears in its place. The **Restore** button reduces the application window size. The **Close** button, located in the right corner of the title bar, closes the application and removes it from the computer's memory.

CAUTION TIP

In order to save hard disk space, Office installs many features and components as you need them. Shortcuts, toolbar buttons, and menu commands for these features appear in the application window or dialog boxes, indicating that the feature is available.

QUICK TIP

Office 2000 file formats (except Access) are compatible with the previous version of Office (Office 97), which means Office 97 users can open Office 2000 files without a converter, although some Office 2000 formatting features will be lost. For a list of Office 2000 formatting features not supported by Office 97, see online Help in each application.

MOUSE TIP

If you are left-handed, you can switch the operation of the left and right mouse buttons in the Mouse Properties dialog box. Double-click the My Computer icon on the desktop, double-click the Control Panel folder, and then double-click the Mouse icon to display the dialog box.

Menu Bar

The **menu bar** is a special toolbar located below the title bar and contains the menus for the application. A **menu** is list of commands. The menus common to Office applications are File, Edit, View, Insert, Format, Tools, Window, and Help. Each application may have additional menus.

The **document Control-menu** icon, located below the application Control-menu icon, contains the Restore, Move, Size, Minimize, Maximize, and Close menu commands for the document window. You can view the document Control menu by clicking the Control-menu icon or by holding down the ALT key and pressing the HYPHEN (-) key.

The **Minimize Window** button reduces the document window to a title-bar icon inside the document area. It appears on the menu bar below the Minimize button in Excel and PowerPoint. (Word documents open in their own application window and use the title bar Minimize button.)

The **Maximize Window** button enlarges the document window to cover the entire application display area and share the application title bar. It appears on the title-bar icon of a minimized Excel workbook or PowerPoint presentation. (Word documents open in their own application window and use the title bar Maximize button.) If the window is already maximized, the Restore Window button appears in its place.

The **Restore Window** button changes the document window to a smaller sized window inside the application window. It appears to the right of the Minimize Window button in Excel and PowerPoint. (Word documents open in their own application window and use the title bar Restore button.)

The **Close Window** button closes the document and removes it from the computer's memory. It appears to the right of the Restore Window or Maximize Window button. (In Word, the Close Window button appears only when one document is open. Otherwise, Word uses the title bar Close button.)

Default Toolbars

The **Standard** and **Formatting toolbars,** located on one row below the menu bar, contain a set of icons called buttons. The toolbar buttons represent commonly used commands and are mouse shortcuts used to perform tasks quickly. In addition to the Standard and Formatting toolbars, each application has several other toolbars available. You can customize toolbars by adding or removing buttons and commands.

When the mouse pointer rests on a toolbar button, a **ScreenTip** appears identifying the name of the button. ScreenTips, part of online Help, describe a toolbar button, dialog box option, or menu command.

Scroll Bars

The **vertical scroll bar,** on the right side of the document area, is used to view various parts of the document by moving, or scrolling, the document up or down. It includes scroll arrows and a scroll box. The **horizontal scroll bar**, near the bottom of the document area, is used to view various parts of the document by scrolling the document left or right. It includes scroll arrows and a scroll box.

Office Assistant

The **Office Assistant** is an animated graphic you can click to view online Help. The Office Assistant may also anticipate your needs and provide advice in a balloon-style dialog box when you begin certain tasks, such as writing a letter in Word.

Taskbar

The **taskbar,** located across the bottom of the Windows desktop, includes the Start button and buttons for each open Office document. The **Start button,** located in the left corner of the taskbar, displays the Start menu or list of tasks you can perform and applications you can use.

You can switch between documents, close documents and applications, and view other items, such as the system time and printer status, with buttons or icons on the taskbar. If you are using Windows 98, other toolbars—such as the Quick Launch toolbar—may also appear on the taskbar.

QUICK TIP

You can use the keyboard to access Office application features. This book lists all keys in uppercase letters, such as the TAB key. This book lists keystrokes as: Press the ENTER key. When you are to press one key and, while holding down that key, to press another key, this book lists the keystrokes as: Press the SHIFT + F7 keys.

1.d Starting Office Applications

You access the Office applications through the Windows desktop. When you turn on your computer, the Windows operating system software is automatically loaded into memory. Once the process is complete, your screen should look similar to Figure 1-2.

The desktop illustrations in this book assume you are using Windows 98 with default settings. Your desktop may not look identical to the illustrations in this book. For more information on using Windows 98 see Appendix A or information provided by your instructor.

FIGURE 1-2
Default Windows 98 Desktop

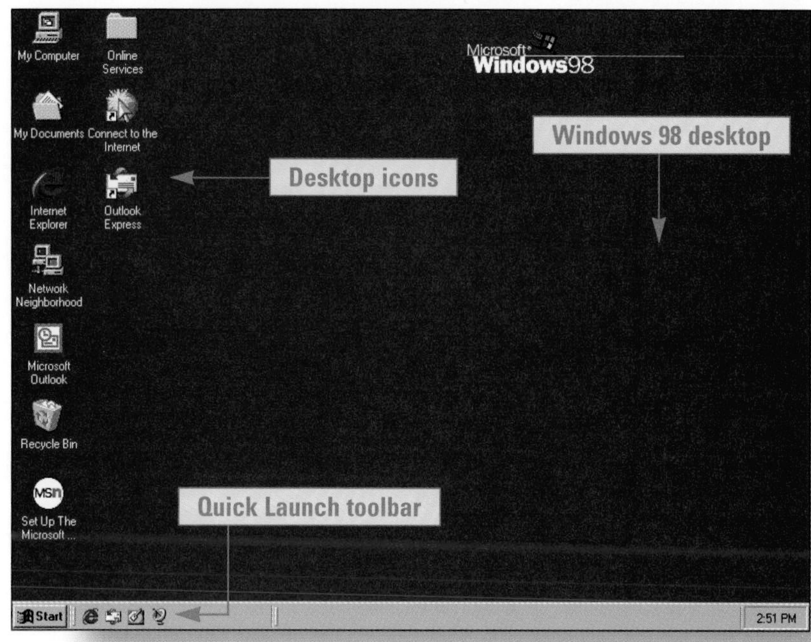

MOUSE TIP

This book uses distinct instructions for mouse operations. **Point** means to place the mouse pointer on the specified command or item. **Click** means to press the left mouse button and then release it. **Right-click** means to press the right mouse button and then release it. **Double-click** means to press the left mouse button twice very rapidly. **Drag** means to press and hold down the left mouse button and then move the mouse on the mouse pad. **Right-drag** means to press and hold down the right mouse button and then move the mouse on the mouse pad. **Scroll** means to use the application scroll bar features or the IntelliMouse scrolling wheel.

You begin by opening the Excel application. To use Start button to open Excel:

Step 1	***Click***	the Start button Start on the taskbar
Step 2	***Point to***	Programs
Step 3	***Click***	Microsoft Excel on the Programs menu

The Excel software is placed into the memory of your computer and the Excel window opens. Your screen should look similar to Figure 1-1.

You can open and work in more than one Office application at a time. When Office is installed, the Open Office Document command and the New Office Document command appear on the Start menu. You can use these commands to select the type of document on which you want to work rather than first selecting an Office application. To create a new Word document without first opening the application:

Step 1	***Click***	the Start button Start on the taskbar
Step 2	***Click***	New Office Document
Step 3	***Click***	the General tab, if necessary

The dialog box that opens should look similar to Figure 1-3.

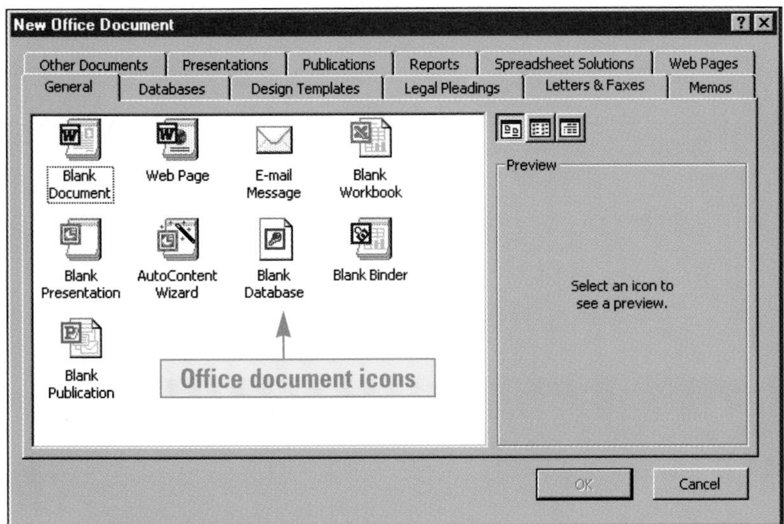

FIGURE 1-3
General Tab in the New Office Document Dialog Box

QUICK TIP

A **dialog box** is a window that contains options for performing specific tasks. The New Office Document dialog box contains **icons** (or pictures) for creating a blank Word document, Web page (in Word), e-mail message (using Outlook or Outlook Express), Excel workbook, PowerPoint presentation, Access database, or Publisher publication. The available icons depends on the Office applications you have installed.

To create a blank Word document:

Step 1	***Click***	the Blank Document icon to select it, if necessary
Step 2	***Click***	OK

The Word software loads into your computer's memory, the Word application opens with a blank document, and a taskbar button appears for the document. Your screen should look similar to Figure 1-4.

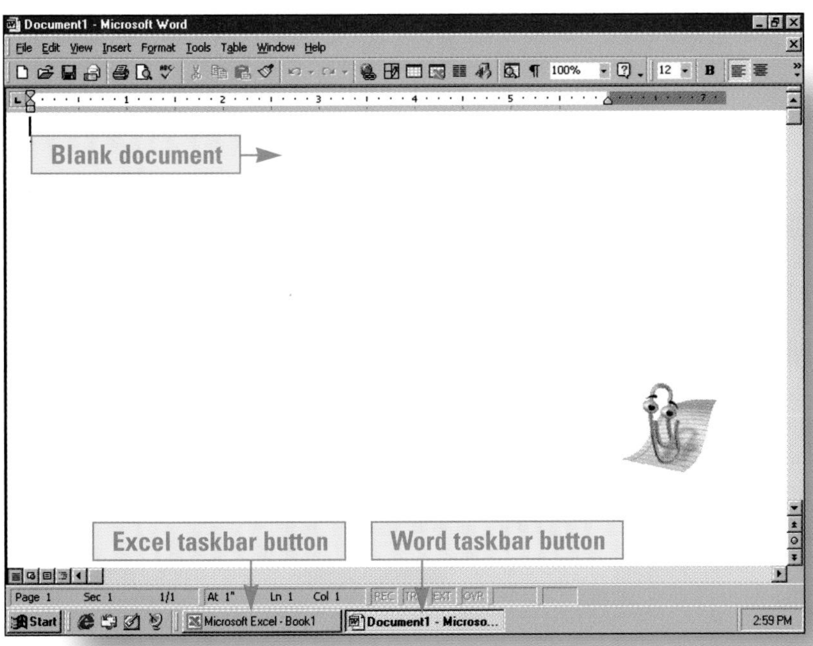

FIGURE 1-4
Word Application Window

chapter one

> **MOUSE TIP**
>
> Double-clicking an icon is the same as clicking it once to select it and then clicking the OK button.

Next you open a blank presentation. To open the PowerPoint application and a blank presentation:

Step 1	***Open***	the New Office Document dialog box using the Start menu
Step 2	***Double-click***	the Blank Presentation icon
Step 3	***Click***	OK in the New Slide dialog box to create a blank title slide, as shown in Figure 1-5

FIGURE 1-5
Blank PowerPoint Presentation

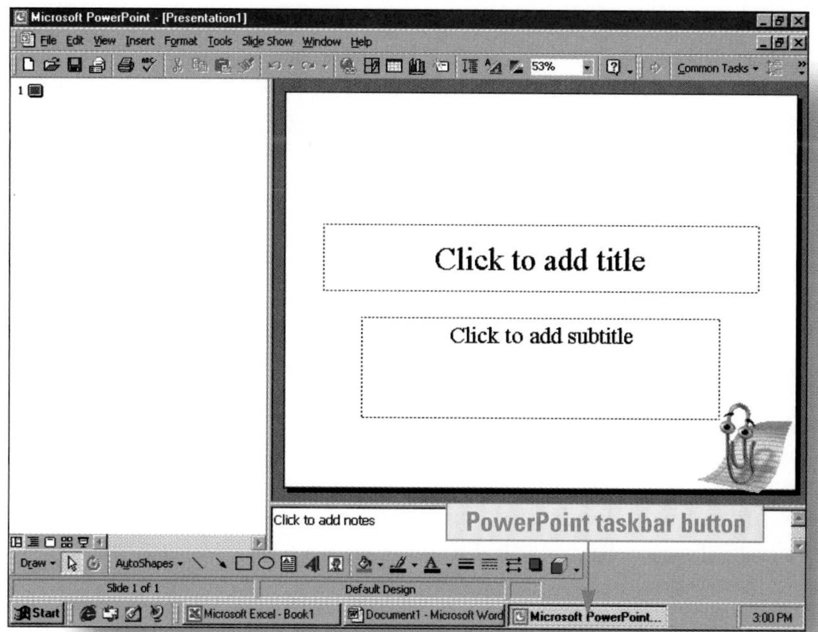

> **QUICK TIP**
>
> You can have multiple Excel workbooks, PowerPoint presentations, and Word documents open at one time. Each open workbook, presentation, and document has its own taskbar button. Your computer's resources determine the number of documents, workbooks, and presentations you can have open at once. You can open only one Access database at a time.

You can also open an Office application by opening an existing Office document from the Start menu. To open an existing Access database:

Step 1	***View***	the Start button on the taskbar
Step 2	***Click***	Open Office Document
Step 3	***Click***	the Look in: list arrow in the Open Office Document dialog box
Step 4	***Switch***	to the disk drive and folder where the Data Files are stored
Step 5	***Double-click***	*International Sales* to open the Access application and database, as shown in Figure 1-6

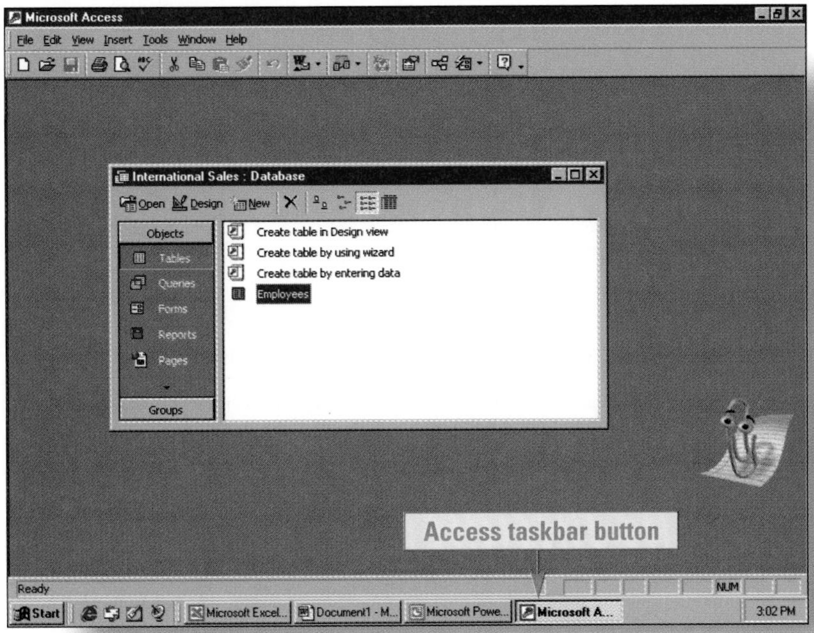

FIGURE 1-6
International Sales Database in Access Window

You can switch between open Office documents by clicking the appropriate taskbar button. To switch to the Excel workbook and then the Word document:

Step 1	***Click***	the Excel button on the taskbar
Step 2	***Observe***	that the Excel window and workbook are visible
Step 3	***Click***	the Word Document1 button on the taskbar
Step 4	***Observe***	that the Word window and document are visible

QUICK TIP

If multiple windows are open, the **active window** has a dark blue title bar. Inactive windows have a light gray title bar.

1.e Getting Help in Office Applications

There are several ways to get help in any Office application. You can display the Office Assistant, get context-sensitive help, or launch your Web browser and get Web-based help from Microsoft.

Using the Office Assistant

The **Office Assistant** is an interactive, animated graphic that appears in the Word, Excel, PowerPoint, and Publisher application windows. When you activate the Office Assistant, a balloon-style dialog box

MENU TIP

You can display the Office Assistant from the Help menu. You can also press the F1 key.

opens containing options for searching online Help by topic. The Office Assistant may also automatically offer suggestions when you begin certain tasks. As you begin to key a personal letter to Aunt Isabel, the Office Assistant automatically asks if you want help writing the letter. To begin the letter:

Step 1	*Verify*	the Word document is the active window
Step 2	*Click*	the Microsoft Word Help button on the Standard toolbar, if the Office Assistant is not visible
Step 3	*Key*	Dear Aunt Isabel: (including the colon)
Step 4	*Press*	the ENTER key

The Office Assistant and balloon appear. Your screen should look similar to Figure 1-7.

FIGURE 1-7
Office Assistant Balloon

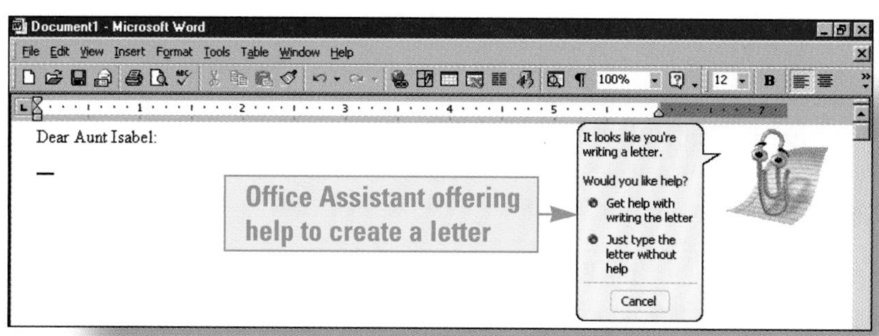

CAUTION TIP

After you cancel the balloon, the letter-writing help options will not appear again until you create a new, blank document.

The Office Assistant balloon contains three options you can click with the mouse. If you click the "Get help with writing the letter" option, the Letter Wizard dialog box opens. A **wizard** is a series of dialog boxes you can use to complete a task step-by-step. If you click the "Just type the letter without help" option or the Cancel option, the balloon closes.

Step 5	*Click*	Cancel to close the balloon

If you prefer to use the Microsoft Help window to access online Help, you can choose to show or hide the Office Assistant or you can turn off the Office Assistant completely. To hide the Office Assistant:

Step 1	*Right-click*	the Office Assistant
Step 2	*Click*	Hide

You can activate the Office Assistant at any time to search online help for specific topics or to customize the Office Assistant. Custom options affect all Office applications. To review the Office Assistant customization options:

Step 1	***Click***	the Microsoft Word Help button on the Standard toolbar
Step 2	***Click***	the Office Assistant to view the balloon, if necessary
Step 3	***Click***	Options in the Office Assistant balloon
Step 4	***Click***	the Options tab, if necessary

MENU TIP

You can hide the Office Assistant by clicking the Hide the Office Assistant command on the Help menu. You can redisplay the Office Assistant by clicking the Show the Office Assistant on the Help menu.

The dialog box that opens should look similar to Figure 1-8.

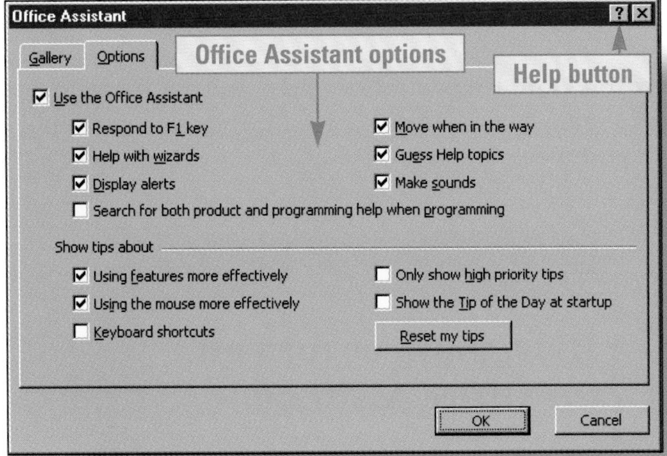

FIGURE 1-8
Options Tab in the Office Assistant Dialog Box

To learn about dialog box options, you can use the dialog box Help button or you can right-click an option. To view the ScreenTip help:

Step 1	***Drag***	the Office Assistant out of the way, if necessary
Step 2	***Right-click***	the Keyboard shortcuts option
Step 3	***Click***	What's This? to view a ScreenTip help message for this option
Step 4	***Press***	the ESC key to close the ScreenTip help message

MOUSE TIP

You can drag the Office Assistant to a new location with the mouse pointer.

The default Office Assistant image is Clippit. But you can select from a gallery of animated images. To view the Office Assistant image options:

Step 1	***Click***	the Gallery tab

Step 2	*Click*	the Next> and <Back buttons to view different image options
Step 3	*Click*	Cancel to close the dialog box without changing any options

You can use the Office Assistant to search an application's online Help. Suppose you want to learn how to turn off the Office Assistant. To search online Help:

Step 1	*Click*	the Office Assistant to activate the balloon
Step 2	*Key*	turn off the Office Assistant in the text box
Step 3	*Press*	the ENTER key to view a list of help options in the balloon dialog box
Step 4	*Click*	the Hide, show, or turn off the Office Assistant option

The Microsoft Word Help window opens and contains information about how to manage the Office Assistant. Your screen should look similar to Figure 1-9.

FIGURE 1-9
Microsoft Word Help Window

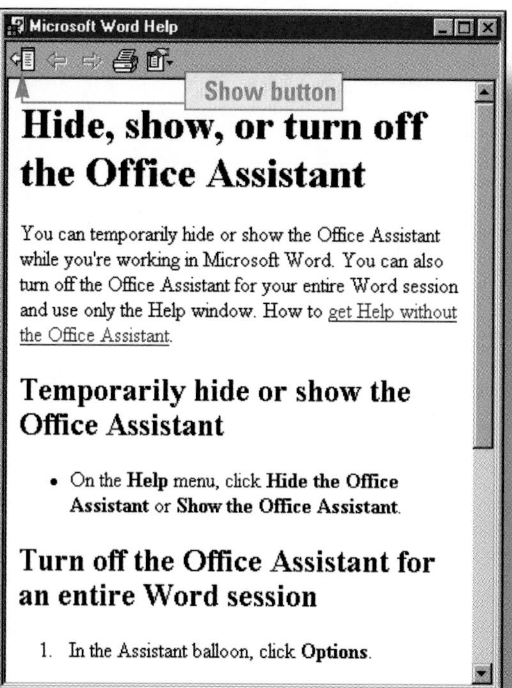

You can scroll the Help window to view all the information. You can click the Show button to view the Contents, Answer Wizard, and Index tabs that access other help topics. If you have Internet access, you can

view a Microsoft Help Web page from inside the Help window. To view the additional tabs:

Step 1	*Click*	the Show button in the Help window, if necessary, to display the Contents, Answer Wizard, and Index tabs
Step 2	*Click*	the Close button in the upper-right corner of the window

Using the Help Menu

The Help menu provides commands you can use to view the Office Assistant or Help window, show or hide the Office Assistant, connect to the Microsoft Web site, get context-sensitive help for a menu command or toolbar button, detect and repair font and template files, and view licensing information for the Office application. To review the Help menu commands:

Step 1	*Click*	Help
Step 2	*Observe*	the menu commands
Step 3	*Click*	in the document area outside the menu to close the Help menu

QUICK TIP

You can press the ESC key to close a menu.

Using What's This?

You can get context-sensitive help for a menu command or toolbar button using the What's This? command on the Help menu. This command changes the mouse pointer to a help pointer, a white mouse pointer with a large black question mark. When you click a toolbar button or menu command with the help pointer, a brief ScreenTip help message appears describing the command or toolbar button. To a ScreenTip help message for a toolbar button:

Step 1	*Press*	the SHIFT + F1 keys
Step 2	*Observe*	that the help mouse pointer with the attached question mark
Step 3	*Click*	the Save button on the Standard toolbar
Step 4	*Observe*	the ScreenTip help message describing the Save button
Step 5	*Press*	the ESC key to close the ScreenTip help message

1.f Closing Office Applications

There are many ways to close the Access, Excel and PowerPoint applications (or the Word application with a single document open) and return to the Windows desktop. You can: (1) double-click the application Control-menu icon; (2) click the application Close button; (3) right-click the application taskbar button and then click the Close command on the shortcut menu; (4) press the ALT + F4 keys; or (5) click the Exit command on the File menu to close Office applications (no matter how many Word documents are open). To close the Excel application from the taskbar:

Step 1	***Right-click***	the Excel button on the taskbar
Step 2	***Click***	Close

You can close multiple applications at one time from the taskbar by selecting the application buttons using the CTRL key and then using the shortcut menu. To close the PowerPoint and Access applications:

Step 1	***Press & Hold***	the CTRL key
Step 2	***Click***	the PowerPoint button and then the Access button on the taskbar
Step 3	***Release***	the CTRL key and observe that both buttons are selected (pressed in)
Step 4	***Right-click***	the PowerPoint or Access button
Step 5	***Click***	Close

Both applications close, leaving only the Word document open. To close the Word document using the menu:

Step 1	***Verify***	that the Word application window is maximized
Step 2	***Click***	File
Step 3	***Click***	Exit
Step 4	***Click***	No in the Office Assistant balloon or confirmation dialog box to close Word without saving the document

Summary

- The Word application provides word processing capabilities for the preparation of text documents such as letters, memorandums, and reports.
- The Excel application provides the ability to analyze numbers in worksheets and for creating financial budgets, reports, charts, and forms.
- The PowerPoint application is used to create presentation slides and audience handouts.
- You can use Access databases to organize and retrieve collections of data.
- Publisher provides tools for creating marketing materials, such as newsletters, brochures, flyers, and Web pages.
- The Outlook application helps you send and receive e-mail, maintain a calendar, "to do" lists, organize the names and addresses of contacts, and perform other information management tasks.
- One major advantage of Office suite applications is the ability to integrate the applications by sharing information between them.
- Another advantage of using Office suite applications is that they share a number of common elements, such as window elements, shortcuts, toolbars, menu commands, and other features.
- You can start Office suite applications from the Programs submenu on the Start menu and from the Open Office Document or New Office Document commands on the Start menu.
- You can close Office applications by double-clicking the application Control Menu icon, clicking the application Close button on the title bar, right-clicking the application button on the taskbar, pressing the ALT + F4 keys, or clicking the Exit command on the File menu.
- You can get help in an Office application by clicking commands on the Help menu, pressing the F1 or SHIFT + F1 keys, or clicking the Microsoft Help button on the Standard toolbar.

Concepts Review

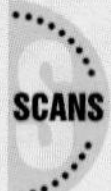

Circle the correct answer.

1. ScreenTips do not provide:
- [a] the name of a button on a toolbar.
- [b] help for options in a dialog box.
- [c] context-sensitive help for menu commands or toolbar buttons.
- [d] access to the Office Assistant.

2. To manage a Web site, you can use:
- [a] Outlook.
- [b] FrontPage.
- [c] PhotoDraw.
- [d] Publisher.

3. The title bar contains the:
- [a] document Control-menu icon.
- [b] Close Window button.
- [c] Standard toolbar.
- [d] application and document name.

4. The Excel application is best used to:
- [a] prepare financial reports.
- [b] maintain a list of tasks to accomplish.
- [c] create newsletters, brochures, and flyers.
- [d] create custom graphics.

Circle **T** if the statement is true or **F** if the statement is false.

T F 1. You use Publisher to create newsletters and brochures.
T F 2. Excel is used to create presentation slides.
T F 3. The default Office Assistant graphic is Clippit.
T F 4. Access is used to create and format text.

Skills Review

Exercise 1

1. Identify each common element of Office application windows numbered in Figure 1-10.

FIGURE 1-10
Excel Application Window

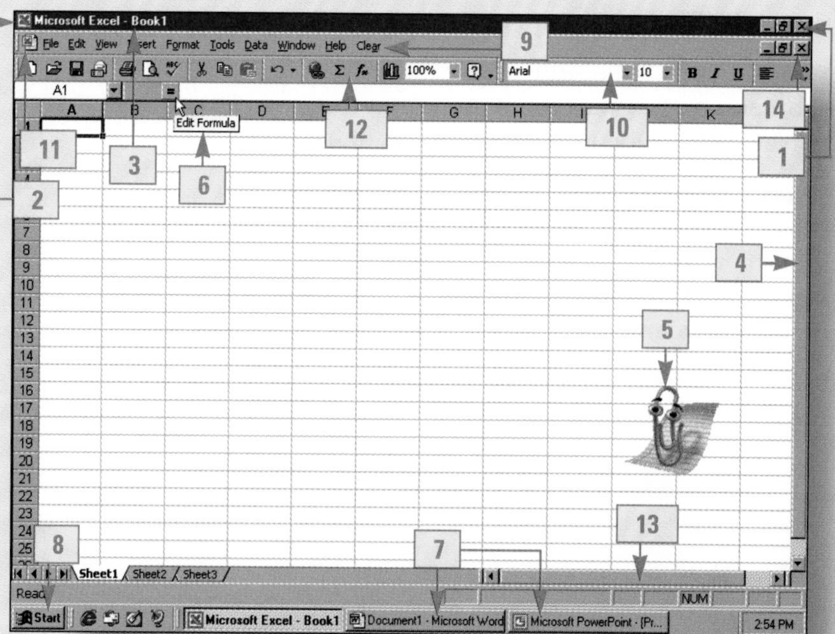

Exercise 2

1. Open the Word application using the Programs command on the Start menu.
2. Close the Word application using the taskbar.

Exercise 3

1. Open the Excel application and then the PowerPoint application using the Programs command on the Start menu.
2. Open the Access application and the *International Sales* database using the Open Office Document command on the Start menu.
3. Switch to the PowerPoint application using the taskbar button and close it using the Close button on the title bar.
4. Close the PowerPoint and Access applications at the same time using the taskbar.

Exercise 4

1. Create a new, blank Word document using the New Office Document command on the Start menu.
2. Create a new, blank Excel workbook using the New Office Document command on the Start menu.
3. Switch to the Word document using the taskbar and close it using the title bar Close button.
4. Close the Excel workbook using the taskbar button.

Exercise 5 

1. Open the Word application using the Start menu.
2. Show the Office Assistant, if necessary, with a command on the Help menu.
3. Hide the Office Assistant with a shortcut menu.
4. Show the Office Assistant with the Microsoft Word Help button on the Standard toolbar.
5. Search online Help using the search phrase “type text.” Open the Type text help page.
6. Click the underlined text typing text to view a help page of subtopics. Scroll and review the help page.
7. Close the Help window. Hide the Office Assistant with a shortcut menu.

Case Projects

Project 1

You are the secretary to the marketing manager of High Risk Insurance, an insurance brokerage firm. The marketing manager wants to know how to open and close the Excel application. Write at least two paragraphs describing different ways to open and close Excel. With your instructor’s permission, use your written description to show a classmate several ways to open and close Excel.

Project 2 

You work in the administrative offices of Alma Public Relations, and the information management department just installed Office 2000 Professional on your computer. Your supervisor asks you to write down and describe some of the Office Assistant options. Open the Options tab in the Office Assistant dialog box. Review each option using the dialog box Help button or the What’s This? command. Write at least three paragraphs describing five Office Assistant options.

Project 3

As the new office manager at Hot Wheels Messenger Service, you are learning to use the Word 2000 application and want to learn more about some of the buttons on the Word toolbars. Open Word and use the What’s This? command on the Help menu to review the ScreenTip help for five toolbar buttons. Write a brief paragraph for each button describing how it is used.

Project 4 

As the acquisitions director for Osiris Books, an international antique book and map dealer, you use Publisher to create the company’s catalogs and brochures. A co-worker, who is helping you with a new brochure, opened Publisher and did not know why the Catalog window appeared. She has asked you for an explanation. Open the Publisher application and review the Catalog window. Close the Catalog window leaving the Publisher window open. Use the Office Assistant to find out more about the Catalog by searching online Help using the keyword “catalog.” Write your co-worker a short note explaining how the Catalog is used.

Working with Menus and Toolbars

Chapter Overview

Office 2000 tries to make your work life easier by learning how you work. The personalized menus and toolbars in each application remember which commands and buttons you use, and add and remove them as needed. In this chapter, you learn how to work with the personalized menus and toolbars, how to customize the menu bar and toolbars, and how to view and customize the Office Shortcut Bar.

Learning Objectives

- Work with personalized menus and toolbars
- View, hide, dock, and float toolbars
- Customize the menu bar and toolbars
- View and customize the Office Shortcut Bar

2.a Working with Personalized Menus and Toolbars

A **menu** is a list of commands you use to perform tasks in the Office applications. Some commands also have an associated image, or icon, shown to the left of a command. A **toolbar** contains a set of icons (the same icons you see on the menus) called **buttons** that you click with the mouse pointer to quickly execute a menu command.

When you first open Excel, Word, or PowerPoint, the menus on the menu bar initially show only a basic set of commands and the Standard and Formatting toolbars contain only a basic set of buttons. These short versions of the menus and toolbars are called **personalized menus and toolbars**. As you work, the commands and buttons you use most frequently are stored in the personalized settings. The first time you select a menu command or toolbar button that is not part of the basic set, it is added to your personalized settings and appears on the menu or toolbar. If you do not use a command for a while, it is removed from your personalized settings and no longer appears on the menu or toolbar. To view the personalized menus and toolbars in PowerPoint:

Step 1	*Click*	the Start button (Start) on the taskbar
Step 2	*Click*	the New Office Document command on the Start menu
Step 3	*Click*	the General tab in the New Office Document dialog box
Step 4	*Double-click*	the Blank Presentation icon
Step 5	*Click*	OK in the New Slide dialog box to create a blank title slide for the presentation
Step 6	*Click*	Tools on the menu bar
Step 7	*Observe*	the short personalized menu containing only the basic commands, as shown in Figure 2-1

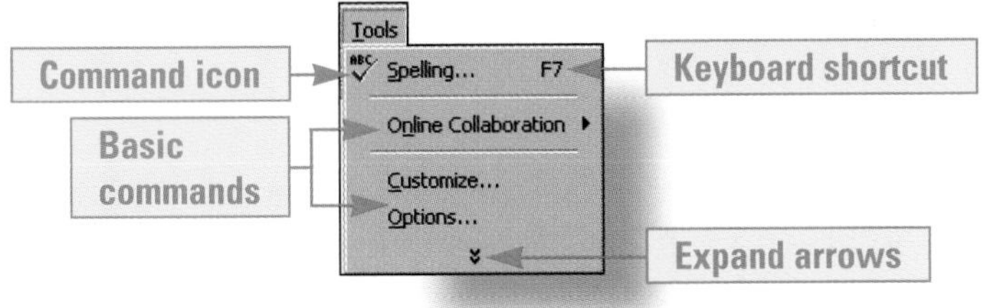

FIGURE 2-1
Personalized Tools Menu

CAUTION TIP

The activities in this chapter assume the personalized menus and toolbars are reset to their default settings. In this chapter, you select menu commands and toolbar buttons by clicking them with the mouse pointer. You learn how to use menu commands and toolbar buttons to perform tasks in the application chapters.

QUICK TIP

FrontPage and Access also provide the personalized menus and toolbars options. When you first open FrontPage, you see the Standard and Formatting toolbars. When you first open Access, you see only the Standard toolbar. Publisher does not provide the personalized menus and toolbars options.

If the command you want to use does not appear on the short personalized menu, you can expand the menu by pausing for a few seconds until the menu expands, clicking the expand arrows at the bottom of the menu, or double-clicking the menu name.

Step 8	***Pause***	until the menu automatically expands, as shown in Figure 2-2

FIGURE 2-2
Expanded Tools Menu

QUICK TIP

You can also use keyboard shortcuts to perform tasks in Office applications. Many of these keyboard shortcuts are shown on the menus to the right of the menu command.

You move a menu command from the expanded menu to the personalized menu, simply by selecting it. To add the AutoCorrect command to the short personalized Tools menu:

Step 1	***Click***	AutoCorrect
Step 2	***Click***	Cancel in the AutoCorrect dialog box to cancel the dialog box
Step 3	***Click***	Tools on the menu bar
Step 4	***Observe***	the updated personalized Tools menu contains the AutoCorrect command, as shown in Figure 2-3

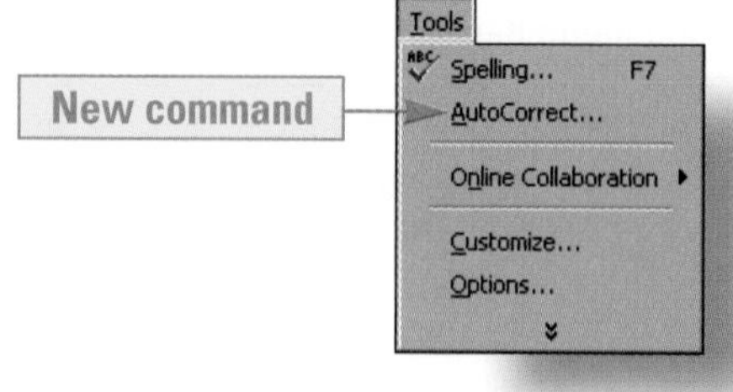

FIGURE 2-3
Updated Personalized Tools Menu

When you first open Word, Excel, or PowerPoint, the Standard and Formatting toolbars appear on one row below the title bar and some default buttons are hidden. You can resize a toolbar to view a hidden button by dragging its **move handle**, the gray vertical bar at the left edge of the toolbar, with the **move pointer,** a four-headed black arrow. To resize the Formatting toolbar:

Step 1	***Move***	the mouse pointer to the move handle on the Formatting toolbar
Step 2	***Observe***	that the mouse pointer becomes a move pointer
Step 3	***Drag***	the Formatting toolbar to the left until nine Formatting toolbar buttons are visible
Step 4	***Observe***	that you see fewer buttons on the Standard toolbar

The buttons that don't fit on the displayed area of a toolbar are collected in a More Buttons list. To view the remaining the Standard toolbar default buttons:

Step 1	***Click***	the More Buttons list arrow on the Standard toolbar
Step 2	***Observe***	the default buttons that are not visible on the toolbar, as shown in Figure 2-4

FIGURE 2-4
More Buttons List

Step 3	***Press***	the ESC key to close the More Buttons list

CAUTION TIP

When updating the personalized Standard or Formatting toolbar with a new button, a button that you have not used recently might move to the More Buttons list to make room for the new button.

If you want to display one of the default buttons on a personalized toolbar, you can select it from the More Buttons list. To add the Format Painter button to the personalized Standard toolbar:

Step 1	***Click***	the More Buttons list arrow on the Standard toolbar
Step 2	***Click***	the Format Painter button
Step 3	***Observe***	that the Format Painter button is turned on and added to the personalized Standard toolbar, as shown in Figure 2-5

FIGURE 2-5
Updated Personalized Standard Toolbar

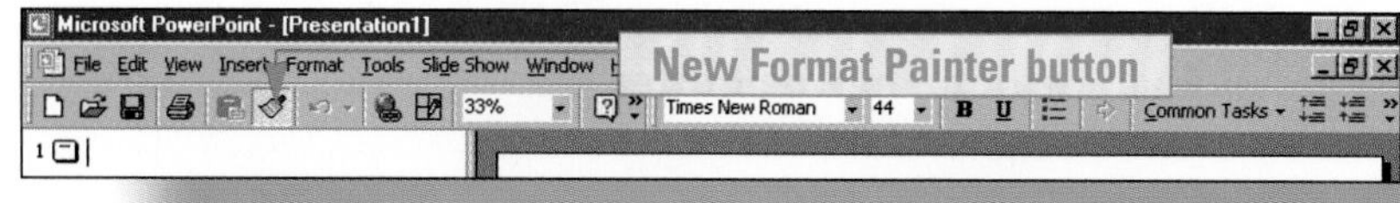

Step 4	*Click*	the Format Painter button  on the Standard toolbar to turn it off

C

If you want to view all the menu commands instead of a short personalized menu and all the default toolbar buttons on the Standard and Formatting toolbars, you can change options in the Customize dialog box. To show all the toolbar buttons and menu commands:

Step 1	*Click*	Tools
Step 2	*Click*	Customize
Step 3	*Click*	the Options tab, if necessary

The dialog box that opens should be similar to Figure 2-6.

FIGURE 2-6
Options Tab in the Customize Dialog Box

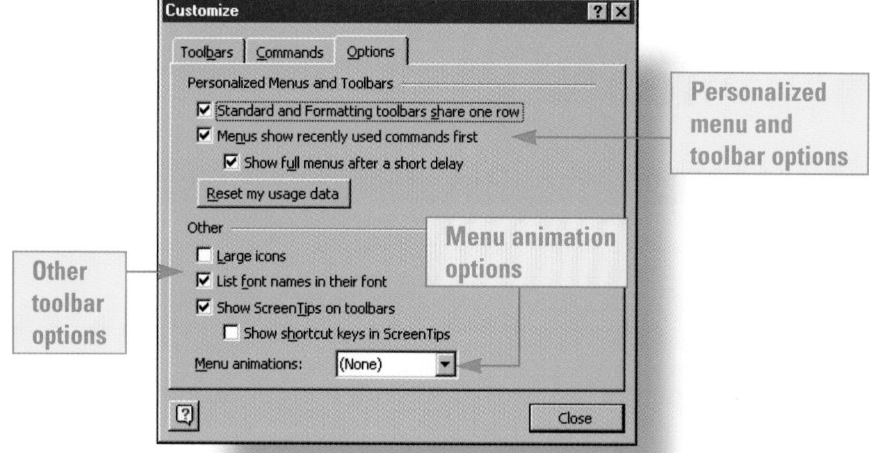

QUICK TIP

If you do not want the short personalized menus to expand automatically when you pause, remove the check mark from the Show full menus after a short delay check box. Then, to show the full menu, double-click the menu or click the expand arrows at the bottom of the menu.

Step 4	*Click*	the Standard and Formatting toolbars share one row check box to remove the check mark and reposition the Formatting toolbar below the Standard toolbar
Step 5	*Click*	the Menus show recently used commands first check box to remove the check mark and show the entire set of commands for each menu
Step 6	*Click*	Close to close the dialog box

Step 7	*Observe*	the repositioned Standard and Formatting toolbars
Step 8	*Click*	Tools to view the entire set of Tools menu commands
Step 9	*Press*	the ESC key

You can return the menus and toolbars to their initial (or **default**) settings in the Customize dialog box. To reset the default menus and toolbars:

Step 1	*Open*	the Options tab in the Customize dialog box
Step 2	*Click*	the Standard and Formatting toolbars share one row check box to insert a check mark
Step 3	*Click*	the Menus show recently used commands first check box to insert a check mark
Step 4	*Click*	Reset my usage data
Step 5	*Click*	Yes to confirm you want to reset the menus and toolbars to their default settings
Step 6	*Close*	the Customize dialog box
Step 7	*Observe*	that the Tools menu and Standard toolbar are reset to their default settings

CAUTION TIP

When you choose the Menus show recently used commands first option, it affects all the Office applications, not just the open application.

Resetting the usage data to the initial settings does not change the location of toolbars and does not remove or add buttons to toolbars you have customized in the Customize dialog box.

2.b Viewing, Hiding, Docking, and Floating Toolbars

Office applications have additional toolbars that you can view when you need them. You can also hide toolbars when you are not using them. You can view or hide toolbars by pointing to the Toolbars command on the View menu and clicking a toolbar name or by using a shortcut menu. A **shortcut menu** is a short list of frequently used menu commands. You view a shortcut menu by pointing to an item on the screen and clicking the right mouse button. This is called right-clicking the item. The commands on shortcut menus vary—depending on where you right-click—so that you view only the most frequently used commands for a particular task. An easy way to view or hide toolbars is with a shortcut menu. To view the shortcut menu for PowerPoint toolbars:

Step 1	*Right-click*	the menu bar, the Standard toolbar, or the Formatting toolbar
Step 2	*Observe*	the shortcut menu and the check marks next to the names of currently visible toolbars, as shown in Figure 2-7

FIGURE 2-7
Toolbars Shortcut Menu

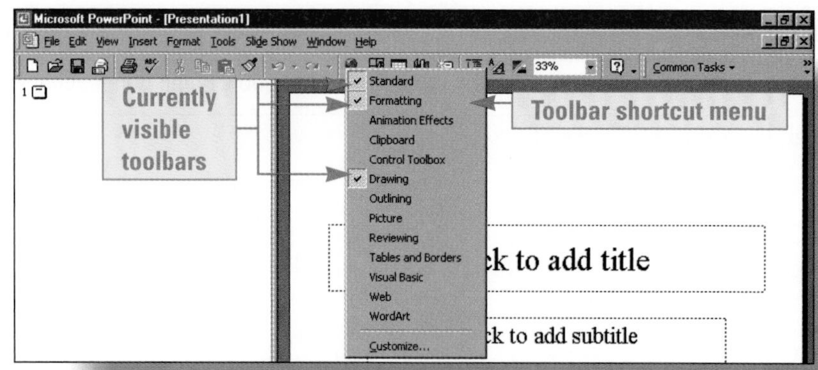

QUICK TIP

Some of the toolbars that appear on the toolbars list vary from Office application to application.

Step 3	***Click***	Tables and Borders in the shortcut menu
Step 4	***Observe***	that the Tables and Borders toolbar appears on your screen

The Tables and Borders toolbar, unless a previous user repositioned it, is visible in its own window near the middle of your screen. When a toolbar is visible in its own window it is called a **floating toolbar** and you can move and size it with the mouse pointer just like any window. When a toolbar appears fixed at the screen boundaries, it is called a **docked toolbar**. The menu bar and Standard and Formatting toolbars are examples of docked toolbars. In PowerPoint, the Drawing toolbar is docked above the status bar. You can dock a floating toolbar by dragging its title bar with the mouse pointer to a docking position below the title bar, above the status bar, or at the left and right boundaries of your screen. To dock the Tables and Borders toolbar below the Standard and Formatting toolbars:

Step 1	***Position***	the mouse pointer on the blue title bar in the Tables and Borders toolbar window
Step 2	***Drag***	the toolbar window slowly up until it docks below the Standard and Formatting toolbars

Similarly, you float a docked toolbar by dragging it away from its docked position toward the middle of the screen. To float the Tables and Borders toolbar:

Step 1	***Position***	the mouse pointer on the Tables and Borders toolbar move handle until it becomes a move pointer
Step 2	***Drag***	the Tables and Borders toolbar down toward the middle of the screen until it appears in its own window

When you finish using a toolbar, you can hide it with a shortcut menu. To hide the Tables and Borders toolbar:

Step 1	***Right-click***	the Tables and Borders toolbar
Step 2	***Click***	Tables and Borders to remove the check mark and hide the toolbar

2.c Customizing the Menu Bar and Toolbars

Recall that you can add a button to a personalized toolbar by clicking the More Buttons list arrow on the toolbar and then selecting a button from the list of default buttons not currently visible. You can also add and delete buttons and commands on the menu bar or other toolbars with options in the Customize dialog box. To customize the menu bar:

Step 1	***Right-click***	any toolbar (the menu bar, Standard toolbar, or Formatting toolbar)
Step 2	***Click***	Customize
Step 3	***Click***	the Commands tab, if necessary

The dialog box on your screen should look similar to Figure 2-8.

QUICK TIP

Remember, the menu bar is also a toolbar. You customize the menu bar and other toolbars the same way.

The Commands tab in the Customize dialog box contains a list of category names and a list of commands available for the selected category. You can view a description of a command by selecting it and clicking the Description button. When you find the command you want to add, drag it from the dialog box to the menu bar or another visible toolbar.

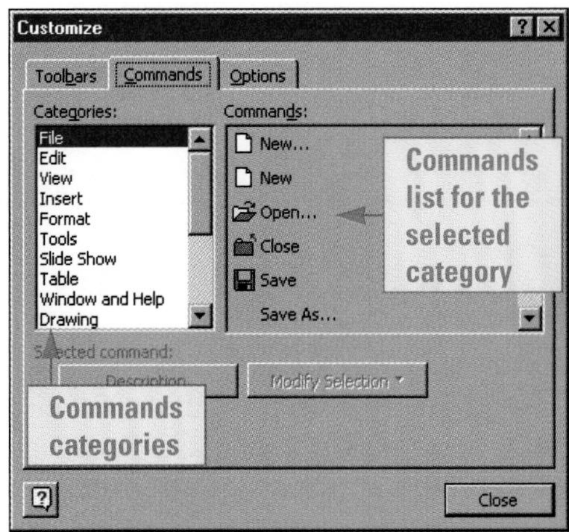

FIGURE 2-8
Commands Tab in the Customize Dialog Box

You add a button on the menu bar to route the active presentation to other users on the network via e-mail.

MOUSE TIP

You can add hyperlinks (the path to another document) to toolbar buttons. For more information, see online Help.

Step 4	*Verify*	that File is selected in the Categories: list
Step 5	*Click*	Routing Recipient in the Commands: list (scroll the list to view this command)
Step 6	*Click*	Description to view the ScreenTip
Step 7	*Press*	the ESC key to close the ScreenTip
Step 8	*Drag*	the Routing Recipient command to the right of Help on the menu bar
Step 9	*Click*	Close to close the dialog box and add the Routing Recipient button to the menu bar
Step 10	*Position*	the mouse pointer on the Routing Recipient icon to view the ScreenTip, as shown in Figure 2-9

FIGURE 2-9
Button Added to Menu Bar

You can remove a button from a toolbar just as quickly. To remove the Routing Recipient button from the menu bar:

Step 1	*Open*	the Customize dialog box
Step 2	*Drag*	the Routing Recipient button from the menu bar into the dialog box
Step 3	*Close*	the dialog box
Step 4	*Close*	the PowerPoint application and return to the Windows desktop

QUICK TIP

You can reset toolbars back to their original buttons and create new custom toolbars with options on the Toolbars tab in the Customize dialog box.

You can view toolbar buttons in a larger size (for high-resolution monitors), show keyboard shortcuts in the button's ScreenTip, and add animation to menus with options in the Options tab in the Customize dialog box. **Menu animation** refers to the movement the menu makes as it opens on your screen.

2.d Viewing and Customizing the Office Shortcut Bar

The **Office Shortcut Bar** is a toolbar that you can open and position on your Windows desktop to provide shortcuts to Office applications and tasks. It can contain buttons for the New Office Document and Open Office Document commands on the Start menu, shortcut buttons to create various Outlook items like the New Task button, and buttons to open Office applications installed on your computer.

You can view and use the Office Shortcut Bar as needed or you can choose to have it open each time you start your computer. To view the Office Shortcut Bar:

Step 1	***Click***	the Start button [Start] on the taskbar
Step 2	***Point to***	Programs
Step 3	***Point to***	Microsoft Office Tools
Step 4	***Click***	Microsoft Office Shortcut Bar
Step 5	***Click***	No in the Microsoft Office Shortcut Bar dialog box to not open the Office Shortcut Bar each time you start your computer

The Office Shortcut Bar appears docked in the upper-right corner of your Windows desktop. Your screen should look similar to Figure 2-10.

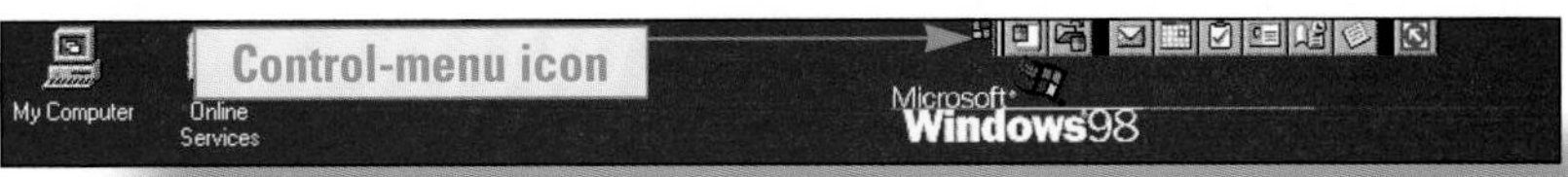

FIGURE 2-10
Office Shortcut Bar

Step 6	***Right-click***	the Office Shortcut Bar Control-menu icon

The Office Shortcut Bar Control-menu contains commands you can use to customize or close the Office Shortcut Bar. If your Shortcut Bar does not already contain buttons to open the individual Office applications, you may want to customize it for the Office applications you use frequently. To open the Customize dialog box:

Step 1	***Click***	Customize
Step 2	***Click***	the Buttons tab

The dialog box on your screen should look similar to Figure 2-11.

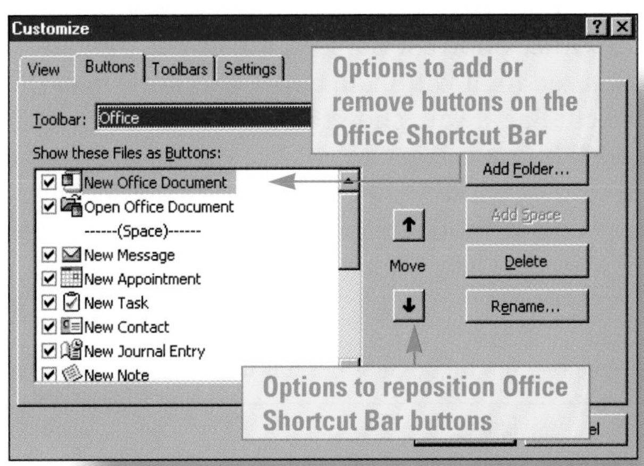

FIGURE 2-11
Buttons Tab in the Customize Dialog Box

CAUTION TIP

The activities in this section assume that the Office Shortcut Bar does not open automatically when you start your computer or contain Office application buttons.

QUICK TIP

The AutoHide command hides the Office Shortcut Bar and displays only a thin border where the Office Shortcut Bar resides. When you position the mouse pointer on the thin border, the Office Shortcut Bar appears. When you move the mouse pointer away from the border, the Office Shortcut Bar hides again.

QUICK TIP

You can enlarge the Shortcut Bar buttons by clicking the Large Buttons check box; this inserts a check mark on the View tab in the Customize dialog box. You can place the Shortcut Bar in its own window, and then move and size the window by clicking the Auto Fit into Title Bar area check box; this removes the check mark on the View tab in the Customize dialog box.

The shortcut button for a particular application or file is visible on the Office Shortcut Bar if a check mark appears in the check box to the left of the application icon in the Show these Files as Buttons: list. To add a shortcut button that opens the Word application:

Step 1	*Scroll*	the Show these Files as Buttons: list to view the check boxes for the Office applications
Step 2	*Click*	the Microsoft Word check box to insert a check mark
Step 3	*Observe*	that a button for the Word application immediately appears on the Office Shortcut Bar

You can easily reposition a button on the Office Shortcut Bar by moving the item into the Show these Files as Buttons: list. To reposition the Word button to the right of the Open Office Document button:

Step 1	*Click*	the Microsoft Word application name to select it in the list
Step 2	*Click*	the Move up arrow until the Microsoft Word application and check box appear immediately below the Open Office Document icon and check box
Step 3	*Observe*	that the Word button on the Office Shortcut Bar is repositioned

You can also delete an application button from the Office Shortcut Bar. To remove the Word application button:

Step 1	*Click*	the Microsoft Word check box to remove the check mark
Step 2	*Move*	the Microsoft Word check box back to its original position above the Excel check box by selecting it and clicking the Move down arrow
Step 3	*Click*	OK

By default, the Office Shortcut Bar is in the upper-right corner of your screen and sized to fit within an application title bar. This means that Office Shortcut Bar always shows on top of the active application's title bar with small buttons. You can enlarge the buttons and place the Shortcut Bar in its own window so you can move it elsewhere on the screen. You can also hide and redisplay the Shortcut Bar as needed. To close the Office Shortcut Bar:

Step 1	*Right-click*	the Office Shortcut Bar Control-menu icon
Step 2	*Click*	Exit

Summary

- When you first start Word, Excel, or PowerPoint, you see personalized menus containing basic commands. As you use different commands, they are automatically added to the personalized menu. Commands that are not used for some time are removed from the personalized menus.
- When you first start Word, Excel, or PowerPoint, the Standard and Formatting toolbars share one row below the menu bar. You can reposition the Formatting toolbar to view more or fewer toolbar buttons. The remaining default toolbar buttons that are not visible on the toolbars can be added from the More Buttons list.
- FrontPage and Access also provide the personalized menus and toolbars options.
- You can turn off or reset the personalized menus and toolbars in the Options tab of the Customize dialog box.
- You can hide or view toolbars as you need them by using a shortcut menu.
- Toolbars can be docked at the top, bottom, or side of the screen or they can remain floating on the screen in their own window.
- You can customize toolbars by adding or deleting buttons and commands, displaying larger-sized buttons, and turning on or off the display of ScreenTips, or adding keyboard shortcut keys to ScreenTips.
- The menu bar is a special toolbar that can be customized just like other toolbars.
- The Office Shortcut Bar is a customizable toolbar you can position on the desktop and contains shortcuts for opening Office documents and applications.

Commands Review

Action	Menu Bar	Shortcut Menu	Toolbar	Keyboard
To display or hide toolbars	View, Toolbars	Right-click a toolbar, click the desired toolbar to add or remove the check mark		ALT + V, T
To customize a toolbar	View, Toolbars, Customize	Right-click a toolbar, click Customize		ALT + V, T, C

Concepts Review

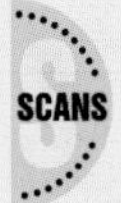

Circle the correct answer.

1. A menu is:
- [a] a set of icons.
- [b] a list of commands.
- [c] impossible to customize.
- [d] never personalized.

2. The Options tab in the PowerPoint Customize dialog box does not include an option for:
- [a] turning on or off ScreenTips for toolbar buttons.
- [b] turning on or off Large icons for toolbar buttons.
- [c] adding animation to menus.
- [d] docking all toolbars.

3. A toolbar is:
- [a] a list of commands.
- [b] always floating on your screen.
- [c] a set of icons.
- [d] never docked on your screen.

4. When you right-click an item on your screen, you see:
- [a] the Right Click toolbar.
- [b] animated menus.
- [c] expanded menus.
- [d] a shortcut menu.

Circle **T** if the statement is true or **F** if the statement is false.

T F 1. The Standard and Formatting toolbars must remain on the same row.

T F 2. When updating docked personalized toolbars, some buttons may be automatically removed from view to make room for the new buttons.

T F 3. Resetting your usage data affects your toolbars regardless of their size or position.

T F 4. You cannot add animation to menus.

Skills Review

Exercise 1

1. Open the Word application.

2. Open the Options tab in the Customize dialog box and reset the usage data, have the Standard and Formatting toolbars share one row, and the menus show recently used commands first.

3. Add the Show/Hide button to the personalized Standard toolbar using the More Buttons list.

4. Add the Font color button to the personalized Formatting toolbar using the More Buttons list.
5. Open the Customize dialog box and reset your usage data in the Options tab.
6. Close the Word application.

Exercise 2 C

1. Open the Excel application.
2. Open the Options tab in the Customize dialog box and reset the usage data, have the Standard and Formatting toolbars share one row, and the menus show recently used commands first.
3. View the personalized Tools menu.
4. Add the AutoCorrect command to the personalized Tools menu.
5. Reset your usage data.
6. Close the Excel application.

Exercise 3

1. Open the Office Shortcut Bar. (Do not set it to automatically open when you start your computer.)
2. Customize the Office Shortcut Bar to add the Word, Excel, and PowerPoint shortcut buttons or remove them if they already appear.
3. Customize the Office Shortcut Bar to have large buttons and position it in its own window vertically at the right side of the desktop.
4. AutoFit the Office Shortcut Bar to the title bar with small buttons.
5. Remove the Word, Excel, and PowerPoint application shortcut buttons or add them back, if necessary.
6. Close the Office Shortcut Bar.

Exercise 4

1. Open the Word application.
2. Add the Clear command icon from the Edit category to the menu bar.
3. Reset the menu bar back to its default from the Toolbars tab in the Customize dialog box.
4. Close the Word application.

Exercise 5

1. Open the Excel application.
2. View the Drawing, Picture, and WordArt toolbars using a shortcut menu.
3. Dock the Picture toolbar below the Standard and Formatting toolbars.
4. Dock the WordArt toolbar at the left boundary of the screen.
5. Close the Excel application from the taskbar.
6. Open the Excel with the New Office Document on the Start menu. (*Hint:* Use the Blank Workbook icon.)
7. Float the WordArt toolbar.
8. Float the Picture toolbar.

9. Hide the WordArt, Picture, and Drawing toolbars using a shortcut menu.

10. Close the Excel application.

Case Projects

Project 1

As secretary to the placement director for the XYZ Employment Agency, you have been using Word 97. After you install Office 2000, you decide you want the menus and toolbars to behave just like they did in Word 97. Use the Office Assistant to search for help on "personalized menus" and select the appropriate topic from the Office Assistant list. (*Hint:* You may need to view all the topics presented in the Office Assistant balloon.) Review the Help topic you select and write down the steps to make the personalized menus and toolbars behave like Word 97 menus and toolbars.

Project 2

You are the administrative assistant to the controller of the Plush Pets, Inc., a stuffed toy manufacturing company. The controller recently installed Excel 2000. She prefers to view the entire list of menu commands rather than the personalized menus and asks for your help. Use the Office assistant to search for help on "full menus" and select the appropriate topic in the Office Assistant balloon. Review the topic and write down the instructions for switching between personalized menus and full menus.

Project 3

As administrative assistant to the art director of MediaWiz Advertising, Inc. you just installed PowerPoint 2000. Now you decide you would rather view the complete Standard and Formatting toolbars rather than the personalized toolbars and want to learn a quick way to do this. Use the Office Assistant to search for help on "show all buttons" and select the appropriate topic from the Office Assistant balloon. Review the topic and write down the instructions for showing all buttons using the mouse pointer. Open an Office application and use the mouse method to show the complete Standard and Formatting toolbars. Turn the personalized toolbars back on in the Customize dialog box.

Project 4

You are the training coordinator for the information technology (IT) department at a large international health care organization, World Health International. The information technology department is planning to install Office 2000 on computers throughout the organization within the next two weeks. Your supervisor, the IT manager, asks you to prepare a short introduction to the Office 2000 personalized menus and toolbars to be presented at next Monday's staff meeting. He wants you to emphasize the advantages and disadvantages of using the personalized menus and toolbars. Write down in at least two paragraphs the advantages and disadvantages of using the personalized menus and toolbars.

Working With Others Using Online Collaboration Tools

Chapter Overview

In today's workplace many tasks are completed by several co-workers working together as part of a team called a workgroup. Office applications provide tools to assist workgroups in sharing information. In this chapter you learn about scheduling and participating in online meetings and conducting Web discussions with others in your workgroup.

Learning Objectives

- Schedule an online meeting
- Participate in Web discussions

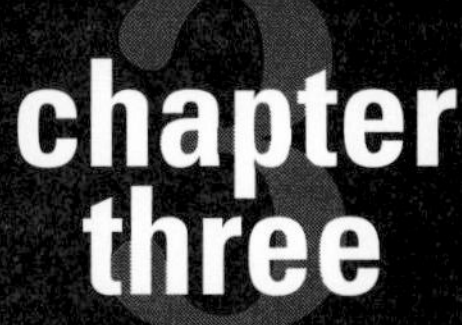

CAUTION TIP

The activities in this chapter assume you have access to directory servers and Web servers with Office Server Extensions installed, Microsoft NetMeeting, and Outlook with Exchange Server service installed. If you do not have access to the appropriate servers and software, you will be able to read but not do the hands-on activities. Your instructor will provide additional server, e-mail address, NetMeeting, and Outlook instructions as needed to complete the hands-on activities.

3.a Scheduling an Online Meeting

Many organizations assign tasks or projects to several workers who collaborate as members of a **workgroup**. Often these workgroup members do not work in the same office or some members travel frequently, making it difficult for the group to meet at one physical location. Office applications, together with Microsoft NetMeeting conferencing software, provide a way for workgroup members to participate in online real-time meetings from different physical locations—just as though everyone were in the same meeting room. In an online meeting, participants can share programs and documents, send text messages, transfer files, and illustrate ideas.

You can schedule an online meeting in advance using Outlook or you can invite others to participate in an online meeting right now by opening NetMeeting directly from Word, Excel, PowerPoint, and Access and calling others in your workgroup. To participate in an online meeting, invitees must have NetMeeting running on their computers.

Calling Others from Office Applications Using NetMeeting

Suppose you are working on an Excel workbook and want to discuss the workbook with another person in your workgroup. You know that they are running NetMeeting on their computer. You can call them while working in the workbook. To open NetMeeting and place a call from within Excel:

Step 1	*Click*	the Start button Start on the taskbar
Step 2	*Click*	the Open Office Document command on the Start menu
Step 3	*Double-click*	the *International Food Distributors* workbook located on the Data Disk
Step 4	*Click*	Tools
Step 5	*Point to*	Online Collaboration
Step 6	*Click*	Meet Now to open NetMeeting and the Place A Call dialog box

The directory server and list of names and calling addresses in the Place A Call dialog box on your screen will be different, but the dialog box should look similar to Figure 3-1.

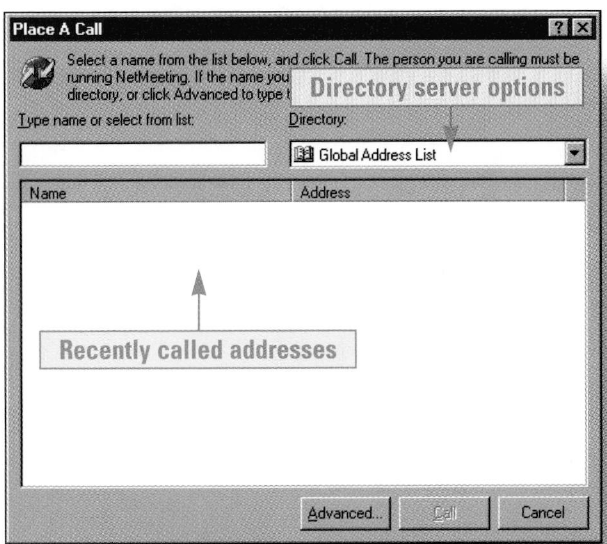

FIGURE 3-1
Place A Call Dialog Box

The person who initiates the meeting call is called the **host**. The person or persons receiving the call are called **participants**. Because you are initiating a call about the open Excel workbook, you are the host for this meeting. You can select a specific directory server and then select the participant to call from a list of persons logged onto the server or select someone from the list of frequently called NetMeeting participants. The *host* now calls a participant in the list:

Step 1	***Right-click***	the name of the person in the list specified by your instructor and click Call

NetMeeting dials the participant. Depending on the participant's NetMeeting configuration, he or she can automatically accept the call or manually accept or ignore the call. If the NetMeeting configuration is set up to manually answer calls, an announcement appears on the participant's screen, allowing him or her to click a button to accept or decline the call.

For the activities in this chapter, the participant's NetMeeting software is configured to automatically accept incoming calls. When the call is accepted, the *International Food Distributors* workbook and the Online Meeting toolbar automatically display on the participant's screen, even if the participant does not have Excel installed. Only the host needs to have the application installed and the file available. Both the *host's* and the *participant's* screens should look similar to Figure 3-2.

The host has **control** of the *International Foods Distributors* workbook when the meeting starts, which means the host can turn on or off collaboration at any time, controlling who can edit the document. When collaboration is turned on, any one participant can control the workbook for editing. When collaboration is turned off,

FIGURE 3-2
Host's and Participant's Screens

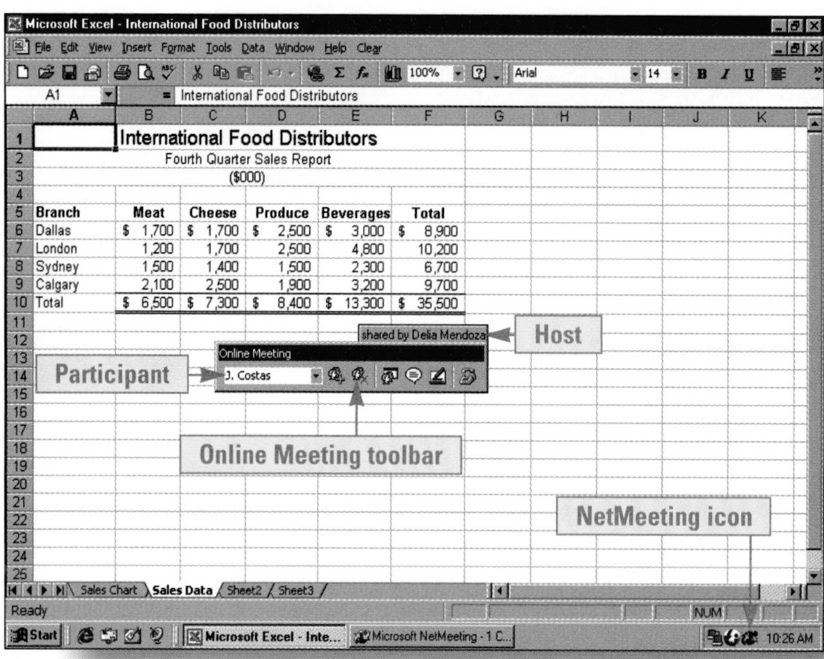

QUICK TIP

Only the host of the meeting can use all the features on the Online Meeting toolbar.

only the host can edit the workbook but all participants can see it. The *host* now turns on collaboration:

Step 1	*Click*	the Allow others to edit button on the Online Meeting toolbar

The first time a participant wants to take control of the workbook, they double-click it. The host can regain control of the workbook at any time simply by clicking it. To regain control of the workbook after the first time they control it, a participant also clicks it. The initials of the person who currently controls the workbook appear beside the mouse pointer. The *participant* takes control of the workbook for the first time to edit it:

CAUTION TIP

When someone else controls a document during an online meeting, you cannot use your mouse pointer to access commands or edit the document until you regain control of it.

Step 1	*Double-click*	the workbook to take control and place your user initials beside the mouse pointer
Step 2	*Click*	Tools
Step 3	*Click*	Options
Step 4	*Click*	the View tab
Step 5	*Click*	the Gridlines check box to remove the check mark
Step 6	*Click*	OK to turn off the gridlines in the workbook

The *host* regains control of the workbook:

Step 1	*Click*	the workbook to regain control and place your initials beside the mouse pointer
Step 2	*Turn on*	the gridlines on the View tab in the Options dialog box

The **Whiteboard** is a tool that participants can use to illustrate their thoughts and ideas. Only the host can display the Whiteboard during an online meeting that originates from within an Office application. All participants can draw on the Whiteboard at the same time only when the host turns off collaboration. The *host* turns off collaboration:

Step 1	*Click*	the workbook to regain control, if necessary
Step 2	*Click*	the Allow others to edit button to turn off collaboration
Step 3	*Click*	the Display Whiteboard button on the Online Meeting toolbar

Your screen should look similar to Figure 3-3.

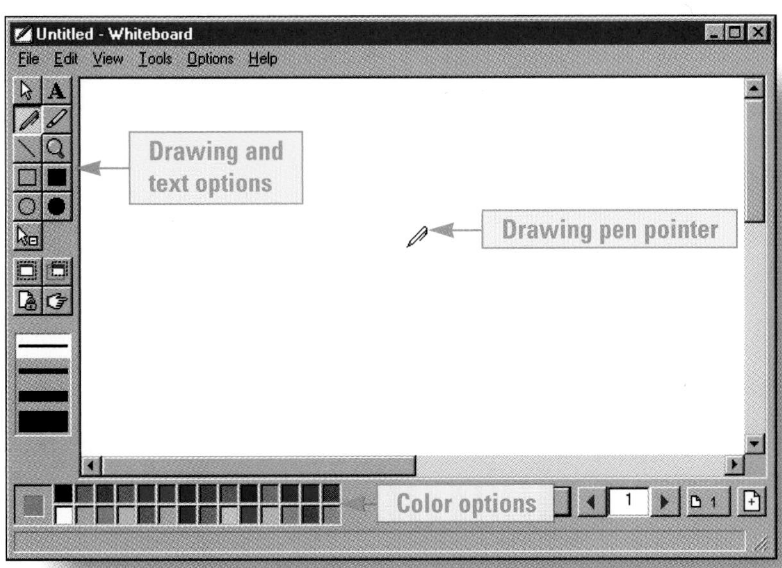

FIGURE 3-3
Whiteboard Window

All participants, including the host, add text, draw shapes, add color, and insert additional pages in the Whiteboard window. The host can save and print Whiteboard pages. The host and participant explore using the drawing, text, and color options for the Whiteboard. First, the *host* selects a color and draws a shape:

QUICK TIP

When collaboration is turned off, meeting participants can use **Chat** to send and respond to keyed messages in real time. With a sound card and a camera attached to their computer, the host and participants in an online meeting can both hear and see one another. For more information on using Chat, audio, and video in online meetings see NetMeeting online Help.

QUICK TIP

The meeting host can turn off collaboration when someone else has control of the document by pressing the ESC key.

MENU TIP

The host can send a copy of the active document to all participants by clicking the File menu, pointing to Send To, and clicking the Online Meeting Recipient command. All participants then receive the file as an e-mail attachment. The host can send the document to one participant by clicking the E-mail button on the Standard toolbar and attaching the document file to an e-mail message.

CAUTION TIP

Only the host can save and print the document during an online meeting. If a participant in control attempts to print or save the workbook, it is printed at the host's printer and saved to the host's hard disk or originating server.

Step 1	***Click***	Red in the color options
Step 2	***Draw***	a shape by dragging the drawing pen pointer in the Whiteboard drawing area

The *participant* now takes control of the drawing pen, selects a color, and draws a shape:

Step 1	***Click***	the Whiteboard to take control of the drawing pen
Step 2	***Click***	Blue in the color options and draw a shape

The *host* and the *participant*:

Step 1	***Continue***	to share the Whiteboard and explore the different Whiteboard options
Step 2	***Click***	the Close button on the Whiteboard window title bar to close the Whiteboard

Each participant can disconnect from the meeting at any time by clicking the End Meeting button on the Online Meeting toolbar. The host can also disconnect any participant by first selecting the participant from the Participants List button and then clicking the Remove Participants button on the Online Meeting toolbar. The host can also end the meeting, which disconnects all the participants. The *host* ends the meeting:

Step 1	***Click***	the End Meeting button on the Online Meeting toolbar
Step 2	***Close***	the Excel application and workbook from the taskbar without saving changes

Scheduling Online Meetings in Advance Using Outlook

As a host, you can schedule online meetings in advance using Outlook directly or from inside other Office applications. Suppose you are putting the finishing touches on a PowerPoint presentation and want to schedule an online meeting in advance with other workgroup members. You can do this from inside the PowerPoint application. To open a PowerPoint presentation and invite others to an online meeting:

Step 1	*Open*	the PowerPoint application and the *International Food Distributors* presentation located on the Data Disk using the Open Office Document command on the Start menu
Step 2	*Click*	Tools
Step 3	*Point to*	Online Collaboration
Step 4	*Click*	Schedule Meeting

The Outlook Meeting window opens, similar to Figure 3-4.

This window provides all the options for setting up the meeting. You address the message to one or more e-mail addresses, key the subject of the meeting, and select the directory server where the meeting will be held. You also select the date and time of the meeting. The current document is selected as the Office document to be reviewed and a meeting reminder is set to be delivered to the host and attendees 15 minutes prior to the scheduled meeting.

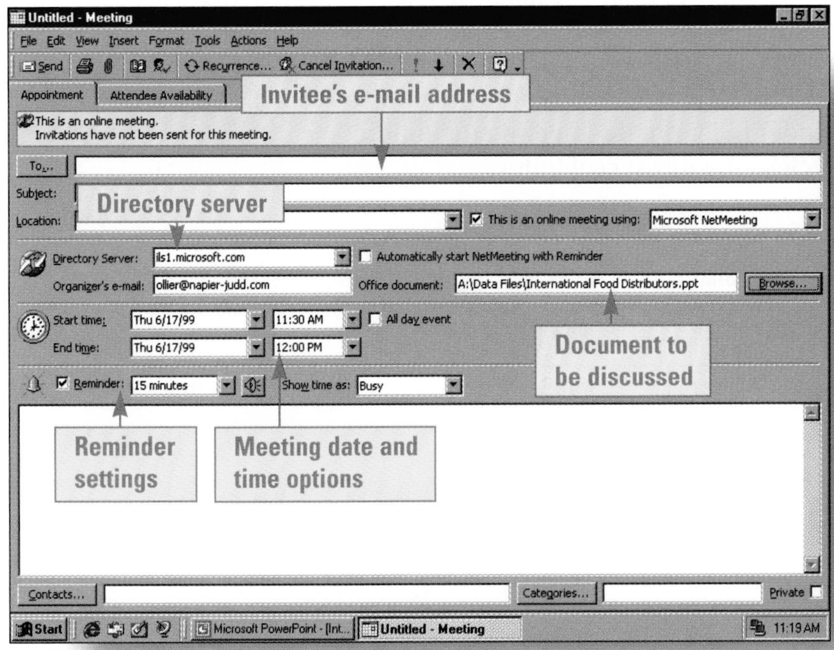

FIGURE 3-4
Outlook Meeting Window

As long as all invitees are using Outlook for their scheduling, you can determine the best time to schedule the meeting by clicking the Attendee Availability tab and inviting others from the Outlook global address book. To review the Attendee Availability tab:

Step 1	*Click*	the Attendee Availability tab

Step 2	*Observe*	the meeting scheduling options you can use to compare each invitee's free and busy times from their Outlook calendars and select the best meeting time
Step 3	*Click*	the Appointment tab

You send the completed meeting invitation by clicking the Send button on the Standard toolbar. Each invitee receives an e-mail message with the meeting information. They can choose to accept, decline, or tentatively accept the invitation by clicking a button inside the message window. If they accept, an Outlook appointment item is added to their calendar. Because you are the host, an appointment item is automatically added to your Outlook calendar. If invitees accept, decline, or accept tentatively, you receive an e-mail notification of their attendance choice and your meeting appointment item is updated to show who is attending and who declined.

Fifteen minutes prior to the scheduled online meeting (if Outlook is running on your computer) a meeting reminder message opens on your screen. If you are the meeting's host, you click the Start this NetMeeting button in the reminder window to begin the meeting. If you are an invited participant, you click the Join the Meeting button in the reminder window to join the meeting or you click the Dismiss this reminder to ignore the meeting invitation.

To close the message window without sending a message:

Step 1	*Click*	the Close button [X] on the message window title bar
Step 2	*Click*	No
Step 3	*Close*	the PowerPoint application and presentation

3.b Participating in Web Discussions

Web discussions provide a way for workgroup members to review and provide input to the same document by associating messages, called **discussion items**, with the document. Discussion items are saved in a database separate from the associated document. This enables the group to consider multiple discussion items related to the same document; it also allows the document to be edited without affecting any discussion items. Discussion items are **threaded**, which means that replies to an item appear directly under the original item. Discussion items are saved as they are entered and are available immediately when the associated document is opened.

QUICK TIP

For more information on scheduling meetings using Outlook, see Outlook online Help.

CAUTION TIP

Special software called Office Server Extensions must be installed on a Web server before discussion items can be created and stored there. For more information on Office Server Extensions software, see the documentation that accompanies Office or online Help.

Suppose you are working on a Word document and want to solicit input from others in your workgroup. Instead of sending a copy to everyone in the workgroup or routing a single copy to everyone, you decide to use the Web discussion feature. To start a Web discussion:

Step 1	***Open***	the Word application and the *Dallas Warehouse Audit* document located on the Data Disk using the Open Office Document command on the Start menu
Step 2	***Click***	Tools
Step 3	***Point to***	Online Collaboration
Step 4	***Click***	Web Discussions

After you connect to your discussion server, the Web Discussions toolbar opens docked above the status bar. See Figure 3-5.

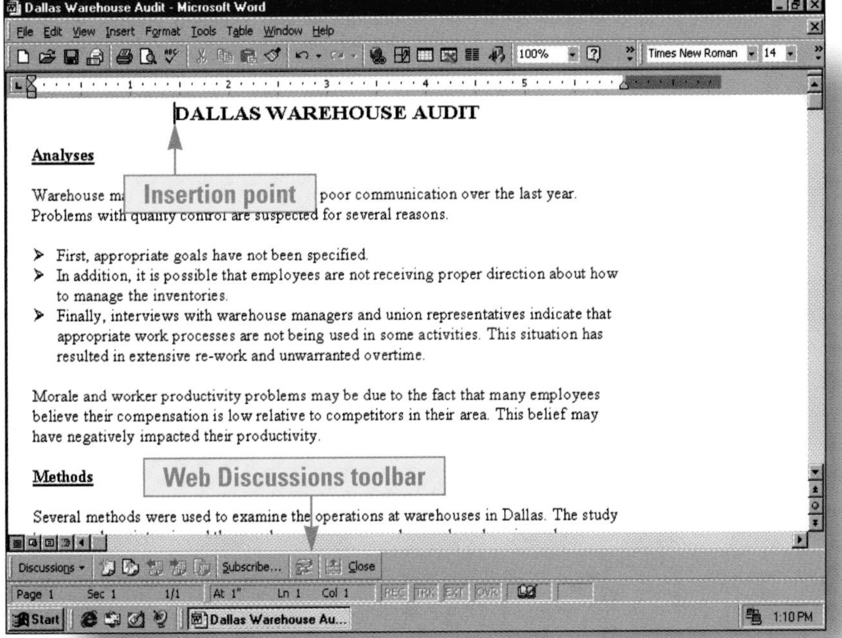

FIGURE 3-5
Document with Web Discussions Toolbar

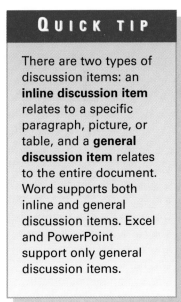

> **QUICK TIP**
>
> There are two types of discussion items: an **inline discussion item** relates to a specific paragraph, picture, or table, and a **general discussion item** relates to the entire document. Word supports both inline and general discussion items. Excel and PowerPoint support only general discussion items.

First, you add a general discussion item identifying the issues to be discussed in the document. To add a general discussion item:

Step 1	***Press***	the CTRL + HOME keys to move the keying position (called the insertion point) to the top of the document
Step 2	***Click***	the Insert Discussion about the Document button on the Web Discussions toolbar

The dialog box that opens should look similar to Figure 3-6.

chapter three

FIGURE 3-6
Enter Discussion Text Dialog Box

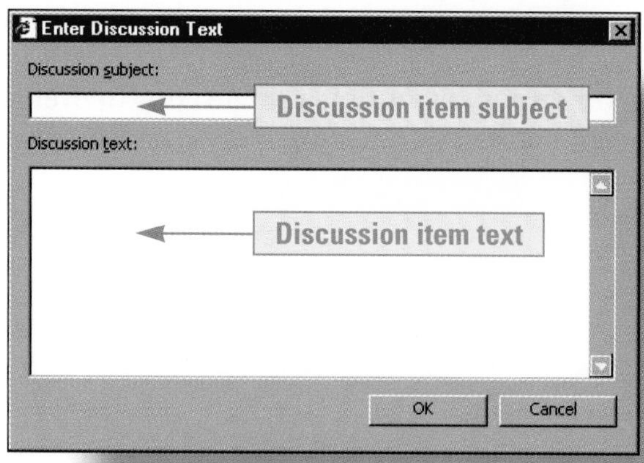

Step 3	***Key***	Problems in Dallas in the Discussion subject: text box
Step 4	***Press***	the TAB key to move the insertion point (the keying position) to the Discussion text: text box
Step 5	***Key***	We have only three weeks to resolve the problems in Dallas.
Step 6	***Click***	OK

The Discussion pane opens and contains information about the active document, the text of the discussion item, and an Action button. You use the Action button to reply to, edit, or delete a discussion item. Your screen should look similar to Figure 3-7.

FIGURE 3-7
Document with Discussion Pane

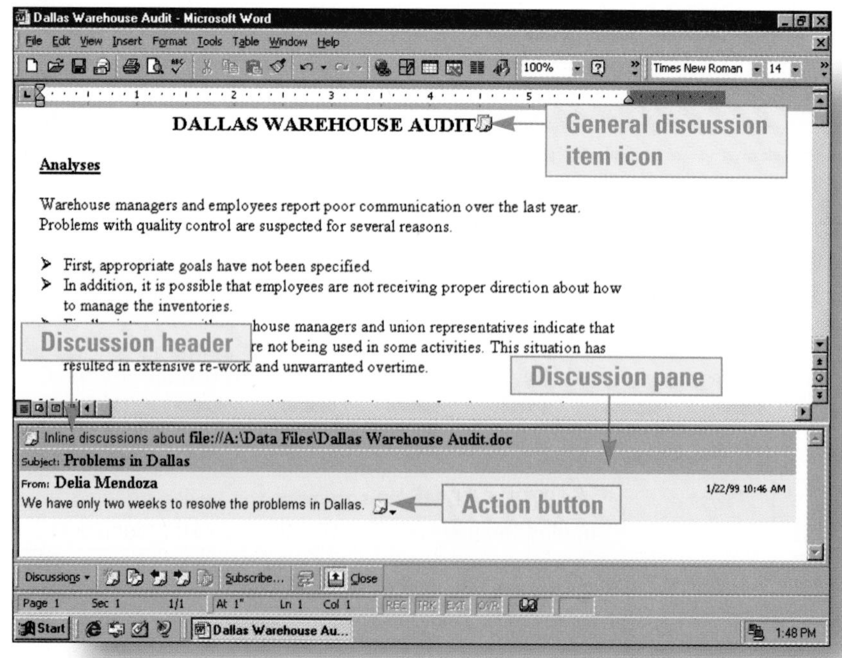

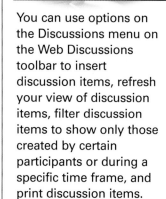

You can use options on the Discussions menu on the Web Discussions toolbar to insert discussion items, refresh your view of discussion items, filter discussion items to show only those created by certain participants or during a specific time frame, and print discussion items.

Next you add an inline discussion item to a specific paragraph. To close the Discussion pane and add an inline discussion item:

Step 1	*Click*	the Show/Hide Discussion Pane button on the Web Discussions toolbar
Step 2	*Click*	at the end of the first bulleted item ending in "specified." to reposition the insertion point
Step 3	*Click*	the Insert Discussion in the Document button on the Web Discussions toolbar
Step 4	*Key*	Goals in the Discussion subject: text box
Step 5	*Key*	Doesn't Yong's group have responsibility for setting warehouse goals? in the Discussion text: text box
Step 6	*Click*	OK

The inline discussion item icon appears at the end of the bulleted text and the Discussion pane opens. Your screen should look similar to Figure 3-8.

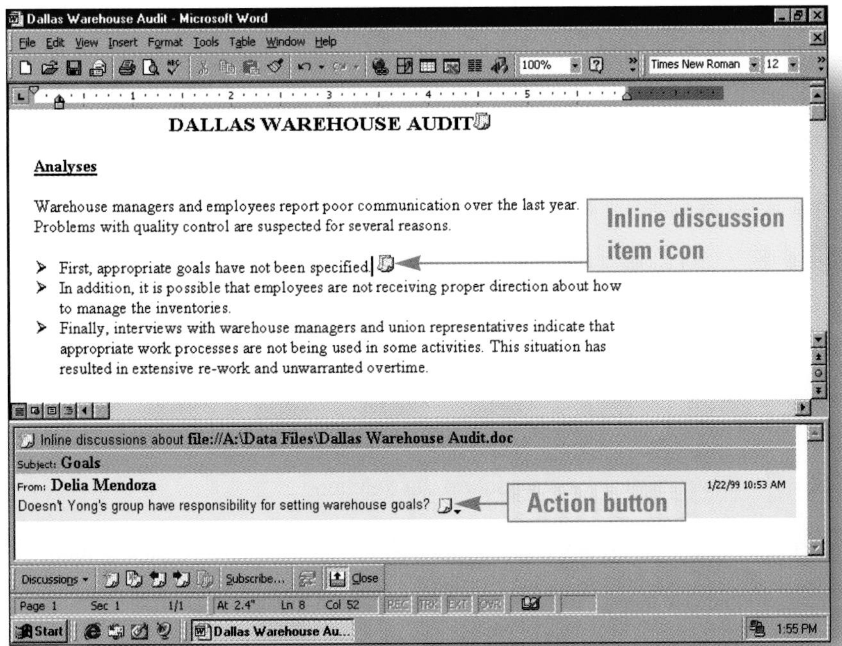

FIGURE 3-8
Inline Discussion Item

Step 7	*Click*	the Show/Hide Discussion Pane button on the Web Discussions toolbar to close the Discussion pane

CAUTION TIP

You can modify a document that contains threaded discussions. If you make changes in an area that is not associated with a discussion item, the inline and general discussions are not affected. If you change or delete part of the document associated with a discussion item, any inline discussions are deleted but general discussions are not affected. If you move, rename, or delete a document, all inline and general discussions are lost.

Others in the workgroup can now open the *Dallas Warehouse Audit* document, log on to the discussion server, and review the inline and general discussion items. They can reply to existing items and create new items. They can edit or delete any discussion items they create. Now assume you are a different member of the workgroup and you just opened the *Dallas Warehouse Audit* document, logged on to the discussion server, and want to participate in the discussion. To thread a reply to the inline discussion item at the end of the bulleted list:

Step 1	***Press***	the CTRL + HOME keys to move the insertion point to the top of the document
Step 2	***Click***	the Next button twice on the Web Discussions toolbar to select the second discussion item and open the Discussion pane
Step 3	***Click***	the Action button in the Discussion pane
Step 4	***Click***	Reply
Step 5	***Key***	Yong's group is currently understaffed and behind schedule. in the Discussion text: text box
Step 6	***Click***	OK to thread your reply immediately below the original discussion item
Step 7	***Close***	the Discussion pane

When discussion items are no longer useful, you can delete them. To open the Discussion pane and delete the discussion items:

Step 1	***Double-click***	the general discussions item at the end of the document title to open the Discussion pane and view the discussion item
Step 2	***Click***	the Action button
Step 3	***Click***	Delete
Step 4	***Click***	Yes to confirm the deletion
Step 5	***Click***	the Next button on the Web Discussions toolbar
Step 6	***Delete***	the first inline discussion item
Step 7	***Delete***	the second inline action item
Step 8	***Click***	Close on the Web Discussions toolbar to close the discussions session
Step 9	***Close***	the Word application and the document without saving any changes

CAUTION TIP

Selecting and deleting the discussion item icons in a document does not remove the discussion items from the server.

QUICK TIP

Users can subscribe to an e-mail notice of changes to folders and documents stored on a server that also has the Office Server Extension software installed. When you subscribe to a folder or document, you can be notified when a new document is added to the folder, when a document is modified, renamed, moved, or deleted, or whenever a discussion item is added to or deleted from a document. You select the notification period: Within a few minutes, Once a day, or Once a week. For more information on Web Subscriptions, see online Help.

Summary

- You can work with others to complete tasks using Office applications' online collaboration tools: NetMeeting and Web Discussions.
- You can use the NetMeeting conferencing software directly from inside Office applications to host or participate in an online meeting.
- During an online meeting using NetMeeting, participants can take turns editing the current document when the meeting's host turns on collaboration.
- When collaboration is turned off, participants in a NetMeeting online meeting can use the Whiteboard.
- You can chat in real-time during an online meeting and, with a sound card and camera, both see and hear other attendees.
- You can schedule a meeting in advance, either using Outlook or from inside Office applications.
- Another way to work with others on a document is to participate in a Web discussion by associating text comments, called discussion items, with a specific document.
- Inline discussion items relate to specific paragraphs, pictures, or tables in a document. General discussion items relate to the entire document. Only the Word application supports inline discussion items.

Commands Review

Action	Menu Bar	Shortcut Menu	Toolbar	Keyboard
Schedule a meeting using NetMeeting inside Office applications	Tools, Online Collaboration, Meet Now			ALT + T, N, M
Schedule a meeting in advance using Outlook inside Office applications	Tools, Online Collaboration, Schedule Meeting			ALT + T, N, S
Participate in Web Discussions from inside Office applications	Tools, Online Collaboration, Web Discussions			ALT + T, N, W

Concepts Review

Circle the correct answer.

1. Workgroup members:
- [a] always work in the same physical location.
- [b] never travel on business.
- [c] always work independently of each other.
- [d] often work in different physical locations or travel frequently.

2. A participant in an online meeting:
- [a] can turn collaboration on and off.
- [b] controls access to the Whiteboard.
- [c] can save and print to their own hard drive or printer.
- [d] is the person receiving the call.

3. The first time a participant takes control of a document during an online meeting, the participant must:
- [a] open the Chat window.
- [b] click the document.
- [c] double-click the document.
- [d] press the CTRL + HOME keys.

4. NetMeeting participants use the Whiteboard to:
- [a] key real-time text messages.
- [b] share and edit documents.
- [c] add inline discussion items.
- [d] illustrate their ideas and thoughts.

Circle **T** if the statement is true or **F** if the statement is false.

T T 1. To participate in an online meeting, invitees must be running NetMeeting on their computer.

T F 2. When collaboration is turned on, the host of an online meeting always maintains control of the active document.

T F 3. To gain control of a document during collaboration, participants must double-click it.

T F 4. The active document can be printed and saved to any participant's printer, hard disk, or server during an online meeting.

You must be connected to the appropriate directory and discussion servers and have NetMeeting and Outlook running with Exchange server to complete these exercises. Your instructor will provide the server and e-mail address information and any NetMeeting and Outlook instructions needed to complete these exercises.

Skills Review

Exercise 1

1. Open the Word application and the *Dallas Warehouse Audit* document located on the Data Disk.
2. Invite three other people to an online meeting now.
3. Take turns making changes to the document.
4. End the meeting. Close the Word application and document without saving any changes.

Exercise 2

1. Open the Excel application and the *International Food Distributors* workbook located on the Data Disk.

2. Invite four other people to an online meeting next Thursday at 2:00 PM.
3. Open Outlook and read their automatic meeting reply messages.
4. Open the Outlook appointment item created for the message and view the updated attendee information.
5. Delete the appointment item and send a message to all attendees canceling the meeting.
6. Close Outlook. Close the Excel application and workbook without saving any changes.

Exercise 3

1. Open the PowerPoint application and the *International Food Distributors* presentation located on the Data Disk.
2. Create a general Web discussion item using the text "This is an important presentation."
3. Close the Web discussion and the PowerPoint application and presentation without saving any changes.

Exercise 4

1. Open the PowerPoint application and the *International Food Distributors* presentation located on the Data Disk.
2. Reply to the general discussion item using the text "What is the project due date?"
3. Print the discussion items using a command on the Discussions menu.
4. Delete the general discussion items created for the *International Food Distributors* presentation.
5. Close the Web discussion and the PowerPoint application and presentation without saving any changes.

Case Projects

Project 1

As assistant to the accounting manager at Wilson Art Supply, you are asked to find out how to select a discussion server. Open the Word application and use the Office Assistant to search for discussion server topics using the keywords "Web discussions" and select the appropriate topic from the Office Assistant balloon. Review the topic and write down the instructions for selecting a discussion server.

Project 2

You work in the marketing department at International Hair Concepts, a company that imports professional hairdresser supplies. Your department is going to start scheduling online meetings to collaborate on Word documents and you want to be prepared for potential problems. Open the Word application and use the Office Assistant to find the "troubleshoot online meetings" topic. Write down a list of potential problems and their possible solutions.

Project 3

A co-worker at Merton Partners, a public relations firm, mentions that you can subscribe to documents and folders stored on a Web server and then be notified when changes are made to them. Using Word online Help to search for Web discussion topics; review the topic, "About subscribing to a document or folder on a Web server." Write a paragraph about how subscribing to documents and folders could help you in your work.

Project 4

The Women's Professional Softball Teams annual tournament is in two months and 30 teams from around the world will participate. The director wants to review the schedule (created in Word) at one time with the team representatives in the United States, England, France, Holland, Germany, China, Argentina, Mexico, and Australia. Write at least two paragraphs recommending an online collaboration tool and explaining why this is the best choice.

Introduction to the Internet and the World Wide Web

Learning Objectives

- Describe the Internet and discuss its history
- Connect to the Internet
- Recognize the challenges to using the Internet
- Use Internet Explorer
- Use directories and search engines

chapter four

Chapter Overview

Millions of people use the Internet to shop for goods and services, listen to music, view artwork, conduct research, get stock quotes, keep up-to-date with current events, and send e-mail. More and more people are using the Internet at work and at home to view and download multimedia computer files containing graphics, sound, video, and text. In this chapter you learn about the origins of the Internet, how to connect to the Internet, how to use the Internet Explorer Web browser, and how to access pages on the World Wide Web.

4.a What Is the Internet?

CAUTION TIP

The activities in this chapter assume you are using the Internet Explorer Web browser versions 4.0 or 5.0. If you are using an earlier version of Internet Explorer or a different Web browser, your instructor may modify the following activities.

To understand the Internet, you must understand networks. A **network** is simply a group of two or more computers linked by cable or telephone lines. The linked computers also include a special computer called a **network server** that is used to store files and programs that everyone on the network can access. In addition to the shared files and programs, networks enable users to share equipment, such as a common network printer. See Figure 4-1.

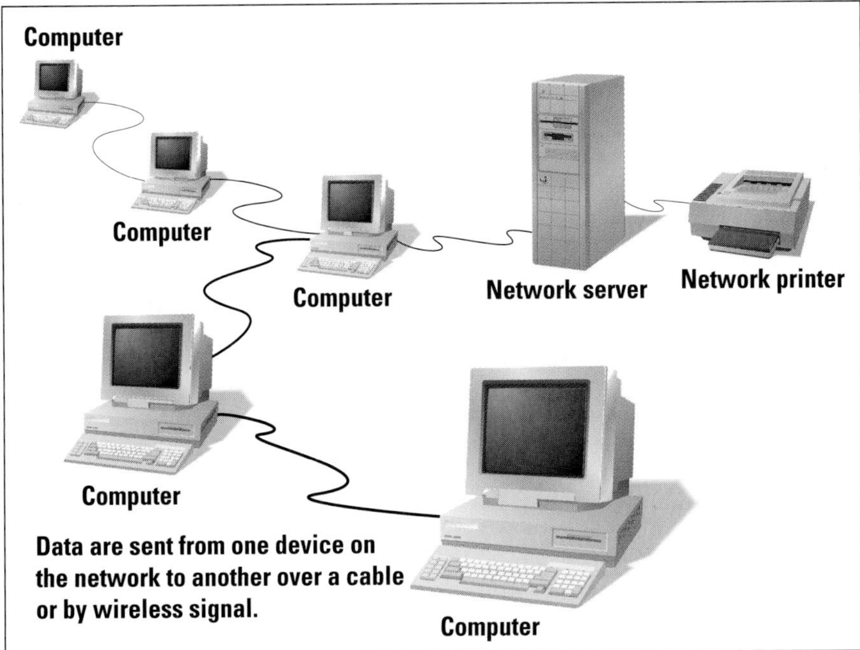
Computer
Computer
Computer
Network server
Network printer
Computer
Data are sent from one device on the network to another over a cable or by wireless signal.
Computer

FIGURE 4-1
Computer Network

The **Internet** is a worldwide collection of computer networks that enables users to view and transfer information between computers. For example, an Internet user in California can retrieve (or **download**) files from a computer in Canada quickly and easily. In the same way, an Internet user in Australia can send (or **upload**) files to another Internet user in England. See Figure 4-2.

The Internet is not a single organization, but rather a cooperative effort by multiple organizations managing a variety of computers.

A Brief History of the Internet

The Internet originated in the late 1960s, when the United States Department of Defense developed a network of military computers called the **ARPAnet**. Quickly realizing the usefulness of such a network,

FIGURE 4-2
The Internet

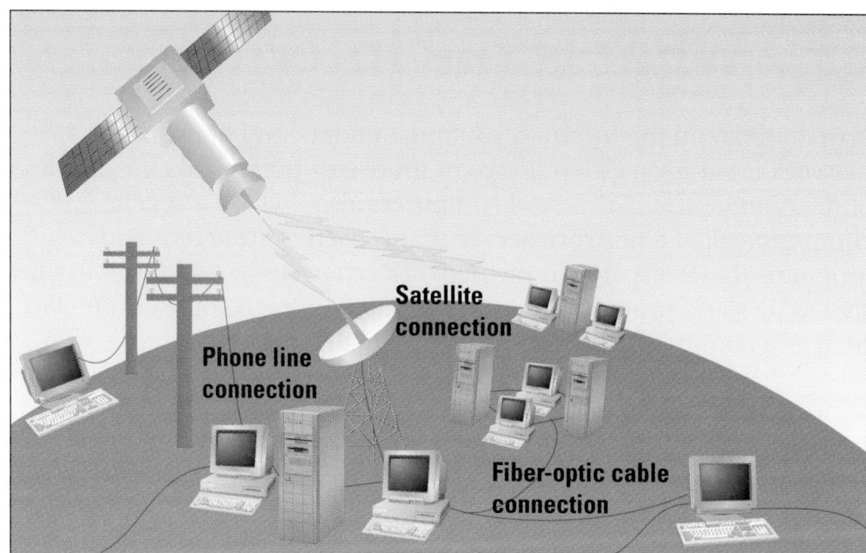

researchers at colleges and universities soon began using it to share data. In the 1980s the military portion of the early Internet became a separate network called the **MILNET**. Meanwhile the National Science Foundation began overseeing the remaining non-military portions, which it called the **NSFnet**. Thousands of other government, academic, and business computer networks began connecting to the NSFnet. By the late 1980s, the term Internet became widely used to describe this huge worldwide "network of networks."

Services Available on the Internet

You find a wide variety of services on the Internet. Table 4-1 explains just some of the options. In this chapter, you learn about using a Web browser and accessing pages on the World Wide Web. Your instructor may provide additional information on other Internet services in the list.

CAUTION TIP

During peak day and evening hours, millions of people are connecting to the Internet. During these hours, you may have difficulty connecting to your host computer or to other sites on the Internet.

4.b Connecting to the Internet

To connect to the Internet you need some physical communication medium connected to your computer, such as network cable or a modem. You also need a special communication program that allows your computer to communicate with computers on the Internet and a Web browser program, such as Microsoft Internet Explorer 5, that allows you to move among all the Internet resources. See Figure 4-3.

TABLE 4-1
Internet Services

Category	Name	Description
Communication	E-mail	Electronic messages sent or received from one computer to another
	Newsgroups	Electronic "bulletin boards" or discussion groups where people with common interests (such as hobbyists or members of professional associations) post messages (called **articles**) that participants around the world can read and respond to
	Mailing Lists	Similar to Newsgroups, except that participants exchange information via e-mail
	Chat	Online conversations in which participants key messages and receive responses on their screen within a few seconds
File Access	FTP	Sending (uploading) or receiving (downloading) computer files via the File Transfer Protocol (FTP) communication rules
Searching Tools	Directories	Tools that help you search for Web sites by category
	Search Engines	Tools to help you find individual files on the Internet by searching for specific words or phrases
World Wide Web (Web)	Web Site	A subset of the Internet that stores files with Web pages containing text, graphics, video, audio, and links to other pages

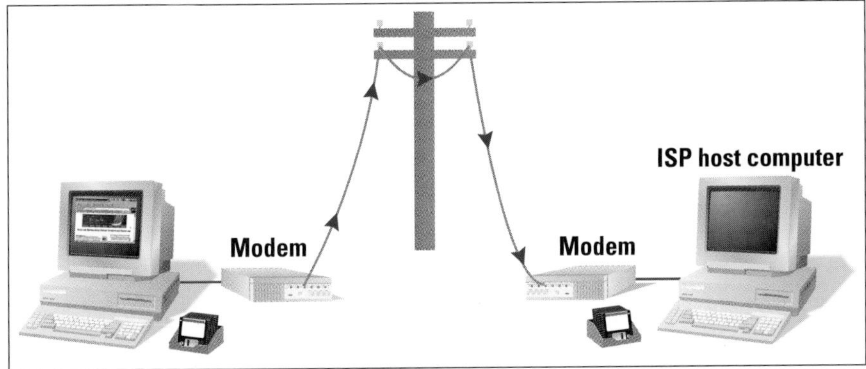

FIGURE 4-3
Internet Connection

Internet Service Providers

After setting up your computer hardware (the network cable or modem) and installing the Internet Explorer Web browser, you must make arrangements to connect to a computer on the Internet. The computer you connect to is called a **host**. Usually, you connect to a host computer via a commercial Internet Service Provider, such as America Online or another company who sells access to the Internet. An **Internet Service Provider (ISP)** maintains the host computer, provides a gateway or entrance to the Internet, and provides an electronic "mail box" with facilities for sending and receiving e-mail. See Figure 4-4.

FIGURE 4-4
Internet Service Providers

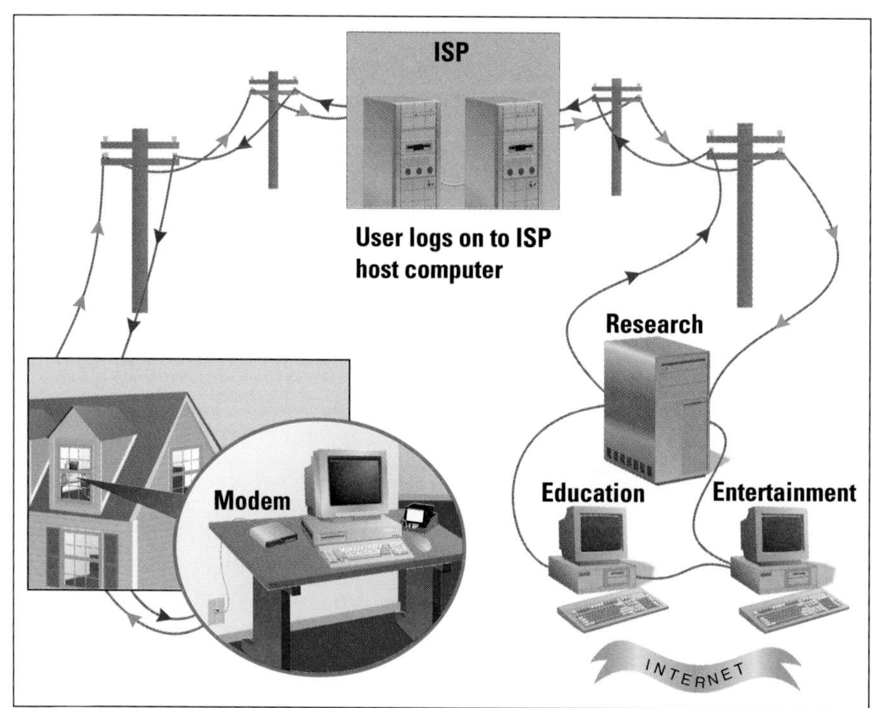

QUICK TIP

USENET is another network that is separate from but closely connected to the Internet. The **USENET** network is a collection of computers that maintain and exchange newsgroup articles or information shared by computer discussion groups.

Large commercial enterprises, colleges, universities, and government institutions may already have a network that is part of the Internet, through which users can connect to the Internet. Many public library systems also provide free Internet access.

Commercial ISPs usually charge a flat monthly fee for unlimited access to the Internet and e-mail services. Many commercial ISPs generally supply the communication program and browser program you need to access the Internet.

Internet Addresses

A unique Internet address or IP address that consists of a series of numbers identifies each host computer on the Internet. Computers on the Internet use these IP address numbers to communicate with each other, but you will probably need to use one only when you install dial-up networking instructions on your computer. The more important address is the host computer's descriptive address. This address specifies the individual computer within a level of organization, or **domain**, on the Internet. For example, a host computer in the math department at a university might be identified as: *raven.math.uidaho.edu* where "raven" identifies the specific computer, "math" identifies the department, "uidaho" identifies the university, and the suffix "edu" identifies that the address is for an educational institution. You'll find that the descriptive host name is much easier to use and remember than the IP address. Table 4-2 identifies the top-level domain (or highest organizational unit on the Internet) names you see as you work with Internet resources. Other top-level domain names are under consideration but not yet in use.

TABLE 4-2
Top-Level Domains

Top-Level Domain	Organization
.com	Commercial enterprise
.gov	Government institution
.edu	Educational institution
.mil	Military institution
.net	Computer network
.org	Other organizations

QUICK TIP

There are several commercial networks that are separate from the Internet. These commercial networks provide users with features such as online newspapers and magazines, chat groups, access to investment activities, computer games, and special-interest bulletin boards as well as Internet access. Popular commercial networks include America Online and the Microsoft Network.

User Names

When you make arrangements to access the Internet via an ISP, you also set up a user name that identifies your account with the ISP. Your user name consists of a name you select and the host's descriptive name. User names can be full names, first initial and last names, nicknames, or a group of letters and numbers. For example, the user name for Beth Jackson who accesses the Internet via a commercial ISP named Decon Data Systems might be: *Beth_Jackson@decon.net* where "Beth_Jackson" is the user's name, and "decon.net" is the descriptive name for the ISP's host computer.

4.c Challenges to Using the Internet

Using the Internet to send e-mail, read and post articles to newsgroups, chat online, send and receive files, and search for information is fun and exciting. However, because people use the Internet all over the world, there is a seemingly endless source of data and information available. The sheer size of the Internet can sometimes be intimidating.

Another potential difficulty is the time it takes for messages and files to travel between computers on the Internet. Communication speeds can be improved by using high-speed modems and special telephone lines. Faster Internet communication via cable is also becoming more widely available.

You should also be aware that the Internet is a cooperative effort, with few widely accepted presentation standards. As a result, the presentation of information on the Internet is varied and inconsistent. Some Web sites are well-designed and easy to use, while some are not. The Internet is a dynamic environment that changes daily with new host computers and Web sites being added and existing ones being removed. This means new or different information is available constantly. Also, old or outdated information may still be available on Web sites that are not properly maintained.

Also, there may be questions about the accuracy of information you find on the Internet. Remember that the Internet is a largely unregulated environment with few, if any, controls over what information is published on the Web or contained in files at FTP sites. It is a good idea to get supporting information from another source before using any information you find on the Internet to make critical business decisions.

Another challenge to using the Internet is the lack of privacy and security for your e-mail and file transmissions. Information sent from one computer to another can travel through many computer systems and networks, where it could be intercepted, copied, or altered. When you access a page on the World Wide Web, it is possible that information such as your e-mail address, which Web pages you view, the type of computer, operating system, and browser you are using, and how you linked to that page can be captured without your knowledge. If you are concerned, you can take advantage of security software that prevents this type of information from being captured.

Certain browser and server programs on Internet computers can encrypt (or scramble) information during transmission and then decrypt (or unscramble) it at its destination. Commercial activities, such as buying an item via credit card or transferring money between bank accounts, can occur in this type of secure environment. However, be advised that much Internet activity takes place in an insecure environment. Government regulations, as well as technological methods to assure privacy and security on the Internet, continue to be developed.

QUICK TIP

Many college and university libraries have Web sites with excellent tips on how to use and evaluate information on the Internet.

INTERNET TIP

To change the start page for the Internet Explorer Web browser, click the Internet Options command on the View menu and then click the General tab. Define the start page by keying the URL in the Address: text box or clicking the Use Current, Use Default, or Use Blank buttons. For more information on designating a start page, see Internet Explorer online Help.

4.d Using Internet Explorer

A **Web browser** is a software application that helps you access Internet resources, including Web pages stored on computers called Web servers. A **Web page** is a document that contains hyperlinks (often called links) to other pages; it can also contain audio and video clips. A **hyperlink** is text or a picture that is associated with the location (path and filename) of another page. To open the Internet Explorer Web browser:

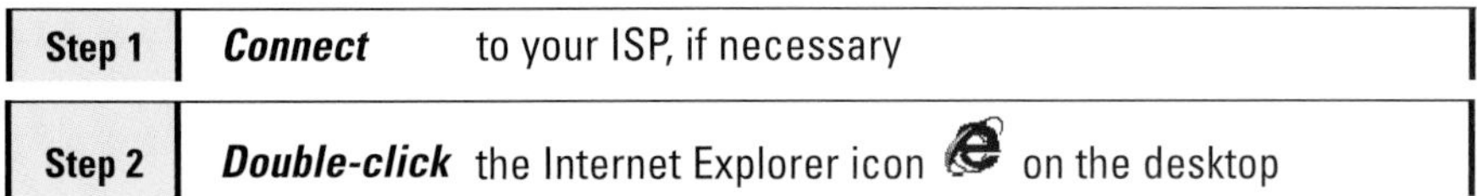

Step 1	***Connect***	to your ISP, if necessary
Step 2	***Double-click***	the Internet Explorer icon on the desktop

When the Web browser opens, a Web page, called the **start page**, loads automatically. The start page used by the Internet Explorer Web browser can be the Microsoft default start page, a blank page, or any designated Web page. Figure 4-5 shows the home page for the publisher of this book as the start page.

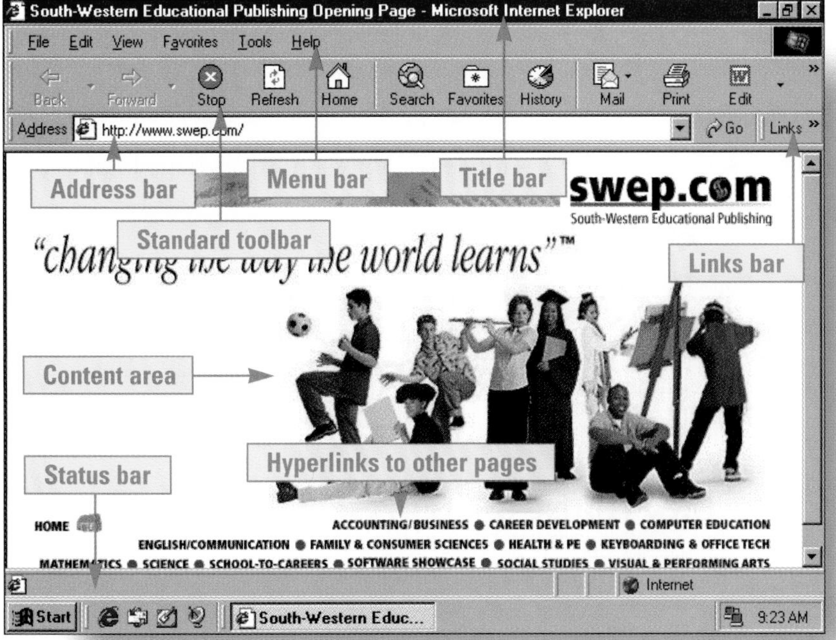

FIGURE 4-5
Internet Explorer Web Browser

Loading a Web Page

Loading a Web page means that the Web browser sends a message to the computer (called a Web server) where the Web page is stored, requesting a copy of the Web page. The Web server responds by sending a copy of the Web page to your computer. In order to load a Web page, you must either know or find the page's **URL** (Uniform Resource Locator)—the path and filename of the page that is the Web page's address. One way to find the URL for a Web page is to use a search engine or directory or you might find a particular company's URL in one of the company's advertisements or on their letterheads and business cards. Examples of URLs based on an organization's name are:

South-Western Educational Publishing	*www.swep.com*
National Public Radio	*www.npr.org*
The White House	*www.whitehouse.gov*

MOUSE TIP

The **Address bar** contains a text box in which you key the path and filename of the Web page you want to load and a drop-down list of recently loaded Web pages and files.

The **Links bar** is a customizable bar to which you can add shortcuts to frequently loaded Web pages.

QUICK TIP

As a Web page loads, the progress bar illustrates the progress of the downloading process. When you place the mouse pointer on a link in the current Web page, its URL appears in the left side of the status bar.

QUICK TIP

When you start keying the URL of a Web page you have previously loaded, the AutoComplete feature automatically adds a suggested URL to the Address bar. You can continue by keying over the suggested URL or you can accept the suggested URL by pressing the ENTER key.

You can try to "guess" the URL based on the organization's name and top-level domain. For example, a good guess for the U.S. House of Representatives Web page is *www.house.gov.*

You can key a URL directly in the Address bar by first selecting all or part of the current URL and replacing it with the new URL. Internet Explorer adds the "http://" portion of the URL for you. To select the contents of the Address bar and key the URL for the U.S. House of Representatives:

Step 1	***Click***	the contents of the Address bar
Step 2	***Key***	www.house.gov
Step 3	***Click***	the Go button or press the ENTER key

In a few seconds, the U.S. House of Representatives page loads. Your screen should look similar to Figure 4-6.

FIGURE 4-6
U.S. House of Representatives Web Page

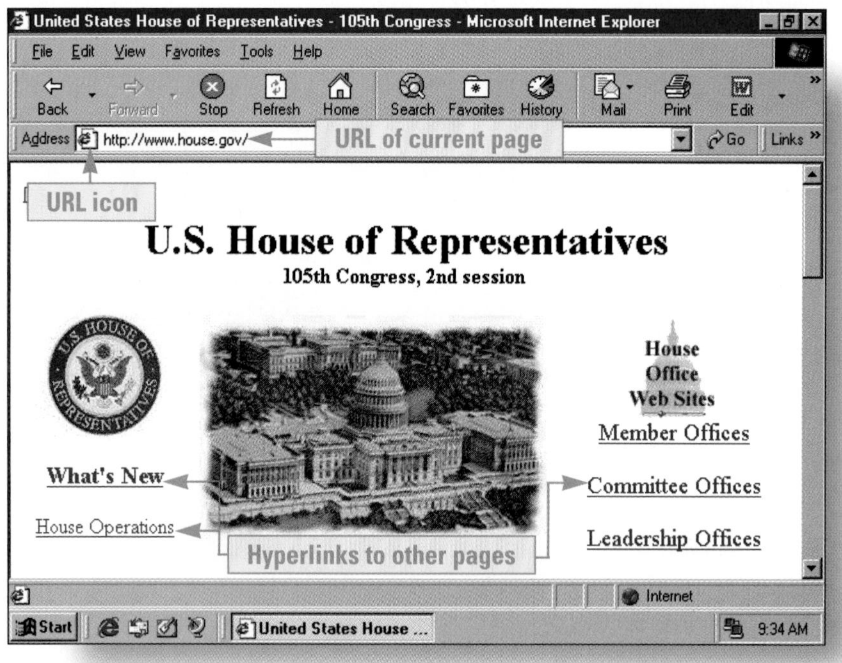

MENU TIP

You can key a URL in the Open dialog box by first clicking the Open command on the File menu.

You can create a favorite by clicking the Favorites command on the menu bar and then clicking Add to Favorites, by right-clicking the background (not a link) on the current Web page and clicking Add to Favorites, or by right-clicking a link on the current Web page and clicking Add to Favorites.

Creating Favorites

Web pages are constantly being updated with new information. If you like a certain Web page or find a Web page contains useful information and plan to revisit it, you may want to save its URL as a **favorite**. Suppose you want to load the U.S. House of Representatives home page frequently. You can create a favorite that saves the URL in a file on your hard disk. Then at any time, you can quickly load this Web page by clicking it in a list of favorites maintained on the Favorites menu.

The URLs you choose to save as favorites are stored in the Favorites folder on your hard disk. You can specify a new or different folder and you can change the name of the Web page as it appears in your list of favorites in this dialog box. To add the U.S. House of Representatives Web page as a favorite:

Step 1	***Click***	Favorites
Step 2	***Click***	Add to Favorites
Step 3	***Click***	OK
Step 4	***Click***	the Home button to return to the default start page

One way to load a Web page from a favorite is to click the name of the favorite in the list of favorites on the Favorites menu. To load the U.S. House of Representatives home page from the Favorites menu:

Step 1	***Click***	Favorites
Step 2	***Click***	the U.S. House of Representatives favorite to load the page
Step 3	***Click***	the Home button to return to the default start page

The Back and Forward buttons allow you to review recently loaded Web pages without keying the URL or using the Favorites list. To reload the U.S. House of Representatives Home page from the Back button list:

Step 1	***Click***	the Back button list arrow on the toolbar
Step 2	***Click***	United States House of Representatives

4.e Using Directories and Search Engines

Because the Web is so large, you often need to take advantage of special search tools, called search engines and directories, to find the information you need. To use some of the Web's numerous search engines and directories, you can click the Search button on the

QUICK TIP

Another way to load a favorite is to use the Favorites button to open the Favorites list in the **Explorer bar**, a pane that opens at the left side of your screen.

CAUTION TIP

Any Web page you load is stored in the Temporary Internet Files folder on your hard disk. Whenever you reload the Web page, Internet Explorer compares the stored page to the current Web page either each time you start the browser or each time you load the page. If the Web page on the server has been changed, a fresh Web page is downloaded. If not, the Web page is retrieved from the Temporary Internet File folder rather than downloaded. To view and change the Temporary Internet File folder options (and other Internet Explorer options), click the Internet Options command on the Tools menu.

> **QUICK TIP**
>
> You can also reload pages from the History folder, which stores the Web pages you load for a specific period of time. You set the number of days to store pages on the General tab in the Options dialog box. Click the History button on the toolbar to open the History list in the Explorer bar.

> **MOUSE TIP**
>
> The Links bar provides shortcuts to various Web pages at the Microsoft Web site. You can also add shortcuts to your favorite Web pages by dragging the URL icon from the Address bar to the Links bar. You can reposition the toolbar, the Address bar, and the Links bar by dragging each one to a new location below the title bar.
>
> You can print the currently loaded Web page by clicking the Print button on the Standard toolbar or the Print command on the File menu.

Standard toolbar to open the Search list in the Explorer bar. To view the Search list:

Step 1	*Click*	the Search button on the toolbar
Step 2	*Observe*	the search list options

Search engines maintain an index of keywords used in Web pages that you can search. Search engine indexes are updated automatically by software called **spiders** (or **robots**). Spiders follow links between pages throughout the entire Web, adding any new Web pages to the search engine's index. You should use a search engine when you want to find specific Web pages. Some of the most popular search engines include AltaVista, HotBot, and Northern Light.

Directories use a subject-type format similar to a library card catalog. A directory provides a list of links to broad general categories of Web sites such as "Entertainment" or "Business." When you click these links, a subcategory list of links appears. For example, if you click the "Entertainment" link you might then see "Movies," "Television," and "Video Games" links. To find links to Web sites containing information about movies, you would click the "Movies" link. Unlike search engines, whose indexes are updated automatically, directories add new Web sites only when an individual or a company asks that a particular Web site be included. Some directories also provide review comments and ratings for the Web sites in their index. Most directories also provide an internal search engine that can only be used to search the directory's index, not the entire Web. You use a directory when you are looking for information on broad general topics. Popular directories include Yahoo and Magellan Internet Guide.

To search for Web pages containing "movie guides:"

Step 1	*Key*	movie guides in the search list text box
Step 2	*Click*	the Search button or press the ENTER key
Step 3	*Observe*	the search results (a list of Web pages in the search list)

The search results list consists of Web page titles as hyperlinks. To load a page from the list, simply click the hyperlink. To close the Explorer bar and search list:

Step 1	*Click*	the Search button on the toolbar

Guidelines for Searching the Web

Before you begin looking for information on the Web, it is a good idea to think about what you want to accomplish, establish a time frame in which to find the information, and then develop a search strategy. As you search, keep in mind the following guidelines:

1. To find broad, general information, start with a Web directory such as Galaxy or Yahoo.
2. To find a specific Web page, start with a search engine such as Alta Vista or HotBot.
3. Become familiar with a variety of search engines and their features. Review each search engine's online Help when you use it for the first time. Many search engine features are revised frequently so remember to review them regularly.
4. Search engines use spider programs to index all the pages on the Web. However, these programs work independently of each other, so not all search engines have the same index at any point in time. Use multiple search engines for each search.
5. **Boolean operators** allow you to combine or exclude keywords when using a search engine. **Proximal operators** allow you specify that search keywords be close together in a Web page. Boolean and proximal operators are words that allow you to specify relationships among search keywords or phrases using (brackets), OR, NOT, AND, NEAR, and FOLLOWED BY. Not all search engines support Boolean and proximal operators, but use them to reduce the scope of your search when they are available. For example, if you are looking for gold or silver and don't want Web pages devoted to music, try searching by the keywords *metals* not *heavy*. To make sure the keywords are in close proximity use the NEAR or FOLLOWED BY proximal operators.
6. Use very specific keywords. The more specific the phrase, the more efficient your search is. For example, use the phrase "online classes" plus the word genealogy (*"online classes" + genealogy)* rather than simply *genealogy* to find Web pages with information about classes in how to trace your family tree.
7. Watch your spelling. Be aware how the search engine you use handles capitalization. In one search engine "pear" may match "Pear", "pEaR", or "PEAR." In another search engine, "Pear" may match only "Pear."
8. Think of related words that might return the information you need. For example, if you search for information about oil, you might also use "petroleum" and "petrochemicals."
9. Search for common variations of word usage or spelling. For example, the keywords deep sea drilling, deepsea drilling, and deep-sea drilling may all provide useful information.
10. The search returns (or **hits**) are usually listed in order of relevance. You may find that only the first 10 or 12 hits are useful. To find more relevant Web pages, try searching with different keywords.

CAUTION TIP

You get varying results when using several search engines or directories to search for information on the same topic. Also, search tools operate according to varying rules. For example, some search engines allow only a simple search on one keyword. Others allow you to refine your search by finding words within quotation marks together, by indicating proper names, or by using special operators such as "and," "or," and "not" to include or exclude search words. To save time, always begin by reviewing the search tool's online Help directions, then proceed with your search.

After you find the desired information, "let the user beware!" Because the Web is largely unregulated, anyone can put anything on a Web page. Evaluate carefully the credibility of all the information you find. Try to find out something about the author and his or her credentials, or the about validity of the origin of the information.

Summary

- A network is a group of two or more computers linked by cable or telephone lines and the Internet is a worldwide "network of networks."
- The Internet began in the late 1960s as the military Internet ARPAnet. By the 1980s the National Science Foundation assumed responsibility for the non-military portions and the term Internet became widely used.
- The World Wide Web is a subset of the Internet that uses computers called Web servers to store documents called Web pages.
- To access the Internet, your computer must have some physical communication medium, such as a cable or dial-up modem and a special communication program.
- An Internet Service Provider (or ISP) maintains a host computer on the Internet. In order to connect to the Internet, you need to connect to the host computer.
- Each host computer has an Internet address or IP address consisting of a series of numbers and a descriptive name based on the computer name and domain of the host. In addition to the host computer IP address and descriptive name, each user has a name that identifies their account at the Internet Service Provider.
- Large commercial enterprises, colleges, and universities may have a computer network on the Internet and can provide Internet access to their employees or students.
- There are many challenges to using the Internet—including the amount of available information, communication speed, the dynamic environment, lack of presentation standards, and privacy/security issues.
- You should carefully evaluate the source and author of information you get from the Internet and confirm any business-critical information from another source.
- Other external networks related to the Internet are large commercial networks, such as America Online, the Microsoft Network, and USENET.
- You use Web browsers, such as Internet Explorer, to load Web pages.
- Web pages are connected by hyperlinks, which are text or pictures associated with the path to another page.
- Directories and search engines are tools to help you find files and Web sites on the Internet.

Commands Review

Action	Menu Bar	Shortcut Menu	Toolbar	Keyboard
Load a Web page	File, Open			ALT + F, O Key URL in the Address bar and press the ENTER key
Save a favorite	Favorites, Add to Favorites	Right-click hyperlink, click Add to Favorites	Drag URL icon to Links bar or Favorites command	ALT + A, A CTRL + D
Manage the Standard toolbar, Address bar, and Links bar	View, Toolbars	Right-click the Standard toolbar, click desired command	Drag the Standard toolbar, Address bar, or Links bar to the new location	ALT + V, T
Load the search, history, or favorites list in the Explorer bar	View, Explorer Bar			ALT + V, E

Concepts Review

Circle the correct answer.

1. To post messages of common interest to electronic bulletin boards, use:
- **[a]** search tools.
- **[b]** e-mail.
- **[c]** file access.
- **[d]** newsgroups.

2. A network is:
- **[a]** the Internet.
- **[b]** a group of two or more computers linked by cable or telephone wire.
- **[c]** a group of two or more computer networks linked by cable or telephone lines.
- **[d]** a computer that stores Web pages.

3. The Internet began as the:
- **[a]** MILNET.
- **[b]** NSFnet.
- **[c]** SLIPnet.
- **[d]** ARPAnet.

4. Which of the following is not a challenge to using the Internet?
- **[a]** chat groups.
- **[b]** dynamic environment and heavy usage.
- **[c]** volume of information.
- **[d]** security and privacy.

Circle **T** if the statement is true or **F** if the statement is false.

T F 1. An IP address is a unique identifying number for each host computer on the Internet.

T F 2. A host computer's descriptive name identifies it by name and organizational level on the Internet.

T F 3. Commercial networks that provide specially formatted features are the same as the Internet.

T F 4. USENET is the name of the military Internet.

Skills Review

Exercise 1

1. Open the Internet Explorer Web browser.

2. Open the Internet Options dialog box by clicking the Internet Options command on the View menu.

3. Review the options on the General tab in the dialog box.

4. Write down the steps to change the default start page to a blank page.

5. Close the dialog box and close the Web browser.

Exercise 2 

1. Connect to your ISP and open the Internet Explorer Web browser.
2. Open the search list in the Explorer bar. Search for Web pages about "dog shows."
3. Load one of the Web pages in the search results list. Close the Explorer bar.
4. Print the Web page by clicking the Print command on the File menu and close the Web browser.

Exercise 3 

1. Connect to your ISP and open the Internet Explorer Web browser.
2. Load the National Public radio Web page by keying the URL, *www.npr.org*, in the Address bar.
3. Print the Web page by clicking the Print command on the File menu and close the Web browser.

Exercise 4 

1. Connect to your ISP and open the Internet Explorer Web browser.
2. Load the AltaVista search engine by keying the URL, *www.altavista.digital.com*, in the Address bar.
3. Save the Web page as a favorite. Search for Web pages about your city.
4. Print at least two Web pages by clicking the Print command on the File menu and close your Web browser.

Case Projects

Project 1

Your supervisor asks you to prepare a fifteen-minute presentation describing the Internet Explorer toolbar buttons. Review the toolbar buttons and practice using them. Write an outline for your presentation that lists each button and describes how it is used.

Project 2

Your manager is concerned about Internet security and wants to know more about Internet Explorer security features. Click the Contents and Index command on the Internet Explorer Help menu to locate and review the topics about security. Write a note to your manager discussing two security topics.

Project 3 

You are working for a book publisher who is creating a series of books about popular movie actors and actresses from the 1920s to the 1950s, including Humphrey Bogart and Lionel Barrymore. The research director asks you to locate a list of movies on the Web that the actors starred in. Use the Explorer bar search list and the Yahoo directory search tool to find links to "Entertainment." Close the Explorer bar and then, working from the Yahoo Web page, click "Movies" within the Entertainment category, scroll down and click the Actors and Actresses link. Search for Humphrey Bogart in the Actors and Actresses portion of the database. Link to the Web page that shows the filmography for Humphrey Bogart. Print the Web page that shows all the movies he acted in. Use the History list to return to the Actors and Actresses search page. Search for Lionel Barrymore, link to and print the filmography for him. Close the Internet Explorer Web browser.

Project 4 

You are the new secretary for the Business Women's Forum. The association's president asked you to compile a list of Internet resources. Connect to your ISP, open Internet Explorer, and search for pages containing the keywords "women in business" (including the quotation marks). From the search results, click the Web page title link of your choice. Review the new Web page and its links. Create a favorite for that page. Use the Back button list to reload the search results and click a different Web page title from the list. Review the Web page and its links. Create a favorite for the Web page. Load and review at least five pages. Return to the default home page. Use the Go menu and the History bar to reload at least three of the pages. Print two of the pages. Delete the favorites you added, and then close Internet Explorer.

Sharing Workbooks with Others

Chapter Overview

Changes in today's software reflect the way the business world works. Documents are shared between departments and among coworkers. Excel workbooks can be edited simultaneously by many different people connected to a network. During the editing process, Excel keeps track of all changes made to a workbook. Workbooks can be distributed electronically, then merged into a single workbook after several people make modifications. You can add comments to cells to clarify results or add an informative note.

Case profile

Each department of Sweet Tooth is responsible for tracking data pertinent to the department. Sales maintains information on how many units are sold and works with production and management to set pricing for each item. At the beginning of each year, you set up a Projected Profit workbook, with estimated income and expense figures. By sharing your workbook, the other departments can update your workbook with real figures as they become available. You can see who made what changes and when, and choose whether to accept those changes.

Learning Objectives

- Protect worksheets and workbooks and use passwords
- Share a workbook
- Track changes
- Change workbook properties
- Merge workbooks
- Create, edit, and remove comments

chapter twelve

12.a Protecting Worksheets and Workbooks and Using Passwords

When sharing a workbook, you may want to prevent other users from changing the data or formatting in that workbook. You do this by enabling workbook protection. If security is a concern, you can add a password to your workbooks as well. You need to distribute the *Sweet Tooth Projected Profit 2000* workbook to several managers in the company. You would like to protect the workbook from unnecessary changes by retaining the work you've done.

To open the workbook:

Step 1	***Open***	the *Sweet Tooth Projected Profit 2000* workbook on your Data Disk
Step 2	***Save***	the workbook as *Sweet Tooth Projected Profit 2000 Revised* in your Data Files folder

Excel provides two ways to protect individual cells from being altered. **Hiding** cells prevents the formula from appearing in the Formula Bar when a user clicks the cell, but still calculates the result as usual. **Locking** cells prevents other users from changing them. To set these options, you use the Format Cells Dialog box, then enable worksheet protection.

To set cell protection options:

Step 1	***Select***	cells B6:F10 and cell F5
Step 2	***Press***	the CTRL + 1 keys to open the Format Cells dialog box
Step 3	***Click***	the Protection tab
Step 4	***Click***	the check box next to Hidden
Step 5	***Click***	OK

The Locked check box is selected by default. Neither option affects the selected cells until you protect the worksheet.

To apply worksheet protection:

Step 1	*Click*	Tools
Step 2	*Point to*	Protection
Step 3	*Click*	Protect Sheet

The Protect Sheet options allow you to protect cell contents, drawing objects, and scenarios. If security is an issue, you can apply a password to prevent anyone who does not have that password from changing the settings.

To apply a password:

Step 1	*Key*	your first name in the Password box (use lowercase letters)

As you enter your password, an asterisk (*) replaces each letter you type, as a security measure.

Step 2	*Click*	OK

Excel prompts you to reenter your password to ensure that you entered it correctly. Passwords are case-sensitive, so *Your Name* is not the same password as *your name*.

Step 3	*Key*	your first name again, exactly as you keyed it before
Step 4	*Click*	OK
Step 5	*Click*	cell F5

Notice you can no longer see the formula in the Formula Bar.

QUICK TIP

You can protect either individual worksheets or the entire workbook. In protecting a workbook, you prevent users from inserting, moving, or deleting worksheets, or even opening the workbook. On the Tools menu, point to Protection, then click Protect Workbook. You can add an optional password, if necessary.

CAUTION TIP

Be sure to remember your password. If you forget it, you may not be able to access your workbook.

Step 6	*Press*	any letter key to change the contents of the cell

Excel notifies you that the cell is protected.

Step 7	*Click*	OK

To remove worksheet protection:

Step 1	*Click*	Tools
Step 2	*Point to*	Protection
Step 3	*Click*	Unprotect sheet
Step 4	*Key*	your password (your first name) exactly as you entered it previously
Step 5	*Click*	OK
Step 6	*Save*	the workbook

QUICK TIP

You can change your user name with the Options dialog box. Click Options on the Tools menu. On the General tab, key your name in the User name box, then click OK.

12.b Sharing a Workbook

To work more efficiently, you can share workbooks with other people. When **sharing** a workbook, you can track modifications to the workbook. You can share a workbook by routing it to other users via e-mail or by working simultaneously with other users on a network. When you collaborate with others via a network, each user is notified when another user has saved changes. You want to share the *Sweet Tooth Projected Profit 2000 Revised* workbook with other departments to collect final data. To share a workbook:

Step 1	*Click*	Tools
Step 2	*Click*	Share Workbook to open the Share Workbook dialog box
Step 3	*Click*	the check box next to Allow changes by more than one user at the same a time

The Share Workbook dialog box on your screen should look similar to Figure 12-1.

MOUSE TIP

The Advanced tab of the Share Workbook dialog box includes advanced tracking options. For more information about these settings, click the Help button, then click the setting about which you want to learn.

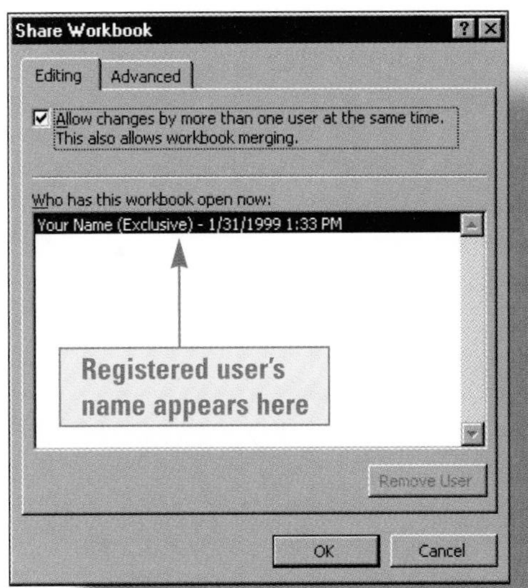

FIGURE 12-1
Share Workbook Dialog Box

> **QUICK TIP**
>
> Limitations exist regarding what changes can and cannot be made to a shared workbook. To obtain a complete list of these limitations, use the Office Assistant.

Step 4	*Click*	OK

An alert box warns you that the workbook will be saved.

Step 5	*Click*	OK

The workbook is saved automatically and the title bar reflects the fact that the workbook is [Shared].

12.c Tracking Changes

Tracking changes allows you to see what changes have been made to a workbook. When you track changes, highlighted borders quickly identify cells whose contents have been edited. When several people work together on the same workbook, each user's changes are assigned a different color, making it easy to see who made changes to different cells. Note that the color assigned to each user's changes may differ each time you open the workbook. To highlight changes:

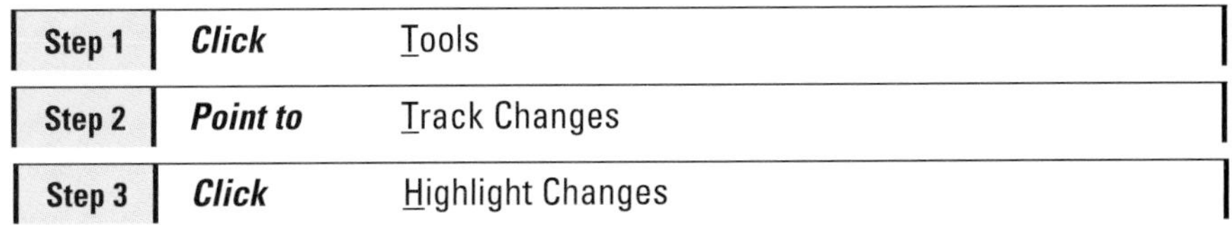

Step 1	*Click*	Tools
Step 2	*Point to*	Track Changes
Step 3	*Click*	Highlight Changes

chapter twelve

The Highlight Changes dialog box, shown in Figure 12-2, allows you to select which changes to show.

FIGURE 12-2
Track Changes Dialog Box

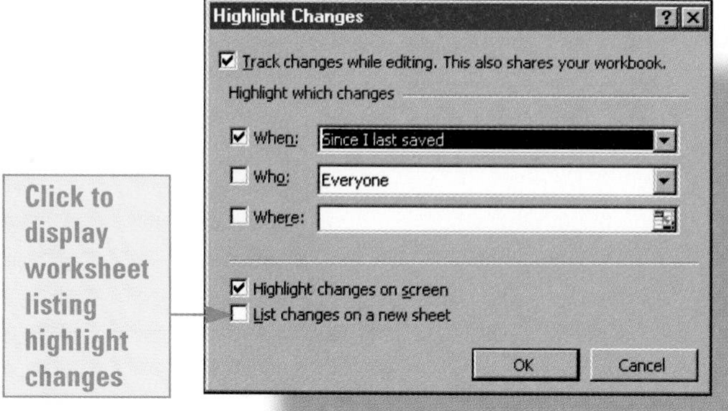

QUICK TIP

When working simultaneously with multiple users, conflicting changes may occur. Excel can either save the latest changes—known as the "whoever saves last, wins" rule—or it can display the Resolve Conflicts dialog box to allow you to select which change to accept. This option appears on the Advanced tab of the Share Workbook dialog box.

Step 4	***Click***	the When: list arrow
Step 5	***Click***	All
Step 6	***Click***	OK

Excel notifies you that it did not find any changes.

Step 7	***Click***	OK
Step 8	***Enter***	10250 in cell B5
Step 9	***Move***	your pointer over cell B5

QUICK TIP

A quick way to enable workbook sharing and track changes simultaneously is to open the Track Changes dialog box, then click the check box next to Track changes while editing.

See Figure 12-3. A ScreenTip indicates the user name of the person who made the change, the date and time when the change was made, and the modification that was made to the cell. The border of the cell changes to a colored border and a small triangle is added in the upper-left corner, indicating that the cell's contents have changed.

FIGURE 12-3
Viewing Changes to a Shared Workbook

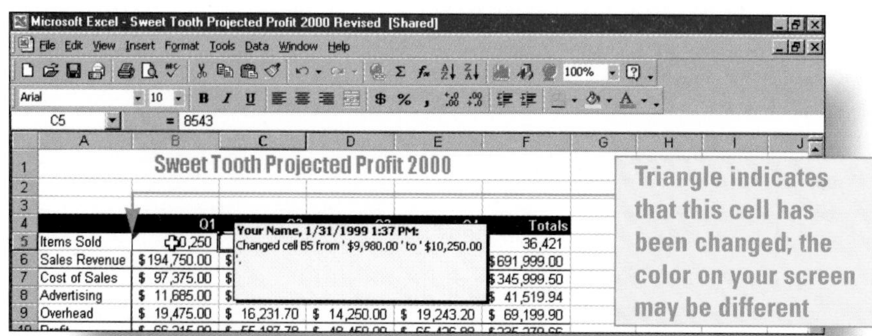

Step 10	*Enter*	10000 in cell C5

You can accept or reject any change to the workbook. To accept or reject changes:

Step 1	*Click*	Tools
Step 2	*Point to*	Track Changes
Step 3	*Click*	Accept or Reject Changes
Step 4	*Click*	OK to save the changes to your workbook

The Select Changes to Accept or Reject dialog box opens. This dialog box allows you to filter the changes made since a certain date, changes made by a certain user, or changes affecting certain cells. The default is to select changes that you haven't reviewed yet.

Step 5	*Click*	OK

When you click OK, the Accept or Reject Changes dialog box opens, allowing you to accept or reject individual or group changes. Your dialog box should look similar to Figure 12-4.

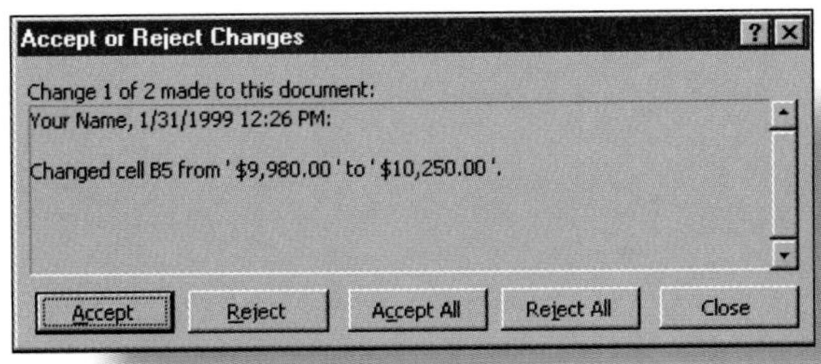

FIGURE 12-4
Accept or Reject Changes Dialog Box

Step 6	*Click*	Accept to accept the first change
Step 7	*Click*	Reject to reject the second change

The value in cell C5 returns to its original value, and the colored triangle and border that indicated a change disappear from the cell.

Step 8	*Save*	the workbook

QUICK TIP

Excel keeps track of changes on a separate worksheet. Normally, this worksheet remains hidden from view, but you can display it by clicking the check box next to List changes on a new sheet in the Highlight Changes dialog box. This history list displays detailed information about all changes made to the workbook because the "track changes" feature was enabled.

QUICK TIP

Click Accept All or Reject All to quickly accept or reject all cells currently being reviewed.

When you disable workbook sharing, you also turn off the track changes feature and erase the History list.

12.d Changing Workbook Properties

Workbook **properties** comprise information about the workbook that can be stored with the workbook. This information includes file size, creation date, company and author name, and date that the workbook was last modified or accessed. You can change some of this information through the workbook Properties dialog box. Before you can change workbook properties, you need to turn off workbook sharing.

To disable workbook sharing:

Step 1	*Click*	Tools
Step 2	*Click*	Share Workbook
Step 3	*Click*	the check box next to Allow changes to remove the check mark
Step 4	*Click*	OK
Step 5	*Click*	Yes after reading the warning about turning off the sharing feature

Now you can change the workbook's properties. To change a workbook's properties:

Step 1	*Click*	File
Step 2	*Click*	Properties
Step 3	*Key*	your name in the Author: box (if it's not already there)
Step 4	*Key*	Sweet Tooth in the Company: box

The dialog box on your screen should look similar to Figure 12-5.

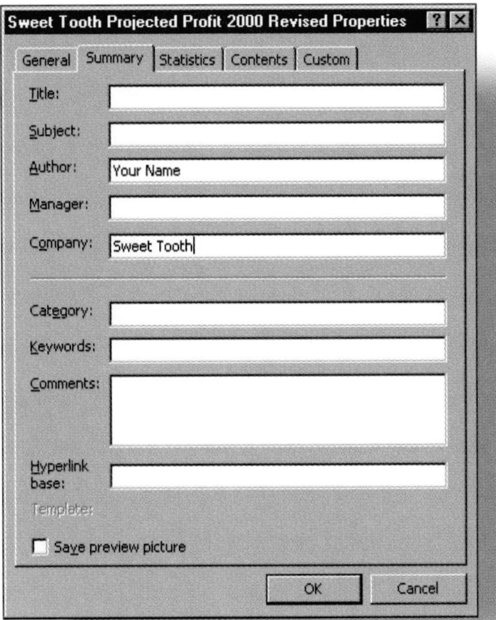

FIGURE 12-5
Workbook Properties Dialog Box

QUICK TIP

You can view a workbook's properties without opening the workbook. In Windows Explorer or in the Open dialog box, right-click any workbook, then click Properties.

Step 5	*Click*	OK
Step 6	*Save & Close*	the workbook

12.e Merging Workbooks

Occasionally, you may need to distribute copies of a shared workbook to users who do not have access to your network. Although you can route the workbook via e-mail, if you must continue editing the workbook simultaneously, this option may not work. In this case, you can save copies of the workbook and distribute them. When other users return these copies to you with their changes, you can incorporate the additional changes into the original workbook by using the Merge workbooks command.

To merge workbooks, you must follow several rules. First, you must create copies of a workbook for which the sharing and track changes features are enabled. Second, each copy must have a unique filename. Third, each workbook must have a common password or no password. Fourth, when you enable workbook sharing, you can specify the length of time for which you want to track changes on the Advanced tab of the Share Workbook dialog box (the default is 30 days). You must merge the copies within this period. For example, if you set the "keep change" history to 30 days, and the workbook copies were made 45 days ago, you can no longer merge the workbooks. If necessary, you can set the "keep change" history to 32,767 days.

When you perform the merge, only the target (workbook receiving the changes) can be open. To create a copy and merge changes:

Step 1	***Open***	the *Sweet Tooth Projected Profit 2001* workbook on your Data Disk

Note that this workbook is designated as being shared.

Step 2	***Save***	the workbook as *Sweet Tooth Projected Profit 2001 Final* in your Data Files folder
Step 3	***Save***	the workbook again as *Sweet Tooth Projected Profit 2001 Revised* in your Data Files folder
Step 4	***Enter***	11000 in cell B5
Step 5	***Enter***	12000 in cell E5
Step 6	***Save & Close***	the workbook
Step 7	***Open***	the *Sweet Tooth Projected Profit 2001 Final* workbook in your Data Files folder
Step 8	***Click***	Tools
Step 9	***Click***	Merge Workbooks
Step 10	***Click***	OK to save the workbook
Step 11	***Select***	the *Sweet Tooth Projected Profit 2001 Revised* workbook in your Data Files Folder
Step 12	***Click***	OK

The changes in the revised (source) workbook become merged into the target workbook. The colored border indicates the changed cells. Your screen should look similar to Figure 12-6.

FIGURE 12-6
Merged Workbooks

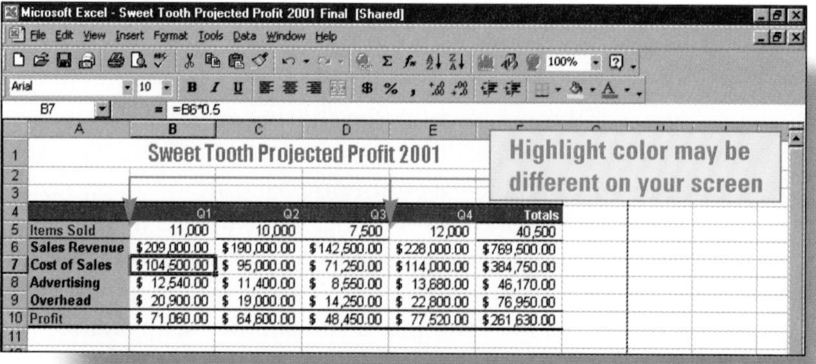

	Q1	Q2	Q3	Q4	Totals
Items Sold	11,000	10,000	7,500	12,000	40,500
Sales Revenue	$209,000.00	$190,000.00	$142,500.00	$228,000.00	$769,500.00
Cost of Sales	$104,500.00	$ 95,000.00	$ 71,250.00	$114,000.00	$384,750.00
Advertising	$ 12,540.00	$ 11,400.00	$ 8,550.00	$ 13,680.00	$ 46,170.00
Overhead	$ 20,900.00	$ 19,000.00	$ 14,250.00	$ 22,800.00	$ 76,950.00
Profit	$ 71,060.00	$ 64,600.00	$ 48,450.00	$ 77,520.00	$261,630.00

Step 13	*Save*	the workbook

12.f Creating, Editing, and Removing Comments

To clarify information in your workbooks, you can add comments to individual cells. Comments might explain how a formula was set up, why you made a certain assumption, or question a colleague about the value of a particular cell. Comments are identified by a small, red triangle in the upper-right corner of a cell.

To add a comment:

Step 1	*Right-click*	cell F10
Step 2	*Click*	Insert Comment

A comment note appears, similar to Figure 12-7.

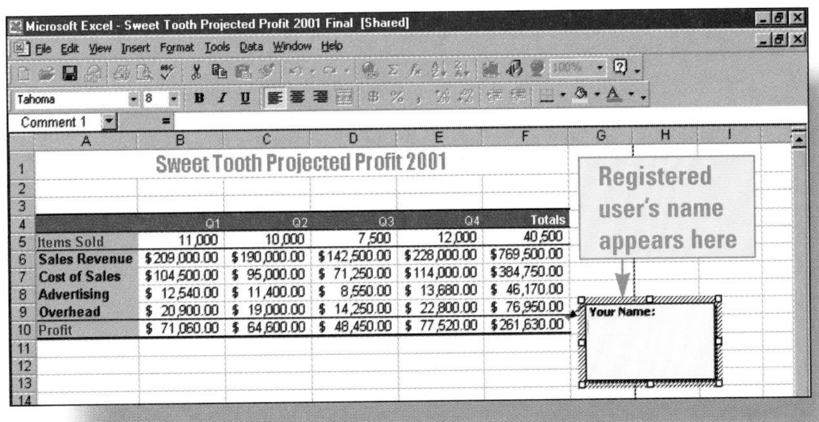

FIGURE 12-7
Adding a Comment

Step 3	*Key*	Merged Sweet Tooth Projected Profit 2001 Revised workbook on DATE
Step 4	*Click*	cell F10 to close the comment

Comment boxes appear when you hover the pointer over the cell.

MENU TIP

To insert a comment, click Comment from the Insert menu.

To view all comments on a worksheet, click Comments on the View menu. The Reviewing toolbar opens, and you can then use this toolbar to add, edit, delete, and display comments.

MOUSE TIP

To delete a comment from a worksheet, right-click the cell with the comment, then click Delete comment.

To read a comment:

Step 1	*Move*	your pointer over cell F10

The comment appears as a ScreenTip. You can also modify comments in a worksheet. To modify a comment:

Step 1	*Right-click*	cell F10
Step 2	*Click*	Edit comment
Step 3	*Replace*	DATE with the current date
Step 4	*Click*	cell F10
Step 5	*Save & Close*	the workbook

QUICK TIP

You can print worksheet comments by printing them at the end of the print report or as they are displayed on the page. On the Sheet tab of the Page Setup dialog box, click the Comments list arrow, then select an option.

Sharing workbooks can be a good way to boost productivity by allowing multiple users to work on and modify the same workbook simultaneously. Tracking changes is an easy way to monitor changes to your workbooks.

Summary

- Protect a workbook from changes by enabling protection. You can also add a level of security by providing password protection to a worksheet or workbook.
- Multiple users can edit a workbook simultaneously on a network. While a workbook is shared, certain features remain unavailable, such as chart and drawing tools.
- Track changes to see which modifications have been made and who made them.
- Merge workbooks to combine information from multiple copies of a shared workbook.
- Add comments to clarify information or to act as a reminder.

Commands Review

Action	Menu Bar	Shortcut Menu	Toolbar	Keyboard
Protect a worksheet	Tools, Protection, Protect Sheet			ALT + T, P, P
Unprotect a worksheet	Tools, Protection, Unprotect Sheet			ALT + T, P, P
Protect a workbook	Tools, Protection, Protect Workbook			ALT + T, P, W
Unprotect a workbook	Tools, Protection, Unprotect Workbook			ALT + T, P, W
Share a workbook	Tools, Share workbook			ALT + T, H
Highlight changes	Tools, Track changes, Highlight changes			ALT + T, T, H
Accept or reject changes	Tools, Track changes, Accept or Reject changes			ALT + T, A
Merge workbooks	Tools, Merge Workbooks			ALT + T, W
Add a comment	Insert, Comment	Insert Comment		ALT + I, M
Edit a comment	Insert, Edit Comment	Edit Comment		ALT + I, E
Delete a comment		Delete Comment		
Hide a comment		Hide Comment		
Show a comment	View, Comments	Show Comment		ALT + V, C

Concepts Review

Circle the correct answer.

1. **When you hide formulas using worksheet protection:**
   [a] formulas do not calculate.
   [b] the formula is displayed but not the calculated value.
   [c] formulas calculate but are not displayed in the Formula Bar.
   [d] formulas display and calculate as usual.

2. **You can identify modified cells using Track Changes by a colored:**
   [a] border and triangle in the upper-right corner.
   [b] border and triangle in the upper-left corner.
   [c] triangle in the upper-right corner.
   [d] triangle in the upper-left corner.

3. **You can identify comments by a colored:**
   [a] border and triangle in the upper-right corner.
   [b] border and triangle in the upper-left corner.
   [c] triangle in the upper-right corner.
   [d] triangle in the upper-left corner.

4. **To select view options for changes, click Tools, then:**
   [a] Merge Workbook.
   [b] Share Workbook.
   [c] Track Changes, Highlight changes.
   [d] Track Changes, Accept or Reject changes,

5. **The History list shows:**
   [a] the results of a Solver operation.
   [b] the results of a Goal Seek operation.
   [c] all changes that have been made to a shared workbook.
   [d] a list of recently accessed files.

6. **When merging workbooks:**
   [a] both workbooks can be open.
   [b] only the target workbook can be open.
   [c] only the source workbook can be open.
   [d] neither of the workbooks has to be open.

7. **You can use comments to:**
   [a] point out important information.
   [b] remind yourself or someone else to do something.
   [c] explain a cell's function or value.
   [d] all of the above.

8. **Workbook properties:**
   [a] cannot be modified.
   [b] contain fields of additional data that are stored with the workbook.
   [c] cannot be displayed unless the workbook is open.
   [d] can be displayed only outside of Excel.

9. **When should you use Merge workbooks instead of another method of viewing changes to a workbook?**
   [a] When several users are sharing the file on the network.
   [b] When another user does not have access to the network, but you must continue working on the workbook at the same time.
   [c] When you need to route a workbook to several users in a certain order.
   [d] Merging workbooks is just as easy as sharing a single workbook.

10. **In Excel, you can protect:**
   [a] worksheets, but not workbooks.
   [b] only selected cells.
   [c] selected cells, entire worksheets, or entire workbooks.
   [d] only worksheets in which changes are highlighted.

Circle **T** if the statement is true or **F** if the statement is false.

T F 1. "Whoever saves last, wins" is one way to deal with conflicting changes in a shared workbook.

T F 2. You must enable sharing before multiple users can access a workbook simultaneously.

T F 3. You can track changes without enabling workbook sharing.

T F 4. To view information about a change made to a shared workbook, you must display the History list worksheet.

T F 5. You can view charts in a shared workbook.

T F 6. Excel automatically saves the workbook before enabling the sharing feature.

T F 7. Merged workbooks can be merged anytime regardless of how many days are specified to track changes.

T F 8. You can change workbook properties while sharing is enabled.

T F 9. You can protect a worksheet or workbook without applying a password.

T F 10. To merge workbooks, you must merge copies of a shared workbook.

Skills Review

Exercise 1

1. Create a new workbook.
2. Enter the information shown in the table below. (Enter Division in cell A1.)

Division	Sales Rep	Total Sales
East		
East		
East		
East		
West		
West		
West		
West		
North		
North		
North		
North		
South		
South		
South		
South		

3. Save the workbook as *Division Sales.*
4. Share the workbook.
5. Save the workbook and print it.

Exercise 2 

1. Open the *Division Sales* workbook that you created in Exercise 1.
2. Enable track changes and set the When option to All.
3. In column B, add fictitious sales representative names for each division.
4. In column C, create fictitious sales data between $1,000 and $5,000.
5. Save the workbook as *Division Sales 1* and print it.

Exercise 3

1. Open the *Division Sales 1* workbook that you created in Exercise 2.
2. Display the change History list. (*Hint:* Use the Track Changes dialog box, and make sure the When: list is set to All.)
3. Print the History worksheet.
4. Save the workbook. Note that when you save the workbook, the History list becomes hidden again.

Exercise 4 

1. Open the *Division Sales 1* workbook that you created in Exercise 2.
2. Save the workbook as *Division Sales 2*.
3. Disable workbook sharing.
4. Add a title to the workbook properties, change the Author name to your name, and change the company name to Sweet Tooth.
5. Save the workbook and print it.

Exercise 5 

1. Open the *Division Sales 2* workbook that you created in Exercise 4.
2. Protect the worksheet, and add your last name in small caps as the password.
3. Try to change the value in cell C2 to $3,000.00.
4. Disable worksheet protection, and change the value of cell C2 to $3,000.00.
5. Save the workbook as *Division Sales 3*.

Exercise 6 

1. Open the *Division Sales 3* workbook that you created in Exercise 5.
2. Add a comment to the name of any sales representative who made less than $2,000. Ask for information from the division managers regarding how the sales representative has performed historically. Ask for recommendations on the sales representative's future with the company.
3. Save the workbook as *Division Sales 4*.
4. Enable workbook sharing.
5. E-mail the workbook to yourself as an attachment.

Exercise 7 

1. You should receive an e-mail containing an attached workbook from Exercise 6. (*Hint:* Use your e-mail program to send/receive messages.)
2. Read the comments in the workbook.
3. In column D, write a response comment suggesting future action for each sales representative.
4. Save the workbook with the new name *Division Sales 4a,* and e-mail the modified workbook back to yourself. (Be sure to close this workbook in Excel.)

Exercise 8 

1. If the *Division Sales 4a* workbook is still open, close it.
2. Open the *Division Sales 4* workbook that you created in Exercise 6.
3. After you receive the workbook *Division Sales 4a* that you sent to yourself as an e-mail attachment, merge the *Division Sales 4a* workbook into the *Division Sales 4* workbook.
4. Print the workbook with the comments at the end of the report.
5. Save the workbook as *Division Sales Recommendations.*

Case Projects

Project 1 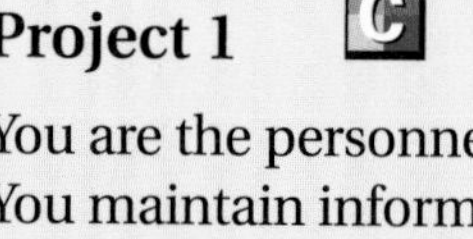

You are the personnel manager for a small company. You maintain information about the company's employees using a worksheet. Create a workbook with fictitious names, home phone numbers, and Social Security numbers for 10 employees. You want to prevent unauthorized users from viewing the contents of this workbook. In addition to protecting worksheets and workbooks, you can add a password to keep users from opening a workbook when you save the file. Use Save As from the File menu to save your workbook as *Employee Info*. Before clicking save, click the Tools menu, then General Options. Add a password consisting of your first name in uppercase letters in the Password to open box.

Project 2 

Your boss is concerned about securing information contained in some workbooks that you are sharing with other staff members. Use the Office Assistant to research how to limit what others can see and change in a shared workbook. Write a half-page summary of your findings, including any steps necessary to hide or protect portions of a workbook from other users. Name your document *Securing Workbook Information.doc.*

Project 3 

As a small business owner just learning Excel, you would like to take a class to help you become familiar with this program more rapidly. Use the Internet to search for businesses offering Excel training in your area. Print a Web page containing contact information for a company near you.

Project 4 

You are looking for a new job where you can apply your Excel skills. Use the Internet to search for jobs (*Hint:* Search for Job Sites first) where Excel is a required skill. Print at least two job descriptions that sound intriguing.

Project 5 

Play a game of Othello using a shared Excel workbook. Open the *Othello* workbook on your Data Disk. Share the workbook, then start a game of Othello. View comments for instructions or ask someone who knows how to play Othello for help. Make sure that both players save their workbooks after each player's turn ends.

Project 6 

You are in charge of documenting and managing workbook files created in your company. You use file properties to make it easy for others to find out information without opening the workbook. Using at least two of the workbooks you created in this chapter or in one of the Skills Review Exercises, edit the file properties by adding a Title, Subject, and Keywords to the workbook file. Save and close the workbooks with new filenames. Open the Open dialog box, click Tools, then click Find to use the Find dialog box to search for one of the keywords you entered in one of the Properties dialog boxes. Be sure to select Keywords in the Property: box in the Find dialog box, and be sure the Look in: box lists the folder where you are storing your Data Files.

Project 7 

You work for a large publishing company tracking sales data for the Computer Books division. Create a worksheet with four fictitious book titles and columns to keep track of the sales data for each quarter of the current year. Add fictitious sales data to your workbook for each book in all quarters. Save the workbook as *Book Sales 1*. Enable Highlight Changes. Save the workbook as *Book Sales 2*. Change the sales data in several cells, then save and close the workbook. Open *Book Sales 1* and merge the changes from *Book Sales 2*. Print a history list of the changes you made.

Project 8 

You are a clerk working in the warehouse of a large shipping company. You have created a custom number format for keeping track of items in your warehouse. Create a workbook with a custom number format that automatically inserts several non-numeric characters. Format the column using your number format. Next, add 5–10 items, then add a comment to one of the entries explaining how to enter data using your custom number format. Finally, enable workbook sharing so others can edit the workbook. Save the workbook as *Warehouse Entries*.

Using Lists in Excel

Chapter Overview

Some workbooks in Excel store lists of data, much as a database does. In this chapter, you learn about the components of a list. To ensure proper data entry in a list, you can specify validation criteria for each column. You can use data forms to enter, edit, find, and delete records from a list. Use AutoFilters or advanced filters to view subsets of a list.

Learning Objectives

- Identify components of a list
- Use data validation
- Use the data form
- Apply data filters

Case profile

You have been asked to create a personnel data list to keep track of information about each of Sweet Tooth's employees. By using data validation, you can ensure that other users will enter the appropriate data in each field. Using data forms and filters, you can then locate specific records.

chapter thirteen

13.a Identifying Components of a List

In earlier chapters, you saw examples of lists in Excel. Sometimes these **lists** are referred to as **databases**. A database stores data in a structure called a **table**, similar to a list in Excel. Each row in a data table contains a unique record, and each column contains entries in a particular field. A **field** contains a collection of characters or numbers, such as a person's name or a phone number. The **field name** identifies the contents of that particular field. A group of field entries is known as a **record**. At the top of the list, or data table, is a **header row**, which identifies the field names used in the table.

The *Sweet Tooth Personnel Data* workbook contains several records that you have already entered. This list contains fields for each employee's last name, first-name initial, division, salary, and "Rec. No.," a field that stores a unique record number for each record in the list. To open the workbook:

Step 1	***Open***	the *Sweet Tooth Personnel Data* workbook on your Data Disk
Step 2	***Save***	the workbook as *Sweet Tooth Personnel Data Revised* to your Data Files folder

Figure 13-1 shows the Sweet Tooth Personnel database.

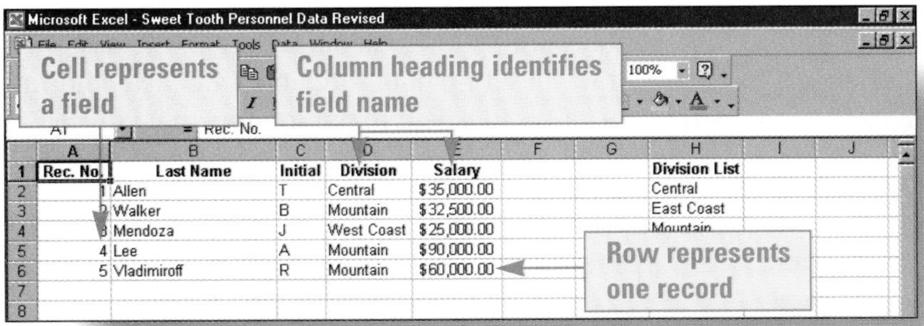

Microsoft Excel - Sweet Tooth Personnel Data Revised

Cell represents a field

Column heading identifies field name

Row represents one record

Rec. No.	Last Name	Initial	Division	Salary			Division List
1	Allen	T	Central	$35,000.00			Central
2	Walker	B	Mountain	$32,500.00			East Coast
3	Mendoza	J	West Coast	$25,000.00			Mountain
4	Lee	A	Mountain	$90,000.00			
5	Vladimiroff	R	Mountain	$60,000.00			

FIGURE 13-1
Typical List in Excel

QUICK TIP

Record numbers are often used in large database tables to speed up indexing and data retrieval. They also provide an easy way to sort the list by the order in which the records were entered into the list.

You must remember some important guidelines when creating lists. First, you should format the header row differently from the rest of the data, using bold, italics, or a different font, so that Excel recognizes that it is the header row and not just another record. Second, the header row should appear as the first row of your list. Don't separate the header row from the first row of data by inserting a blank row. If necessary, use borders or cell fill to distinguish the header row from the data in the list. Third, each field entry in a field must contain the same type of data. For example, don't place a phone number in the Last Name field of a phone directory list. Take note of the following guidelines as well:

- Create only one list per worksheet. If you need more than one list, use a separate worksheet for each new list. This strategy helps you avoid the potential problem of mixing lists when you perform a sort.
- Always leave one column and one row blank on both sides and above and below a list. Excel can then automatically detect the list boundaries, saving you the hassle of selecting the list, or else make sure it starts in row 1 and column A for sorting, outlining, and AutoFormat operations.
- Avoid using spaces at the beginning of a field entry. Spaces affect the sort order of a list, because the space character comes before alphabetic characters. Entries that have spaces as their first character are placed at the top of a sorted list.
- Format data in a column in a consistent manner. Don't make some names bold and others italic.
- Never place critical data to the left or right of a list. When filters are later applied to the list, you may not be able to see important data.
- Always include a record number field so as to give each record a unique record number. This strategy enables you to return the list to its original entry order after you've performed other sort operations.

13.b Using Data Validation

You want to ensure that anyone who uses the *Sweet Tooth Personnel Data Revised* workbook enters the correct data in each field. For example, the Salary field should contain only numerical data. To help the user meet these expectations, you will set up data validation for each column. **Data validation** restricts the entry in a field to parameters that you set. You can, for example, apply data validation to each field in a list to restrict the entry to specific types of data.

You want to limit the entry in the record number field to whole numbers between 1 and 999. To use data validation:

Step 1	*Select*	cells A7:A10
Step 2	*Click*	Data
Step 3	*Click*	Validation
Step 4	*Click*	the Allow: list arrow on the Settings tab

Figure 13-2 shows the Allow: list.

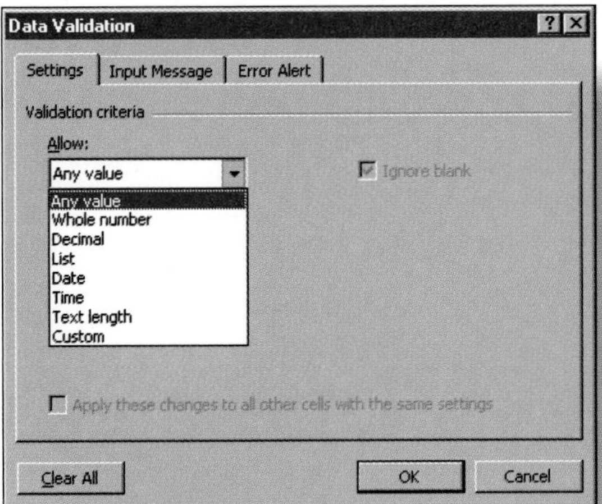

FIGURE 13-2
Allow List on the Settings Tab of the Data Validation Dialog Box

Each choice in the list restricts the data in the selected cells to different types. For example, the Whole number validation option restricts entry to whole numbers, and the Decimal validation option allows entry of any numerical value. The List validation option permits you to supply a list of valid entries from which the user can select one choice from a drop-down list. The Text length validation option allows you to limit the number of characters that can be entered in a field.

Step 5	***Click***	Whole number from the Allow: list

The options on the Settings tab change for each validation option in the Allow list. For whole numbers, you specify an operator (less than, greater than, between, and so on) and minimum and maximum values to restrict which numerical values are permitted.

Step 6	***Select***	between from the Data: list
Step 7	***Key***	1 in the Minimum: box
Step 8	***Key***	999 in the Maximum: box

You want to ensure that every new record receives a record number. By default, Excel does not count blank entries as invalid.

Step 9	***Click***	the check box next to Ignore blank to deselect it

Input messages display entry instructions, to make it easier for the user to understand what should be entered into a field.

To add an input message to the selected cells:

Step 1	*Click*	the Input Message tab
Step 2	*Key*	Record Number in the Title: box
Step 3	*Press*	the TAB key to move to the Input message: box
Step 4	*Key*	Enter a whole number between 1 and 999.

Your dialog box should look similar to Figure 13-3.

FIGURE 13-3
Input Message Tab

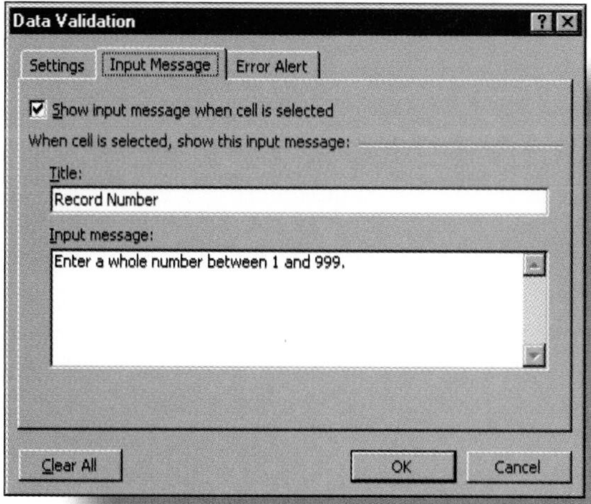

When the user enters invalid data, you can have the worksheet display one of three types of error messages. To set the error messages:

Step 1	*Click*	the Error Alert tab
Step 2	*Verify*	that the Show error alert after invalid data is entered check box is checked
Step 3	*Click*	the Style: list arrow

Each option produces a different type of error message alert box. The Stop style generates an alert box that contains Retry and Cancel buttons. The Warning style alert box contains Yes and No buttons. The Information style alert box contains OK and Cancel buttons. As you will not allow the entry of invalid data into the worksheet, you will prompt the user to enter the correct entry or cancel the operation.

Step 4	*Click*	Stop
Step 5	*Key*	Record Number in the Title: box

Step 6	***Press***	the TAB key to move to the Error message: box
Step 7	***Enter***	You must enter a whole number between 1 and 999.

Your dialog box should look similar to Figure 13-4.

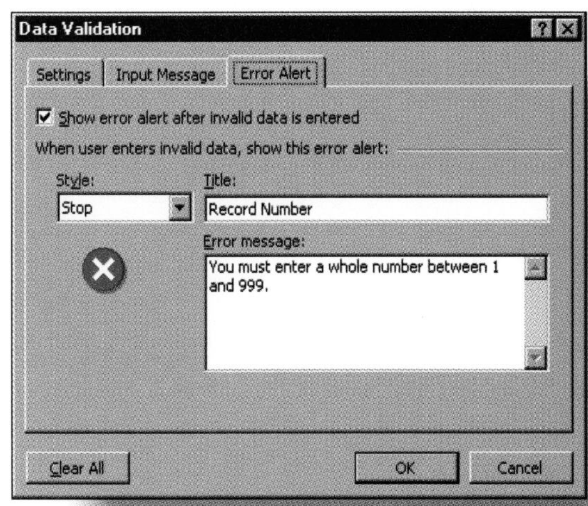

FIGURE 13-4
Error Alert Tab

Step 8	***Click***	OK

The dialog box closes, and the input message that you just created appears near the selected cells. Next, test the new data validation rules. To test data validation:

QUICK TIP

If you have the Office Assistant open, the Input Message appears in an Office Assistant dialog balloon instead of next to the cell.

Step 1	***Activate***	cell A7

The Input Message appears, similar to Figure 13-5.

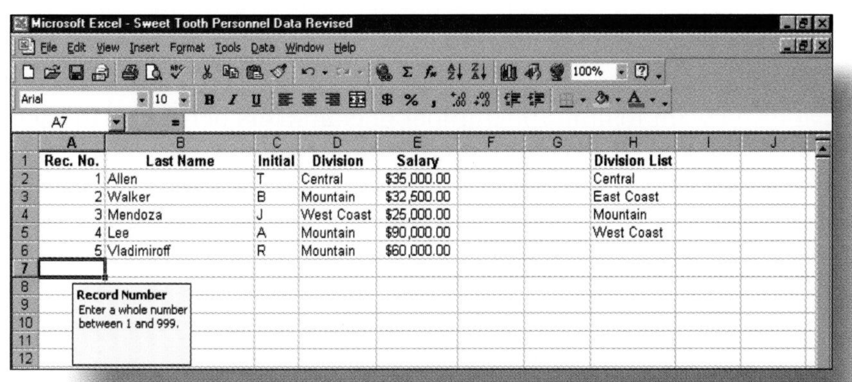

FIGURE 13-5
Input Message

Step 2	*Key*	1000
Step 3	*Press*	the ENTER key

The error message box you created appears, similar to Figure 13-6.

FIGURE 13-6
Invalid Entry Dialog Box

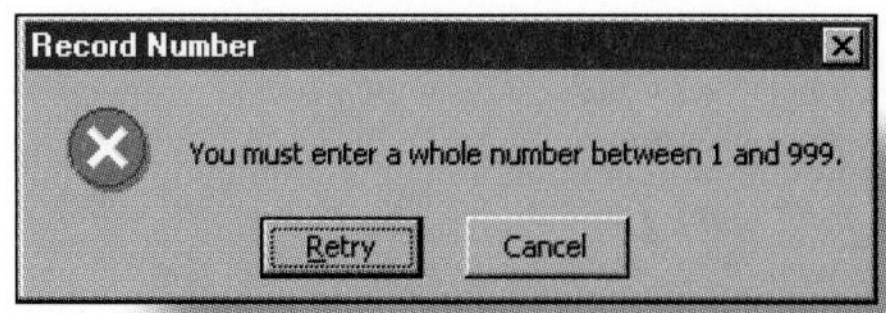

Step 4	*Click*	Retry
Step 5	*Key*	6
Step 6	*Press*	the TAB key

This entry is valid and accepted. Next, you enter validation criteria for each of the other fields. Table 13-1 briefly describes the type of validation criteria you will use.

TABLE 13-1
Setting Validation Criteria

Field Name	Validation Characteristic Settings	Input Message	Error Alert
Last Name	Text length maximum of 20 characters	Yes	Stop
Initial	Text length maximum of 1 character	Yes	Stop
Division	Select from a list	Yes	Stop
Salary	Decimal number should not exceed $75,000 without special authorization	Yes	Information

For the Last Name and Initial fields, you want users to enter only text, and you want to limit the number of characters permitted in each field. To set data validation for the Last Name column:

Step 1	*Select*	cells B7:B10
Step 2	*Click*	Data

Step 3	*Click*	Validation
Step 4	*Click*	the Settings tab
Step 5	*Select*	Text length from the Allow: list
Step 6	*Key*	1 in the Minimum: box
Step 7	*Key*	20 in the Maximum: box
Step 8	*Click*	the Ignore blank check box to clear the check mark
Step 9	*Click*	the Input Message tab
Step 10	*Key*	Last Name in the Title: box
Step 11	*Key*	"Limit last name to 20 characters. Abbreviate if necessary." in the Input message: box (do not key the quotation marks)
Step 12	*Click*	the Error Alert tab
Step 13	*Select*	Stop from the Style: list
Step 14	*Key*	Last Name in the Title: box
Step 15	*Key*	"Please limit last name to 20 characters. Abbreviate if necessary." in the Error message: box
Step 16	*Click*	OK
Step 17	*Enter*	Rawlins in cell B7

QUICK TIP

If you set data validation for a range of cells but later need to update the validation settings, you can have the update apply to all cells with similar data validation settings. Select any cell that contains the data validation setting you wish to change, then open the Data Validation dialog box to modify the setting. On the Settings tab, check the box next to Apply these changes to all other cells with the same settings.

Next, you add the validation criteria for the Initial column. To add the validation criteria for the Initial column:

Step 1	*Select*	cells C7:C10
Step 2	*Open*	the Data Validation dialog box
Step 3	*Select*	Text length from the Allow: list on the Settings tab
Step 4	*Key*	1 in the Minimum: box
Step 5	*Key*	1 in the Maximum: box
Step 6	*Click*	the Ignore blank check box to clear it
Step 7	*Click*	the Input Message tab
Step 8	*Key*	Initial in the Title: box
Step 9	*Key*	"Enter first initial of employee's first name." in the Input message: box

Step 10	*Click*	the Error Alert tab
Step 11	*Key*	Initial in the Title: box
Step 12	*Key*	"You must enter a one-character initial." in the Error message: box
Step 13	*Click*	OK
Step 14	*Enter*	J in cell C7

QUICK TIP

To prevent changes to data validation, choose Protection on the Tools menu, then click Protect Sheet. Verify that the Contents box is checked before you click OK.

The next field, Division, contains only four valid entries. You can create a list of these valid entries from which the user can select. To set list validation criteria:

Step 1	*Select*	cells D7:D10
Step 2	*Open*	the Data Validation dialog box
Step 3	*Select*	List from the Allow: list on the Settings tab
Step 4	*Click*	the Collapse Dialog button in the Source: box
Step 5	*Select*	cells H2:H5
Step 6	*Click*	the Expand Dialog button
Step 7	*Verify*	the In-cell dropdown check box is checked
Step 8	*Click*	the Ignore blank check box to remove the check

Your dialog box should look similar to Figure 13-7.

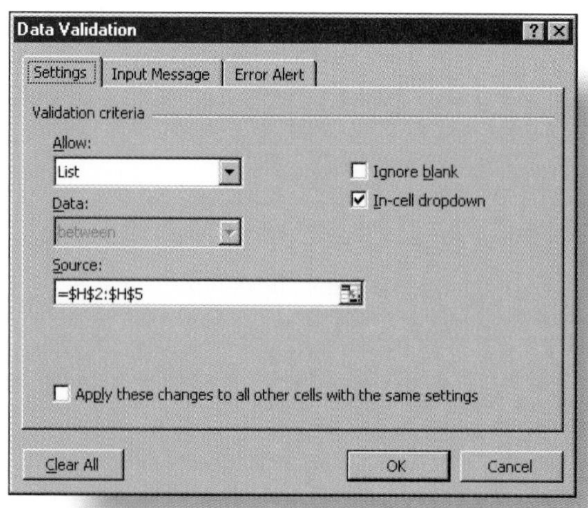

FIGURE 13-7
List Validation Options

Step 9	*Click*	the Input Message tab
Step 10	*Key*	Division in the Title: box
Step 11	*Key*	"Select a Division from the list." in the Input message: box
Step 12	*Click*	the Error Alert tab
Step 13	*Key*	Division in the Title: box
Step 14	*Key*	"You must select an entry from the list." in the Error message: box
Step 15	*Click*	OK
Step 16	*Click*	cell D7
Step 17	*Click*	the list arrow next to cell D7

Your screen should look similar to Figure 13-8.

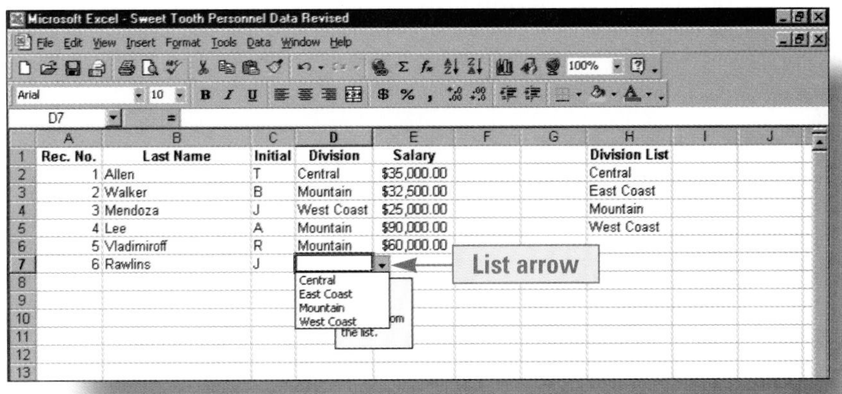

FIGURE 13-8
Using a List to Enter Valid Data in a Field

Step 18	*Click*	East Coast

Using Paste Special to Copy Data Validation Criteria

You do not have to select all cells to which you want to add validation criteria when you set up the data validation. Instead, you can copy the validation criteria using the Paste Special command. Employee salaries are entered as decimal numbers not greater than $75,000; salaries higher than this figure cannot be entered without permission from Amy Lee, Sweet Tooth's president. To enter the validation criteria for the Salary field:

Step 1	*Select*	cell E7

Step 2	*Open*	the Data Validation dialog box
Step 3	*Select*	Decimal from the Allow: list on the Settings tab
Step 4	*Select*	less than or equal to from the Data: list
Step 5	*Key*	75000 in the Maximum: box
Step 6	*Click*	the Ignore blank check box to remove the check
Step 7	*Click*	the Input Message tab
Step 8	*Key*	Salary in the Title: box
Step 9	*Key*	"Enter a salary under $75,000. For salaries over $75,000, get permission from A. Lee." in the Input message: box
Step 10	*Click*	the Error Alert tab

QUICK TIP

To find out more about data validation options, use the Office Assistant.

Because you sometimes need to enter values greater than $75,000, you will use the Information style error alert, which gives you the option of ignoring the validation criteria.

Step 11	*Select*	Information from the Style: list
Step 12	*Key*	Salary in the Title: box
Step 13	*Key*	"Salary must be under $75,000 unless authorized by A. Lee." in the Error message: box
Step 14	*Click*	OK
Step 15	*Click*	cell E7, if necessary
Step 16	*Key*	80000
Step 17	*Click*	the Enter button on the Formula Bar

The Information dialog box displays the error alert message. In this case, you have been authorized to add this salary to the list. Clicking OK accepts the entry; clicking Cancel clears the entry so that you can key another value.

Step 18	*Click*	OK

Next, copy the validation criteria to cells E8:E10. To copy the data validation criteria:

Step 1	*Click*	the Copy button on the Standard toolbar

Step 2	***Select***	cells E8:E10
Step 3	***Right-click***	the selected cells
Step 4	***Click***	Paste Special
Step 5	***Click***	the Validation option button
Step 6	***Click***	OK
Step 7	***Save***	the workbook

Entering Data in a List

You do not have to add data validation to enter data in a list. Nevertheless, data validation is important to ensure that the user enters the appropriate type of data in each field. To enter the rest of the data in the list:

Step 1	***Enter***	the records, as shown in Table 13-2

TABLE 13-2
Additional Records for Sweet Tooth Personnel List

Rec. No.	Last Name	Initial	Division	Salary
7	Munns	R	East Coast	$45,000
8	Greenwood	J	West Coast	$30,000
9	Chin	M	Central	$25,000

When you finish, your screen should look similar to Figure 13-9.

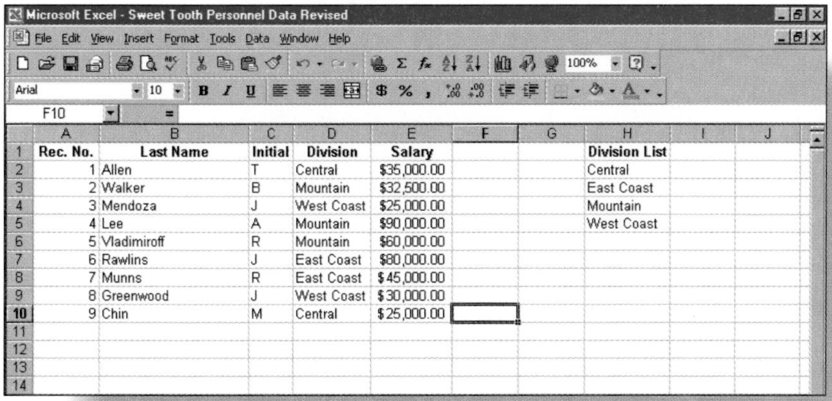

Rec. No.	Last Name	Initial	Division	Salary			Division List
1	Allen	T	Central	$35,000.00			Central
2	Walker	B	Mountain	$32,500.00			East Coast
3	Mendoza	J	West Coast	$25,000.00			Mountain
4	Lee	A	Mountain	$90,000.00			West Coast
5	Vladimiroff	R	Mountain	$60,000.00			
6	Rawlins	J	East Coast	$80,000.00			
7	Munns	R	East Coast	$45,000.00			
8	Greenwood	J	West Coast	$30,000.00			
9	Chin	M	Central	$25,000.00			

FIGURE 13-9
Completed Data List

chapter thirteen

13.c Using the Data Form

An alternative method of entering data in a list is to use a data form. A data form simplifies data entry by allowing the user to enter each field of a record using a simple dialog box, rather than the worksheet itself. You can also use the data form to edit and locate specific records in a list.

Entering Data in a List with a Data Form

You need to add another record to the list. To use a data form to enter a new record:

Step 1	***Activate***	any cell that is part of the list, including the header row
Step 2	***Click***	Data
Step 3	***Click***	Form

The Form dialog box opens, with the worksheet tab name as the title of the dialog box, as shown in Figure 13-10. You can use the scroll bar or the Find Prev and Find Next buttons to scroll through the records.

FIGURE 13-10
Form Dialog Box

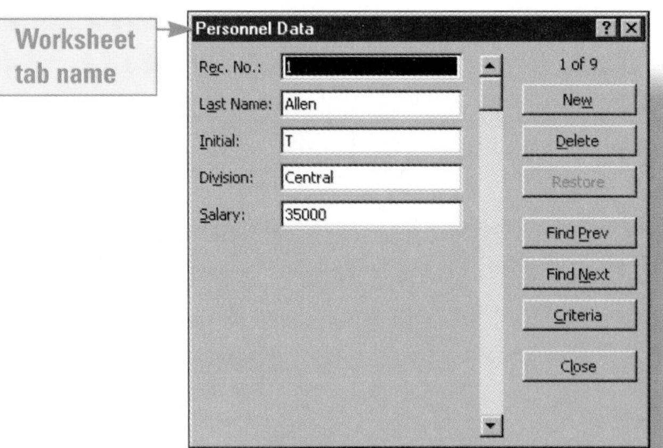

Step 4	***Click***	New
Step 5	***Key***	10 in the Rec. No.: box
Step 6	***Press***	the TAB key
Step 7	***Key***	Tate in the Last Name: box
Step 8	***Press***	the TAB key

Step 9	*Key*	J in the Initial: box
Step 10	*Press*	the TAB key
Step 11	*Key*	Central in the Division: box
Step 12	*Press*	the TAB key
Step 13	*Enter*	65000 in the Salary: box
Step 14	*Press*	the ENTER key

The record is added to the bottom of your list, and a new record is started in the Form dialog box. You can enter a new record at this point or close the Form dialog box.

Step 15	*Click*	Close

CAUTION TIP

One drawback to using the Form dialog box is that data validation criteria are not active with this method of data entry. In other words, you will not see input messages or error alert messages, and the list option is not available.

Finding Specific Records Using the Data Form

The data form allows you to readily locate specific records in a list; however, scrolling through a list of hundreds or thousands to find a certain record would be very time-consuming. You want to review records of Sweet Tooth employees whose annual salaries are $40,000 or more. Using the data form, you can set criteria for the records you want to see. To search for specific records:

Step 1	*Open*	the Form dialog box
Step 2	*Click*	Criteria
Step 3	*Click*	the Salary: box
Step 4	*Key*	>40000
Step 5	*Click*	Find Next

The first record meeting the criteria appears in the Form dialog box.

Step 6	*Click*	Find Next

The next record meeting the criteria appears in the Form dialog box.

Step 7	*Click*	Find Next four more times

QUICK TIP

You can use the Find Prev button to step back through the records meeting the specified criteria.

The computer indicates that no more records meet your criteria by making a sound. To clear the criteria and view all records again:

Step 1	*Click*	Criteria
Step 2	*Click*	Clear
Step 3	*Click*	Form to return to the Form dialog box

Deleting a Record from a List Using the Data Form

Occasionally, you will need to remove records from a list. To delete a record using the data form:

Step 1	*Drag*	the scroll box in the Form dialog box up until 6 of 10 appears in the upper-right corner
Step 2	*Click*	Delete to delete the record for J. Rawlins

MOUSE TIP

You can delete a record by deleting the row in the worksheet or the cells containing the data. Right-click the row number, then click Delete; alternatively, select all cells in the record, right-click the selection, click Delete, then choose the appropriate option.

A confirmation dialog box opens, indicating that the record will be permanently deleted.

Step 3	*Click*	OK

The record is removed from the list.

Step 4	*Click*	Close
Step 5	*Save*	the workbook

13.d Applying Data Filters

Filtering a list allows you to work with a subset of a list. You can use the Find command in the data form to filter the records displayed in the Form dialog box, or you can filter records in the worksheet. When you apply a filter, only those records meeting the specified criteria are displayed. You can format, edit, chart, and print the filtered list. When you have finished, turn the filter off and the rest of the records in the list reappear.

Using AutoFilter

The AutoFilter feature offers a fast, easy way to apply multiple filters to a list. When you apply AutoFilter to a list, a filter list arrow appears next to each of the column labels. Clicking the filter list arrow displays the filter list, which includes the following information:

- Each unique entry in the list
- A Top 10 option that you can customize
- A custom option to apply conditional operators (AND and OR) and logical operators (greater than, equal to, and less than)
- Options to filter for blank or nonblank fields
- An option to show all records

You need to compile a list of the employees in Sweet Tooth's Central division who make less than $40,000 per year.

To apply an AutoFilter:

Step 1	***Activate***	any cell in the list
Step 2	***Click***	Data
Step 3	***Point to***	Filter
Step 4	***Click***	AutoFilter

The AutoFilter list arrows appear next to each column label, as shown in Figure 13-11.

Microsoft Excel - Sweet Tooth Personnel Data Revised

AutoFilter list arrows

D3 = Mountain

	A	B	C	D	E	F	G	H	I	J
1	Rec. N	Last Name	Initi	Division	Salary			Division List		
2	1	Allen	T	Central	$35,000.00			Central		
3	2	Walker	B	Mountain	$32,500.00			East Coast		
4	3	Mendoza	J	West Coast	$25,000.00			Mountain		
5	4	Lee	A	Mountain	$90,000.00			West Coast		
6	5	Vladimiroff	R	Mountain	$60,000.00					
7	7	Munns	R	East Coast	$45,000.00					
8	8	Greenwood	J	West Coast	$30,000.00					
9	9	Chin	M	Central	$25,000.00					
10	10	Tate	J	Central	$65,000.00					

FIGURE 13-11
AutoFilter Applied

Step 5	***Click***	the Filter list arrow in the Division field
Step 6	***Click***	Central
Step 7	***Click***	the Filter list arrow in the Salary field
Step 8	***Click***	(Custom...)

The Custom AutoFilter dialog box opens, as shown in Figure 13-12.

FIGURE 13-12
Custom AutoFilter Dialog Box

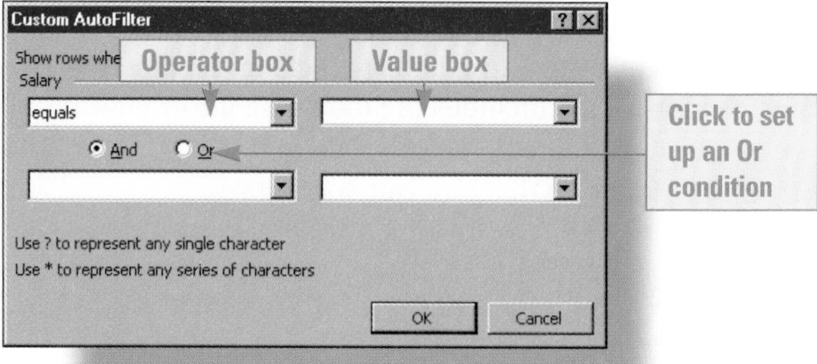

The default in the Custom AutoFilter dialog box is for the And option button to be selected.

Step 9	*Click*	the operator list arrow on the left side of the dialog box
Step 10	*Click*	is greater than or equal to
Step 11	*Click*	the value list arrow on the right side of the dialog box
Step 12	*Click*	$35,000.00
Step 13	*Click*	OK

The list is filtered, as shown in Figure 13-13. Notice that the filter list arrows of the filtered columns and the row headings appear in blue. Filtered rows remain hidden.

FIGURE 13-13
A Filtered List

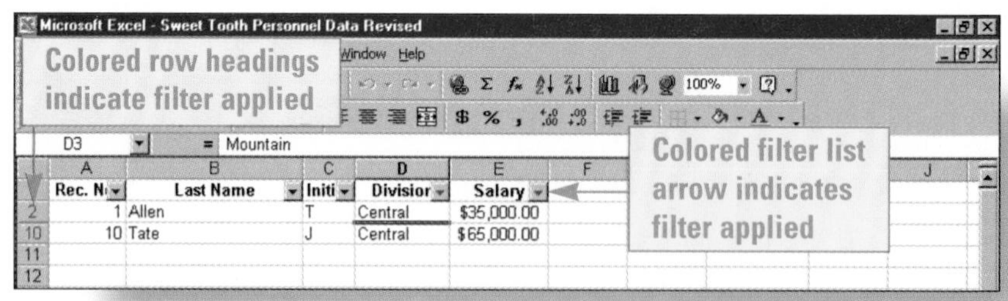

When you want to display all of the records again, use the Show All command.

To clear the filters:

Step 1	*Click*	Data
Step 2	*Point to*	Filter
Step 3	*Click*	Show All

You can also use wildcards in your custom filters. A **wildcard** is used in place of other characters. Suppose you want to filter a list for all last names starting with R. You could enter R* in the Custom AutoFilter dialog box, where the asterisk (*) represents any characters after the R. The question mark (?) can be used in place of a single character. If you used the filter r?n on a list of words, for example, you would see ran and run.

To apply a wildcard filter:

Step 1	*Click*	the Last Name filter arrow
Step 2	*Click*	(Custom...)
Step 3	*Click*	the operator list arrow
Step 4	*Click*	begins with
Step 5	*Key*	m* in the value box
Step 6	*Click*	OK

The list is filtered to show all last names beginning with M. When you have finished filtering a list, you can turn off AutoFilter. To turn off AutoFilter:

Step 1	*Click*	Data
Step 2	*Point to*	Filter
Step 3	*Click*	AutoFilter
Step 4	*Save*	the workbook

You can also use filters that are more advanced.

MOUSE TIP

You can remove the filter from one column by clicking the filter list arrow and selecting (All).

Using Advanced Filters

Another way to filter records is to use advanced filters. Advanced filters allow you to work with multiple AND and OR operators in each field so as to filter a list. These types of filters are more difficult to set up than AutoFilters, however. To take advantage of advanced filters, you must establish a criteria range in the worksheet. The column labels in the criteria range must match the column labels of your list. Rows beneath the column labels in the criteria range indicate the filter criteria. You should also follow these guidelines when using advanced filtering:

- Place the criteria range above or below the rows containing your list data. Do not set up the range in the same rows as the list, because filtered rows remain hidden from view.
- The first row of the criteria range identifies the columns to be filtered. Although its formatting does not have to match that of the column labels in the list you are filtering, the spelling must match exactly.
- Adding multiple criteria in the same row creates an AND condition. For example, to list employees who have an annual salary greater than $40,000 AND who work in the Central division, you would enter >40000 under the column heading Salary and Central under the column label Division; both of these entries would appear in the same row.
- Entering criteria in subsequent rows specifies an OR condition. For example, if you wanted to find all employees who made more than $40,000 OR less than $30,000 per year, you would enter >40000 in one row under the Salary column label and <30000 in the next row under the column label. Each time you add another row to the criteria, you specify another OR condition.

To create a criteria range:

Step 1	***Insert***	six blank rows above row 1
Step 2	***Enter***	Last Name in cell D1
Step 3	***Enter***	Salary in cell E1

Your criteria range now appears above your list. Next, enter the criteria you want to use in your filter. To add criteria to a criteria range:

Step 1	***Enter***	a* in cell D2

This filter will display records that start with the letter "A" in the Last Name field.

Step 2	*Enter*	m* in cell D3
Step 3	*Enter*	>40000 in cell E3

This multiple-column condition will display records that start with the letter "M" in the Last Name field AND have a salary greater than $40,000.

Step 4	*Enter*	g* in cell D4

This complex filter will display records for all employees whose last name starts with A or G, as well as records for any employee whose salary is more than $40,000 and whose last name starts with M.

To apply the advanced filter:

Step 1	*Click*	cell A8

You must select a cell within the list that you want to filter. Excel automatically searches for the header row.

Step 2	*Click*	Data
Step 3	*Point to*	Filter
Step 4	*Click*	Advanced Filter

The Advanced Filter dialog box opens, as shown in Figure 13-14. In this dialog box, you can select the list range and criteria range and specify whether you want to create a copy of the filtered records or filter the list in place. The default is to filter the list in place. The list range is automatically selected.

FIGURE 13-14
Advanced Filter Dialog Box

QUICK TIP

You can use named ranges as references in the Advanced Filter dialog box.

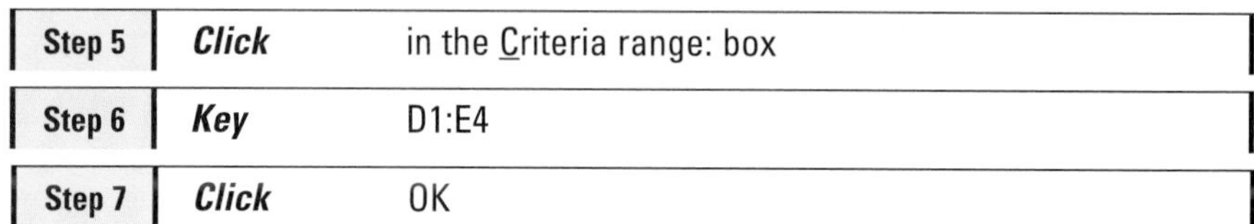

Step 5	***Click***	in the Criteria range: box
Step 6	***Key***	D1:E4
Step 7	***Click***	OK

The list is filtered to produce only records meeting the criteria specified in the criteria range D1:E4, as shown in Figure 13-15.

FIGURE 13-15
Filtered List

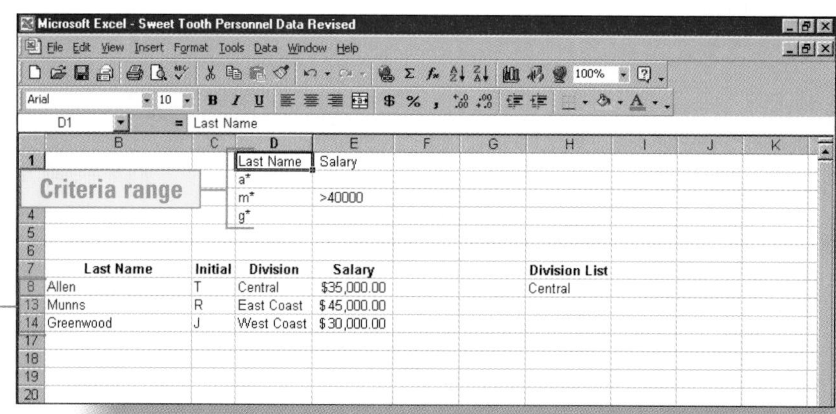

QUICK TIP

To find out about other advanced filtering techniques, use the Office Assistant to search for information about advanced filters and examples of advanced filter criteria.

You can clear the filter to show all records in the list. To show all records:

Step 1	***Click***	Data
Step 2	***Point to***	Filter
Step 3	***Click***	Show All

The complete list is displayed.

Extracting Data

When you use the advanced filter copy option, you leave the original list of data unfiltered and **extract** the records meeting your filter criteria to a new location. You want to extract a list of all employees who make more than $35,000 per year.

To extract data:

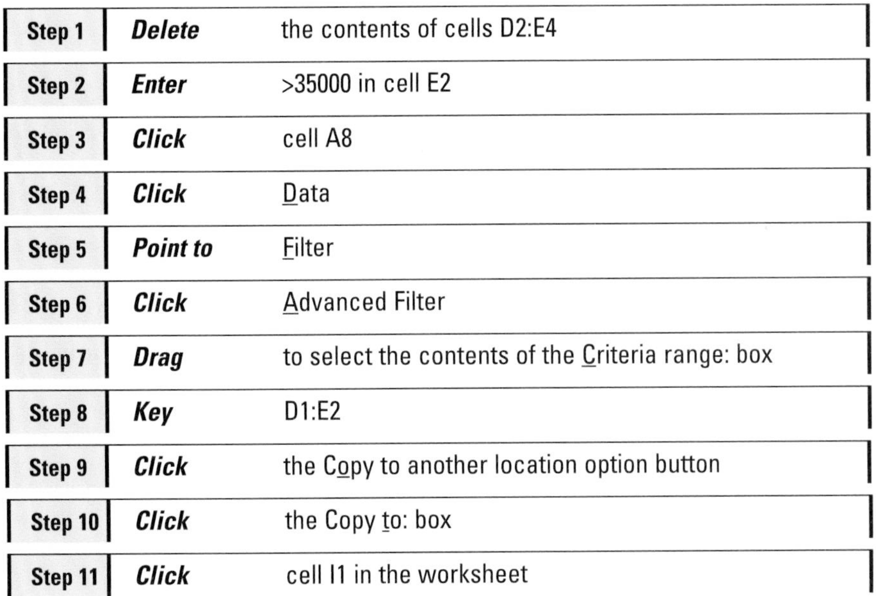

Step 1	*Delete*	the contents of cells D2:E4
Step 2	*Enter*	>35000 in cell E2
Step 3	*Click*	cell A8
Step 4	*Click*	Data
Step 5	*Point to*	Filter
Step 6	*Click*	Advanced Filter
Step 7	*Drag*	to select the contents of the Criteria range: box
Step 8	*Key*	D1:E2
Step 9	*Click*	the Copy to another location option button
Step 10	*Click*	the Copy to: box
Step 11	*Click*	cell I1 in the worksheet

Note that you can copy filtered data only to the active worksheet. Once you have extracted the records, you can move or copy them wherever you like.

Step 12	*Click*	OK
Step 13	*Scroll*	the worksheet to view the extracted data
Step 14	*Increase*	the width of column M to show the data

The filtered records are copied to the new location, starting in cell I1. Notice that the column headings are included with the extracted records, as shown in Figure 13-16.

FIGURE 13-16
Extracted Records

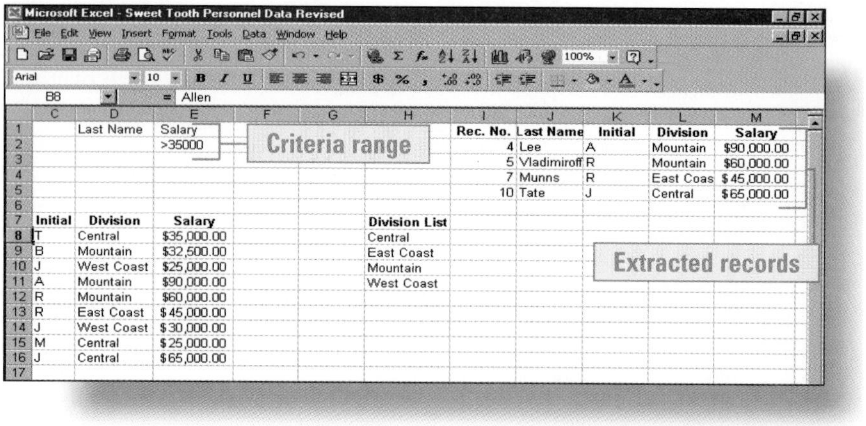

Step 15	***Save & Close*** the workbook

It may take you some time to become comfortable when working with data lists and filters, but these features provide powerful tools for storing and retrieving data.

Summary

- Identify the main components of a list. Know the guidelines for creating lists.
- Enter data in a list. Preselect a list to permit quicker data entry.
- Create data validation criteria to ensure that the user enters proper data in each field of a record.
- Use the data form to add, modify, locate, and delete records.
- Use AutoFilter to add simple filters to a list.
- Use advanced filters to build complex filters using AND and OR operators.
- Extract records from a list for use elsewhere.

Commands Review

Action	Menu Bar	Shortcut Menu	Toolbar	Keyboard
Open the Data Validation dialog box	Data, Validation			ALT + D, L
Use a data form to enter records	Data, Form			ALT + D, O
Apply AutoFilter	Data, Filter, AutoFilter			ALT + D, F, F
Apply an advanced filter	Data, Filter, Advanced Filter			ALT + D, F, A
Show all records	Data, Filter, Show All			ALT + D, F, S

Concepts Review

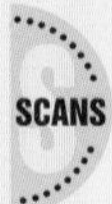

Circle the correct answer.

1. The field name:
- [a] is a collection of characters or numbers that make up one part of a record.
- [b] is the collection of fields that make a complete entry.
- [c] identifies the contents of each column.
- [d] can appear anywhere on the worksheet.

2. A record:
- [a] is a collection of characters or numbers that make up one part of a record.
- [b] is the collection of fields that make a complete entry.
- [c] identifies the contents of each column.
- [d] can appear anywhere on the worksheet.

3. Why should you leave one column and one row blank between the list and any other data on the worksheet?
- [a] This approach makes it easier to return the list to its original sort order.
- [b] Excel can autodetect list boundaries more easily.
- [c] You should not leave blank rows or columns, because spaces affect the sort order of a list.
- [d] It does not matter, as long as you format each field in the same way.

4. Data validation is used to:
- [a] sort fields using criteria you define.
- [b] restrict the data that can be entered in each field.
- [c] search for records containing certain characters.
- [d] make a copy of filtered records in another location.

5. How would you remove the filter from one field in a list that has AutoFilter applied?
- [a] (All)
- [b] (Top 10)
- [c] (Custom...)
- [d] Mountain

6. Multiple criteria in the same row in an advanced filter criteria range indicate:
- [a] an AND condition.
- [b] an OR condition.
- [c] a wildcard character.
- [d] the inclusion of additional fields in the result.

7. Criteria in additional rows beneath a criteria column heading indicate:
- [a] an AND condition.
- [b] an OR condition.
- [c] a wildcard character.
- [d] the inclusion of additional records in the result.

8. Extracted data refers to records:
- [a] meeting filter criteria that are moved from the list.
- [b] meeting filter criteria that are copied from the list.
- [c] not meeting filter criteria.
- [d] that are randomly removed from the database.

9. A data form can be used to:
- [a] add records to a list.
- [b] locate records meeting specific criteria in a list.
- [c] delete records from a list.
- [d] all of the above.

10. One drawback of a data form is that:
- [a] you cannot delete records from a list.
- [b] the data validation criteria are not active.
- [c] you cannot move from record to record.
- [d] you cannot edit records once they are entered.

Circle **T** if the statement is true or **F** if the statement is false.

T F 1. Column headings for advanced filter criteria must be spelled exactly like the column headings in the list you are filtering.

T F 2. "Part No." would be a likely field name in a warehouse database.

T F 3. The terms "record" and "field" refer to the same thing.

T F 4. The term "list" in Excel can often be used interchangeably with "database."

T F 5. Spaces at the beginning of a field entry affect the sort order of a list.

T F 6. You cannot specify AND or OR conditions using AutoFilters.

T F 7. The header row can be placed anywhere in a list, as long as it is formatted differently than the rest of the list.

T F 8. Filters allow you to work with a subset of records in a list.

T F 9. When you apply a filter to a list, you hide all other records that don't meet the criteria.

T F 10. When using advanced filters, the top row of the criteria area must contain column headings spelled exactly the same way as the field names in the list you are filtering.

Skills Review

SCANS

Exercise 1

1. Create a new workbook.

2. Use the following field names to create a product list for use in the warehouse: Part No.; Description; Manufacturer; Cost; Quantity; and Value. Start your entries in cell A8.

3. Select 15 rows per column. Use data validation to set the rules in the table below, using the following instructions:

a. Do not allow blank entries for any fields.

b. The valid manufacturer names are Price Mfg., Sunrise Products Inc., Watershed Mfg., and Irontown Mfg.

c. Use a formula in the Value column to calculate the value of stock on hand by multiplying the quantity of each item times the cost.

Field Name	Validation Characteristic	Input Message	Error Alert Type
Part No.	Whole number between 1,000 and 4,999	Yes	Stop
Description	Text limited to 20 characters	Yes	Information
Manufacturer	Use the list of four valid manufacturer names	Yes	Stop
Cost	Decimal number limited to less than $100.00	Yes	Information
Quantity	Whole number limited to less than 1,000	Yes	Stop

4. Review your list setup to make sure that it fits the list guidelines discussed in at the beginning of this chapter.

5. Save the workbook as *Warehouse Parts* and print it.

Exercise 2 

1. Using the *Warehouse Parts* workbook that you created in Exercise 1, enter the data shown in the table below. Calculate the Value column using a formula.

Part No.	Description	Manufacturer	Cost	Quantity	Value
1010	Sugar, 50 lb	Price Mfg.	19.95	333	(use a formula)
1020	Sugar, 125 lb	Price Mfg.	39.95	693	(use a formula)
1030	Molasses	Watershed Mfg.	45.95	282	(use a formula)
2100	Sprinkles, 1,000 gross	Sunrise Products Inc.	70.95	314	(use a formula)
2200	Rainbow Sprinkles, 10 gross	Watershed Mfg.	6.95	838	(use a formula)
2300	Chocolate Sprinkles, 50 gross	Irontown Mfg.	34.95	279	(use a formula)
3001	Flour, 25 lb	Irontown Mfg.	12.95	940	(use a formula)
3002	Flour, 5 lb	Irontown Mfg.	5.95	412	(use a formula)
3003	Wheat flour, 150 lb	Price Mfg.	99.95	758	(use a formula)
4020	Honey, 30 gallons	Sunrise Products Inc.	89.95	687	(use a formula)
4030	Honey, 2 gallons	Sunrise Products Inc.	6.95	769	(use a formula)
4040	Honey, 1 quart	Watershed Mfg.	1.95	930	(use a formula)

2. Resize columns to fit, as necessary.
3. Format columns D and F using the Accounting format, two decimal places.
4. Sort the list by Manufacturer and Cost.
5. Save the workbook as *Warehouse Parts Inventory* and print it.

Exercise 3 

1. Open the *Warehouse Parts Inventory* that you developed in Exercise 2.
2. Use a data form to edit part number 3003. Change the description to Wheat Flour, 175 lb.
3. Use a data form to eliminate part number 4040.
4. Use a data form to add a new record using the information in the table below.

Part No.	Description	Manufacturer	Cost	Quantity
4041	Honey, 25 gallons	Price Mfg.	35.95	750

5. Apply AutoFilters to the list.
6. Using the AutoFilter list arrows, filter the list to find only items manufactured by Price Mfg.
7. Sort the list in order of cost, from lowest to highest.
8. Print the filtered list.
9. Save the workbook as *Warehouse Parts Inventory Filter 1.*

Exercise 4

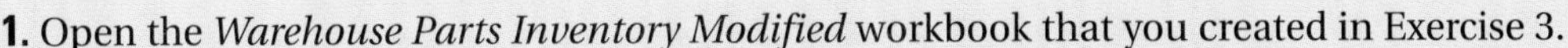

1. Open the *Warehouse Parts Inventory Modified* workbook that you created in Exercise 3.
2. Create an advanced filter criteria that will find any records with a quantity of more than 500 items, or any item that costs less than $30.00 (be sure you don't create an "AND" condition).
3. Filter the list with the criteria set up in step 2.
4. Sort the list by quantity.
5. Print the filtered list.
6. Save the workbook as *Warehouse Parts Inventory Filter 2.*

Exercise 5 

1. Open the *Sweet Tooth Sales Data* workbook on your Data Disk.
2. Apply AutoFilters to the list.
3. Filter the list for all names starting with D or M.
4. Sort the filtered list alphabetically by first name.
5. Use an advanced filter to extract records for sales representatives whose first names begin with D and who work in the Mountain Region. Copy the records starting in cell J1.
6. Resize columns to display all data, if necessary.
7. Set the print area to print only the extracted records.
8. Print the extracted records.
9. Save the workbook as *Sweet Tooth Sales Data Extracted Records.*

Exercise 6 

1. Open the *Sweet Tooth Sales Data Extracted Records* workbook that you created in Exercise 5.
2. Create a new advanced filter to find records of employees whose Gross Sales were less than $3,000 or more than $4,500.
3. Filter the list in place.
4. Sort the filtered list by Gross Sales from highest to lowest.
5. Print the filtered list.
6. Save the workbook as *Sweet Tooth Sales Data Extracted Records 1.*

Exercise 7 

1. Open the *Sweet Tooth Sales Data Extracted Records 1* workbook that you created in Exercise 6.
2. Display all records.
3. Click any cell in the data list, then use a data form to add the following record to the list:

   Mountain South Sun Li $4,500

4. Save the workbook as *Sweet Tooth Sales Data 1.*

Exercise 8

1. Open the *Sweet Tooth Sales Data 1* workbook that you created in Exercise 7.
2. Use a data form to locate the record for all employees whose name starts with W.
3. Use the Find Next button to locate the record for Walter Jacobs.
4. Delete the record.
5. Close the Form dialog box.
6. Print the data list.
7. Save the workbook as *Sweet Tooth Sales Data 2*.

Case Projects

Project 1 

You are reviewing workbooks in use at your company. The personnel data workbook is a mess because no one used data validation when creating the workbook. Use the Office Assistant and what you learned in this chapter to create a document explaining what data validation is and how to set it up for use in a workbook. Include instructions for dealing with text, number, and date entries. Be sure to describe how to set up an input message and an error alert. Save the document as *Data Validation.doc.*

Project 2 

As the personnel director for a small retail sales company, you are in charge of tracking personnel information. Create a list of 15 employees. Include a unique record number for each employee, starting at 1. Each record should include a record number, last name, first initial, hire date (within the last five years), date of last pay increase, current salary, and department (use at least three departments). Use appropriate data validation for each field. Prepare and print a series of sorted reports showing employees sorted by record number, alphabetically by last name, by hire date, by department (alphabetically by last name within each department), and by current salary. Use subtotals to prepare a pie chart showing salary percentages by department. Print the chart. Save the workbook as *Personnel Information.*

Project 3 

Use the Office Assistant to find out how to locate cells that have data validation rules applied. Write a step-by-step summary of this process. Save the document as *Find Data Validation Cells.doc.*

Project 4  

As a financial advisor for personnel in a large corporation, you are constantly asked for investment resources. Use the Internet to locate 6 to 10 sites that provide investment information. Find sites that offer more than just stock quotes, such as investment advice, market trend analysis, financial reports for different companies, and investment research tools. Create a workbook with at least six hyperlinks to these Web sites. Print five Web pages providing investment advice.

Project 5 

Programmers sometimes add “Easter Eggs” to a program. If a user follows a certain sequence of commands, they might see a special message containing the names of the programmers or something else fun. Use the Internet to search for Excel Easter Eggs and see if any of them work with Excel 2000. You could also try searching for Easter Eggs in other programs you use. Print at least one page explaining how to display an Easter Egg.

Project 6 

You are the data manager at a shipping company. Create a workbook to track shipping dates, company names, addresses, and four-digit item numbers. Use a data form to add five records to the list. Print the list and save the workbook as *Shipping*.

Project 7  

Your marketing firm is preparing a commercial that it would like to release in the 10 largest cities in the United States. Use the Internet to find a list of populations of cities in the United States. In a new workbook, set up field names for each city, its state, and its population. Apply data validation to each column. Limit the data in the city field to a text length of 15 characters, the state field to a text length of 2 characters, and the population field to a whole number greater than 1,000,000. Enter the data for the 10 largest cities you can find. Save the workbook as *Population*.

Project 8 

You work at a telemarketing company. Create a list to log the date, time, and duration of each call. Use data validation to restrict the data entry for each cell to the appropriate type of data (limit call length to less than 60 minutes). Enter fictitious data for five calls. Save the workbook as *Phone Log*.

Auditing a Worksheet

Chapter Overview

Auditing tools help you identify relationships between cells. The Auditing toolbar provides tools to identify precedents and dependents, trace errors to their source, and locate invalid data.

Learning Objectives

- Use Range Finder to check and review data
- Identify relationships between precedent and dependent cells
- Trace errors
- Identify invalid data

Case profile

Many of Sweet Tooth's employees use the Excel workbooks you've created, and they also create their own workbooks. As you share workbooks with other workers, you occasionally find errors (not to mention your own *rare* errors) or need to review the sources of values referenced by a certain formula. Using Excel's auditing tools, you can make quick work of tracking down the source of errors or identifying locations where values are used throughout even the most complex worksheets.

chapter fourteen

14

14.a Using Range Finder to Check and Review Data

Whenever you open a workbook created by someone else, it is a good idea to review the worksheet's assumptions and calculations before you begin editing data. **Range Finder** can help you track down references used in formulas. The *Sweet Tooth Projected Profit* workbook contains several errors that should be corrected. To open the file and save it with a new name:

Step 1	***Open***	the *Sweet Tooth Projected Profit with Errors* workbook on your Data Disk
Step 2	***Save***	the workbook as *Sweet Tooth Projected Profit Revised* to your Data Files folder

The Projected Profit worksheet contains projections for income and expenses for the coming year. Rows 17–22 contain multipliers used in some of the formulas on the worksheet to calculate expense amounts. Because the information for the third and fourth quarters consists of projected data, it is italicized. To use Range Finder to revise a formula:

Step 1	***Click***	cell E13 on the Projected Profit worksheet

The formula in cell E13 is supposed to calculate the projected profit for the third quarter, but it currently shows a value of zero (shown as a dash in the Accounting format). The formula refers to empty cells G6 and G8:G12. You could key in the correction so that the formula refers to the correct cells in the column E, but Range Finder can make this type of correction even more easily.

Step 2	***Double-click***	cell E13

Your screen should look similar to Figure 14-1. The formula highlights each cell or range reference, using a different color for each reference to make it easier to identify the reference.

FIGURE 14-1
Use Range Finder to Locate References

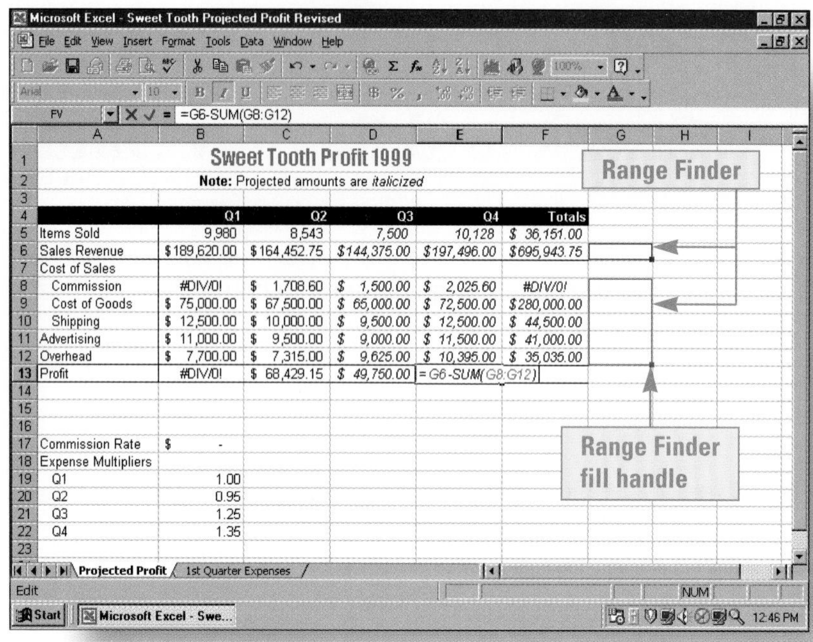

You can see that the references point to the wrong column. To adjust the reference, drag the border to the correct location in column E. If necessary, you can drag the Range Finder fill handle to increase or decrease the size of the range.

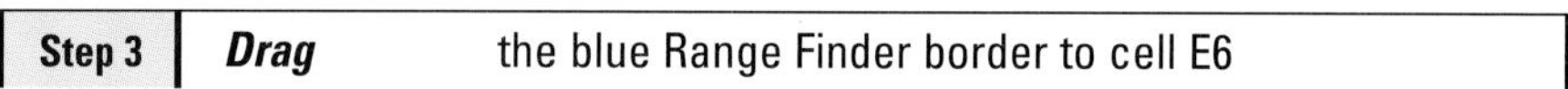

Step 3	***Drag***	the blue Range Finder border to cell E6

As you drag the border, the formula in the Formula Bar adjusts itself automatically.

Step 4	***Drag***	the green Range Finder border to cells E8:E12
Step 5	***Click***	the Enter button ✓ on the Formula Bar

The total $88,575.40 should appear in cell E13.

Step 6	***Save***	the workbook

14.b Identifying Relationships Between Precedent and Dependent Cells

As workbooks grow larger and more complicated, it becomes increasingly difficult to locate and review relationships between cells. Excel provides auditing features to simplify this job.

Tracing Precedents

Precedents are the cells referred to by a formula. You can locate precedents by using the Auditing commands on the Tools menu and on the Auditing toolbar. To show the Auditing toolbar:

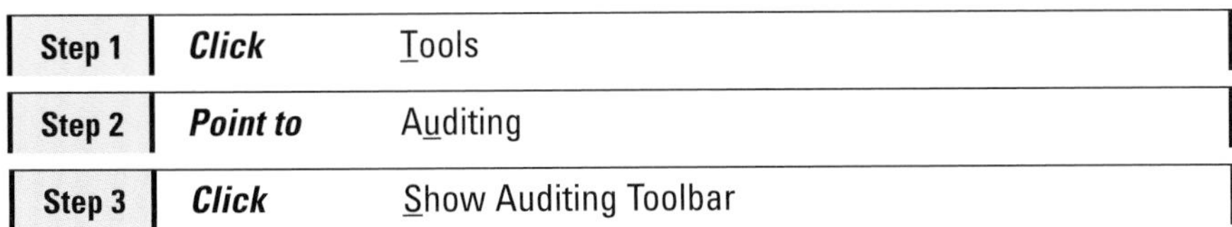

Step 1	*Click*	Tools
Step 2	*Point to*	Auditing
Step 3	*Click*	Show Auditing Toolbar

The formula in cell F6 adds the total Sales Revenue figures for each quarter. To trace the precedents for this formula:

Step 1	*Click*	cell F6
Step 2	*Click*	the Trace Precedents button on the Auditing toolbar

A heavy blue tracer arrow identifies the precedent(s) for this formula. When the precedent consists of a range of cells, the tracer arrow is indicated with a heavy line and the range is highlighted with a blue border. When the precedent consists of a single cell, the tracer arrow is indicated with a thin line. Your screen should look similar to Figure 14-2.

MENU TIP

To trace precedents, point to Auditing on the Tools menu, then click Trace Precedents.

FIGURE 14-2
Tracing Precedents

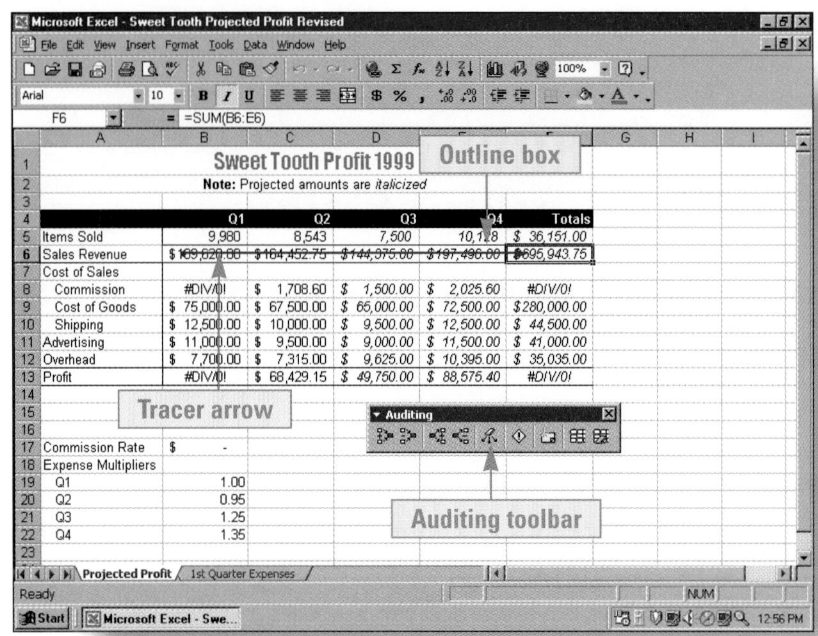

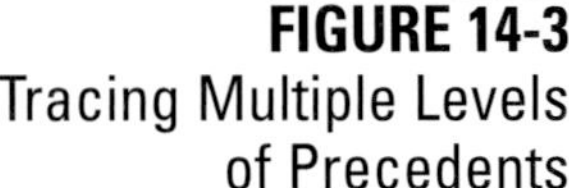

You can jump to a referenced cell using the tracer arrow lines. Double-click an arrow line and the active cell moves back and forth between the referenced cells and the formula.

Many times, the results of a formula are not based on a single level of precedents. For example, the formula in cell F6 refers to the range B6:E6, but the values in this range are derived from still other formulas. To view a second level of precedents:

Step 1	*Click*	the Trace Precedents button on the Auditing toolbar

Your screen should look similar to Figure 14-3.

FIGURE 14-3
Tracing Multiple Levels of Precedents

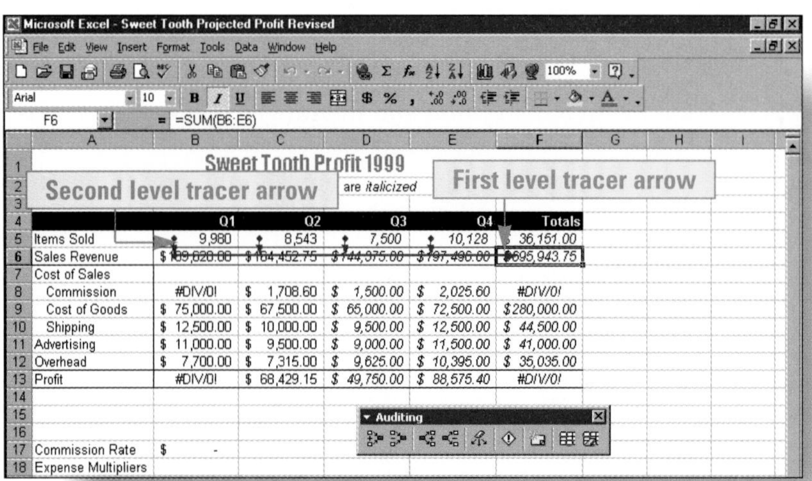

You can continue to click the Trace Precedents button until you have revealed all of the precedent levels. If your computer has a sound card and speakers attached, an alert sound indicates when Excel has reached the last level of precedents. Once you have finished viewing the precedents for a cell, you may want to clear the precedent arrows to view your worksheet more easily. To clear all precedent arrows:

Step 1	*Click*	the Remove All Arrows button on the Auditing toolbar

The arrows are removed from the display.

Tracing Dependents

Dependents are all cells containing formulas that rely on the value of another cell. A cell may be referenced by one or several formulas throughout a workbook. You can locate dependents in the same manner that you located precedents. To trace dependents:

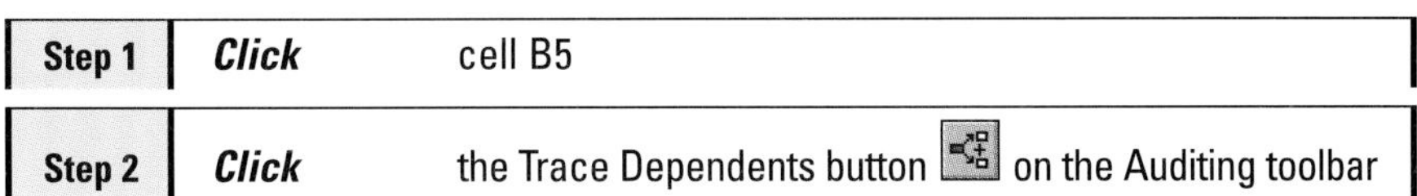

Step 1	*Click*	cell B5
Step 2	*Click*	the Trace Dependents button on the Auditing toolbar

Thin blue tracer arrows point to cells B6, B8, and F5. Each of these cells contains a formula that references cell B5. Your screen should look similar to Figure 14-4.

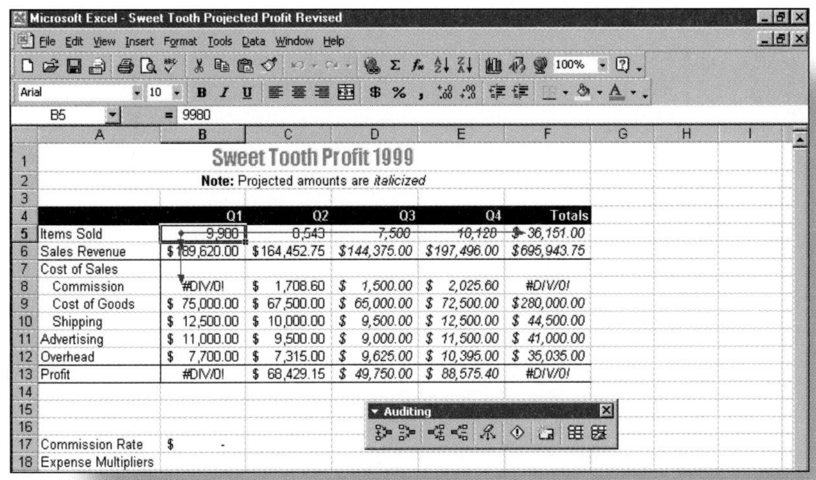

FIGURE 14-4
Tracing Dependents

You can identify multiple levels of dependents by continuing to click the Trace Dependents button on the Auditing toolbar. The number of items sold, which appears in cell B5, is referenced by the formula in cell B8, which calculates the commission expense. This amount is then referenced by still other formulas. Cell B5 is also referenced by the formula in cell B6, which is then referenced by cell F6.

Step 3	*Click*	the Trace Dependents button on the Auditing toolbar

MENU TIP

To remove all precedent and dependent tracer arrows, click Tools, point to Auditing, then click Remove All Arrows.

A second level of tracer arrows is added to the display. A thin blue tracer arrow now points to cell F6. Because the formula in cell B8 contains an error, red tracer arrows point to the two cells that use cell B8 in their formulas. You take care of this error in the next section.

You can remove a single level of arrows rather than removing all arrows at once. To remove a single level of arrows:

Step 1	*Click*	the Remove Dependent Arrows button on the Auditing toolbar

The second level of tracer arrows disappears.

Step 2	*Click*	the Remove Dependent Arrows button on the Auditing toolbar

The first level of tracer arrows disappears.

Tracing Cell Relationships Between Worksheets

As you learned in previous chapters, you can reference cells located on other worksheets as well as those on the current worksheet. Excel's auditing tools help you trace references to these cells. To trace precedents between worksheets:

Step 1	*Click*	cell B12
Step 2	*Click*	the Trace Precedents button on the Auditing toolbar

A worksheet icon and a black tracer arrow appear, indicating that a reference in cell B12 is located on another worksheet. Check the formula in the Formula Bar to verify this relationship. Your screen should look similar to Figure 14-5. You can quickly jump to the referenced cell.

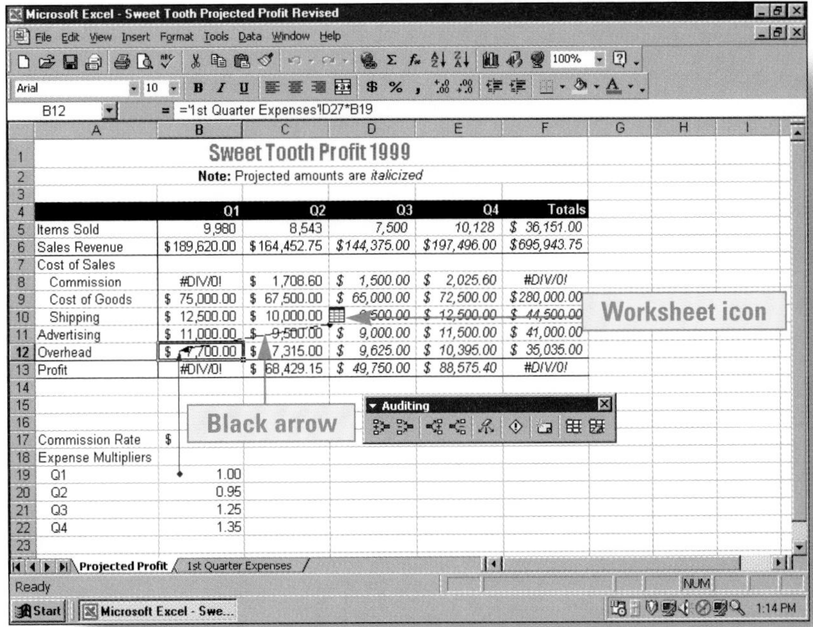

FIGURE 14-5
Tracing Relationships Between Worksheets

Step 3	***Double-click*** the black tracer arrow

The Go To dialog box opens.

Step 4	***Click***	the reference listed at the top of the Go to: list box
Step 5	***Click***	OK

The 1st Quarter Expenses worksheet is activated, and the active cell moves to cell D27. The total in cell D27 is used in cell B12 on the Projected Profit worksheet.

Step 6	***Click***	the Projected Profit worksheet tab
Step 7	***Click***	the Remove All Arrows button on the Auditing toolbar
Step 8	***Save***	the workbook

14.c Tracing Errors

The formulas in cells B8, F8, B13, and F13 display the #DIV/0! error. This error indicates that at least one of these cells contains a formula that attempts to divide a value by zero. To trace and correct the source of this error:

MENU TIP

You can trace errors by clicking Tools, then pointing to Auditing and clicking Trace Error.

Step 1	*Click*	cell F13
Step 2	*Click*	the Trace Error button on the Auditing toolbar

Your screen should look similar to Figure 14-6.

FIGURE 14-6
Tracing Errors

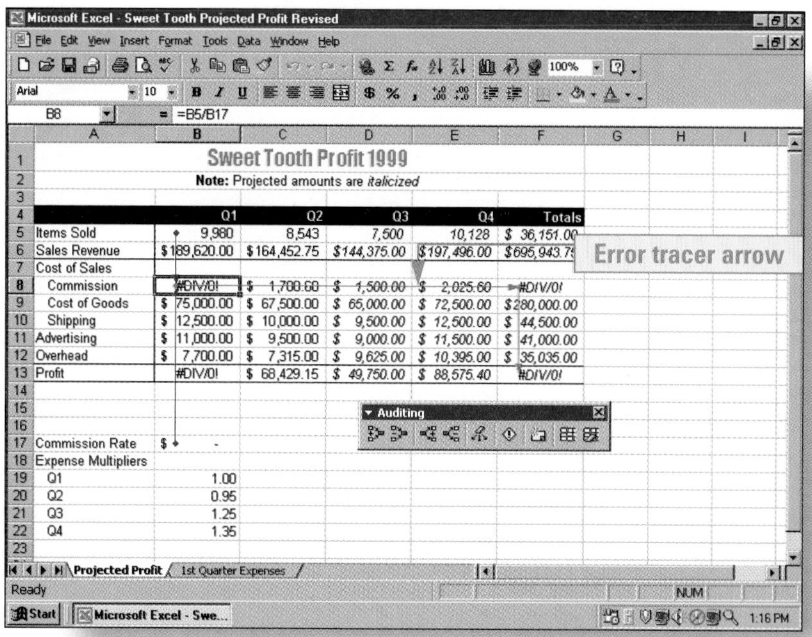

The formula in cell F13 refers to the range F8:F12. Because an error occurs in cell F8, you see a red error arrow. Cell F8 adds the range B8:F8 and therefore a second error arrow stretches back to cell B8. Cell B8 contains a formula that divides the value of cell B5 by the value of cell B17. The blue arrows, as you know, indicate precedents of cell B8. By examining the value of B17, you find the source of the problem—cell B17 contains a value of 0.

Step 3	*Enter*	5 in cell B17

This correction solves the "divide by 0" error in cell B8, and consequently eliminates the problems in cells B13, F8, and F13. Now blue tracer arrows, indicating the formulas are working correctly, replace the red error arrows.

Step 4	*Click*	the Remove All Arrows button on the Auditing toolbar

14.d Identifying Invalid Data

In Chapter 13, you learned how to use data validation when creating lists of data. You also learned about the three different types of error alert messages. Two of the error alert messages—Information and Warning—allow a user to input invalid data, even though the user is informed that the information is invalid. To help you identify cells in a list that contain data violating data validation rules, you can use an auditing command. To find invalid data:

Step 1	*Click*	the 1st Quarter Expenses worksheet tab
Step 2	*Click*	the Circle Invalid Data button on the Auditing toolbar
Step 3	*Scroll*	the worksheet up until you can see row 1

All cells containing invalid data are circled in red. Your screen should look similar to Figure 14-7.

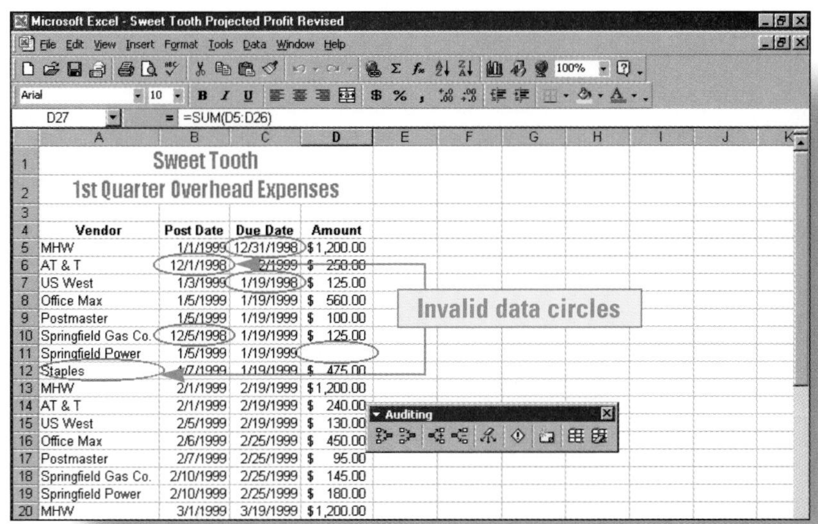

FIGURE 14-7
Identifying Invalid Data

MOUSE TIP

You can turn the circles off by clicking the Clear Validation Circles button on the Auditing toolbar.

chapter fourteen

CAUTION TIP

The invalid data circle should disappear when you select Office Max from the list. But sometimes it doesn't "take," so be sure to key the entry if necessary as we did here.

Step 4	***Click***	cell A12
Step 5	***Click***	the list arrow in cell A12
Step 6	***Select***	Office Max from the list
Step 7	***Key***	Of
Step 8	***Press***	the ENTER key to accept the AutoComplete entry

Office Max is a valid entry. As you correct the errors, the validation circles disappear.

Step 9	***Enter***	1/1/99 in cell B6
Step 10	***Enter***	1/5/99 in cell B10
Step 11	***Enter***	1/31/99 in cell C5
Step 12	***Enter***	1/19/99 in cell C7
Step 13	***Enter***	185 in cell D11
Step 14	***Click***	the Circle Invalid Data button on the Auditing toolbar to double-check for additional errors
Step 15	***Close***	the Auditing toolbar
Step 16	***Save & Close***	the workbook

The Auditing toolbar can be helpful when your worksheets include complicated formulas that use many precedents.

Summary

- Use Range Finder to quickly edit cell references in a formula. Click and drag Range Finder borders to move a reference. Use the Range Finder fill handle to "resize" a range reference.
- Precedents are cells or ranges referenced by a specific formula. Select a cell containing a formula, then use the Trace Precedents tool to identify cells and ranges referenced in that particular formula.
- Dependents are cells containing formulas that depend on the value of a certain cell. Select a cell containing a value or formula, then use the Trace Dependents tool to identify other cells containing formulas that reference that particular cell.
- Use the Trace Error tool to quickly locate the source of a formula error.
- Locate data that violates data validation rules by using the Circle Invalid Data auditing tool.

Commands Review

Action	Menu Bar	Shortcut Menu	Toolbar	Keyboard
Trace precedents	Tools, Auditing, Trace Precedents			ALT + T, U, T
Trace dependents	Tools, Auditing, Trace Dependents			ALT + T, U, D
Trace errors	Tools, Auditing, Trace Error			ALT + T, U, E
Remove all arrows	Tools, Auditing, Remove All Arrows			ALT + T, U, A
Circle invalid data				
Clear validation circles				

Concepts Review

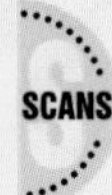

Circle the correct answer.

1. Precedents are cells that:
- [a] are referred to by a formula.
- [b] depend on the value of another cell.
- [c] have blue arrow lines showing the relationship between two cells.
- [d] have red arrow lines showing the source of an error.

2. Dependents are cells that:
- [a] are referred to by a formula.
- [b] depend on the value of another cell.
- [c] have blue arrow lines showing the relationship between two cells.
- [d] have red arrow lines showing the source of an error.

3. Traced errors are indicated by a:
- [a] blue arrow.
- [b] black arrow.
- [c] red arrow.
- [d] blinking cell border.

4. A heavy tracer arrow indicates a:
- [a] serious error.
- [b] multiple-cell reference.
- [c] single-cell reference.
- [d] reference on another worksheet.

5. A black arrow indicates a:
- [a] traced error.
- [b] traced precedent.
- [c] traced dependent.
- [d] precedent or dependent cell located on another worksheet.

6. To locate data that violates data validation, use the:
- [a] Trace Precedents button.
- [b] Trace Error button.
- [c] Trace Dependents button.
- [d] Circle Invalid Data button.

7. To quickly jump to a precedent or dependent in another worksheet that has been traced:
- [a] click the worksheet icon that appears in the worksheet.
- [b] double-click the black tracer arrow.
- [c] drag the black tracer arrow to the worksheet tab.
- [d] double-click the cell to which the black tracer arrow points.

8. You can trace errors in worksheet formulas by:
- [a] clicking the Trace Errors button on the Auditing toolbar.
- [b] double-clicking the tracer arrows until they point to the errors.
- [c] clicking the Find Errors button on the Auditing toolbar.
- [d] dragging the red tracer arrows to the precedent cell.

9. If data in a worksheet has a red circle around it, you should:
- [a] fix the precedent cells.
- [b] reenter the value currently in the cell.
- [c] enter a valid entry in the cell.
- [d] erase the red circles using the Eraser button on the Drawing toolbar.

Circle **T** if the statement is true or **F** if the statement is false.

T F 1. You can view multiple levels of precedents and dependents.

T F 2. It is a good idea to review the relationships between cells when using a workbook prepared by someone else or when using a workbook with which you haven't worked for a long time.

T F 3. You can jump between ends of a tracer arrow by double-clicking the arrow line.

T F 4. You can open the Auditing toolbar by right-clicking a toolbar and clicking Auditing.

T F 5. The #DIV/0! error indicates a number that Excel cannot display.

T F 6. Red arrows indicate precedents and dependents.

T F 7. If a cell containing a formula that results in an error is a precedent of a formula in another cell, both cells will display the error.

T F 8. To move a range with Range Finder, click and drag the Range Finder fill handle.

T F 9. You can use Trace Errors tool to find invalid data entered in a list.

T F 10. As you correct invalid entries in a list, the validation circles disappear.

Skills Review

Exercise 1

1. Open the *Warehouse Inventory Errors* file on your Data Disk.
2. Use the Auditing toolbar to locate cells containing invalid data.
3. Select rows 17–24.
4. Use the Clear All command to clear data validation settings from rows 17–24.
5. Click the Circle Invalid Data button on the Auditing toolbar again.
6. Print the worksheet with the circles displayed.
7. Save the workbook as *Warehouse Inventory Errors 1.*

Exercise 2

1. Open the *Warehouse Inventory Errors 1* file that you created in Exercise 1.
2. Use the Auditing toolbar to circle invalid entries.
3. Correct the errors using data that is compatible with the validation rules.
4. Save the workbook as *Warehouse Inventory Fixed* and print it.

Exercise 3

1. Open the *Fee Calculator Errors* file on your Data Disk.
2. Click cell H7.
3. Use auditing tools to trace the #NAME? error to its source.
4. The formula in cell C3 refers to a named range, percentage, that does not exist in the worksheet. Edit the formula to properly refer to cell C2. If necessary, check the formula in the cell to the right of cell 3.
5. Save the workbook as *Fee Calculator Errors Fixed 1* and print it.

Exercise 4

1. Open the *Fee Calculator Errors Fixed 1* file that you created in Exercise 3.
2. Click cell H7.
3. Use Range Finder to correct the formula so that it adds cells H3:H6.
4. Save the workbook as *Fee Calculator Errors Fixed 2* and print it.

Exercise 5 

1. Open the *Fee Calculator Errors Fixed 2* file that you created in Exercise 4.

2. Trace the source of the #DIV/0! error in cell B10.

3. Change the value of the erroneous cell to 5.

4. Remove the arrows.

5. Print the worksheet.

6. Save the workbook as *Fee Calculator Fixed 3.*

Exercise 6 

1. Open the *XYZ Accounting* file on your Data Disk.

2. Click cell B2 and trace its precedents.

3. Print the worksheet with the arrows displayed.

4. Double-click the black arrow line.

5. Select the reference to the San Diego tab and click OK.

6. Print the worksheet.

7. Save the workbook as *XYZ Accounting 1.*

Exercise 7 

1. Open the *XYZ Accounting 1* file that you created in Exercise 6.

2. Click cell E5 on the San Diego worksheet.

3. Display the first-level precedents for cell E5.

4. Display the second-level precedents for cell E5.

5. Print the worksheet.

6. Save the workbook as *XYZ Accounting 2.*

Exercise 8 

1. Open the *XYZ Accounting 2* file that you created in Exercise 7.

2. Activate cell B2 on the Summary tab.

3. Trace all dependents of cell B2.

4. Print the worksheet.

5. Save the workbook as *XYZ Accounting 3.*

Case Projects

Project 1

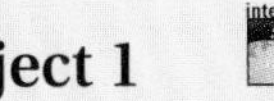

Use the Web toolbar to connect to your favorite search engine. Most search engines have a News section. Locate and read two articles one specifically about business or technology, and a subject of some interest to you (non-sports-related!). Print both articles.

Project 2

Some of your clients work with other spreadsheet applications that use the R1C1 cell reference style. Use the Office Assistant to research the R1C1 reference style. Write a description of the differences between the two styles, and how to use absolute and relative cell references in R1C1 style. Include instructions on how to change Excel to use the R1C1 reference style. Save the document as *R1C1 Instructions.doc.*

Project 3

Use the Office Assistant to look up "circular references." Write an explanation of circular reference, explaining how to turn on the Circular Reference toolbar and how to resolve the problem. Save the document as *Circular References.doc.*

Project 4

You are in charge of hiring new employees for the accounting division. Part of your hiring procedure is to test applicants using a workbook containing several errors, to see how they resolve the problems. Create a workbook similar to the one used in this chapter, using your own row and column headings, and data. Create erroneous formulas using incorrect references, named ranges that don't exist, circular references, and a divide by 0 error. Trace the source of each of your errors, and document them in another section of the worksheet. Save your workbook as *Error Test.*

Project 5

A popular method of transferring files on the Internet is FTP. Use an Internet search engine to find out what FTP stands for. Print a Web page containing a simple explanation of FTP. The article may suggest several FTP programs you can download, or you may need to use the search engine again to locate FTP programs. Find at least one FTP program you can download and print the page you find it on.

Project 6

Use the Internet to see if you can find out who invented the first spreadsheet application. Print a page explaining who invented it, why it was invented and what it was called.

Automating Excel with Macros

Chapter Overview

Many tasks you perform in Excel can be very repetitive. Macros can record these steps, then play them back automatically and much more rapidly than you could do normally. In this chapter, you record and edit macros. You even learn how to program a dialog box that gets text from a user to use in your macro.

Learning Objectives

- Record a macro
- Run a macro
- Edit a macro
- Use workbooks containing macros
- Add Visual Basic functions to a macro

Case profile

Every time you create a new worksheet for Sweet Tooth, you spend precious time keying a worksheet title and formatting it the same way you do all other worksheet titles. You can streamline this tedious process to a couple of mouse clicks by recording a macro to do the work for you.

15

chapter fifteen

15.a Recording a Macro

A **macro** is a set of instructions that automatically executes a set of commands. Using macros, you can automate repetitive tasks. For example, you format Sweet Tooth's worksheet titles with the Impact font, 16 point size, red color, and centered across several cells. This formatting is a perfect candidate for a simple macro: repetitive, specific commands that you use over and over again. Other good candidates for macros include tasks such as adding headers and footers to a print report, creating charts, sorting lists, and setting up worksheets.

Macros are written or recorded in a programming language called Visual Basic. Visual Basic is used in all of the Office 2000 applications. It is fairly easy to learn, and if you take the time to learn its basics, you can create macros that work in Word, Access, PowerPoint, or Excel.

Now, take a deep breath. Yes, we said "programming." And yes, you're going to do it. Keep a few things in mind: (1) Programming is not just for geeks anymore; and (2) by learning how to do a little bit of programming (deep breath), you can actually lighten your workload and free yourself to do other things.

The simplest way to create a macro is to record it. When you record a macro, Excel takes note of every command you use and every keystroke you press. The first macro you record adds Sweet Tooth's company title to a worksheet using the company's preferred font style, size, color, and alignment. To start recording a macro:

Step 1	*Create*	a new, blank workbook
Step 2	*Click*	Tools
Step 3	*Point to*	Macro
Step 4	*Click*	Record New Macro

The Record Macro dialog box opens. Macros can be stored as part of the current workbook or in a hidden workbook called the Personal Macro Workbook.

Step 5	*Key*	Sweet_Tooth_Title in the Macro name: box

Macro names cannot contain spaces, so use the underscore (_) character instead.

Step 6	*Select*	This Workbook from the Store Macro in: list box

QUICK TIP

When creating macros, a very helpful technique is to write down or practice each step in the task you want to automate. When you are sure that you have written down all of the steps involved, begin recording your macro.

If you want your recorded macros to be available whenever you use Excel, store them in the Personal Macro Workbook.

Step 7	*Drag*	to select all of the text in the Description: box
Step 8	*Key*	Create and format a worksheet title

The Shortcut key: box allows you to assign a shortcut key to the macro. For now, leave this box blank. Your dialog box should look similar to Figure 15-1.

FIGURE 15-1
Record Macro Dialog Box

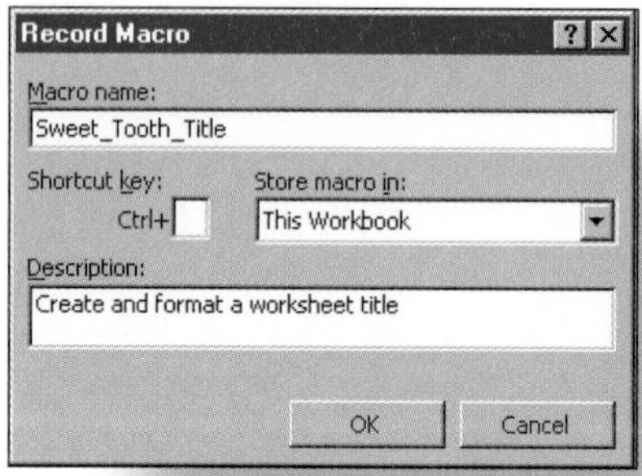

Step 9	*Click*	OK

The Stop Recording toolbar appears, and Recording appears in the status bar, as shown in Figure 15-2.

FIGURE 15-2
Stop Recording Toolbar

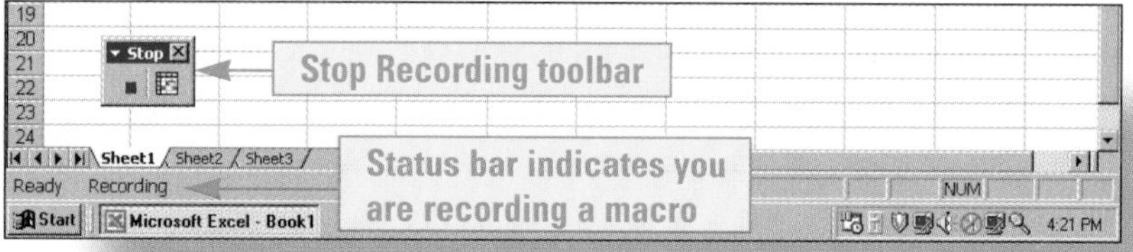

Now enter and format the titles you want on your worksheet. To enter the titles:

Step 1	*Enter*	Sweet Tooth in cell A1
Step 2	*Enter*	<Add a subtitle in cell A2> in cell A2 (include the brackets)
Step 3	*Select*	cells A1:F1
Step 4	*Click*	the Merge and Center button on the Formatting toolbar

Step 5	*Repeat*	steps 3 and 4 with cells A2:F2
Step 6	*Select*	cells A1:A2
Step 7	*Open*	the Format Cells dialog box by pressing the CTRL + 1 keys
Step 8	*Click*	the Font tab
Step 9	*Select*	Impact from the Font: list
Step 10	*Select*	16 from the Size: list
Step 11	*Select*	Red from the Color: palette
Step 12	*Click*	OK
Step 13	*Activate*	cell A1
Step 14	*Click*	the Stop Recording button  on the Stop Recording toolbar

Your macro is saved as part of the workbook, and the Stop Recording toolbar closes.

QUICK TIP

If you want to see additional information about recording macros, use Microsoft Visual Basic Help from the Visual Basic Editor.

15.b Running a Macro

C

To test the macro, you must run it. You can use the Macro dialog box to run macros stored in any currently open workbook or macros stored in your Personal Macro Workbook. To run the macro:

Step 1	*Click*	the Sheet2 worksheet tab
Step 2	*Click*	Tools
Step 3	*Point to*	Macro
Step 4	*Click*	Macros

The Macro dialog box opens.

Step 5	*Click*	Sweet_Tooth_Title from the list of available macros

MENU TIP

The Personal Macro workbook is hidden by default. You can hide other open workbooks or view hidden workbooks. To hide a workbook, click Window, then Hide. To view a hidden workbook, click Window, then Unhide.

The description that you keyed when you recorded the macro appears at the bottom of the dialog box. Your dialog box should look similar to Figure 15-3.

FIGURE 15-3
Macro Dialog Box

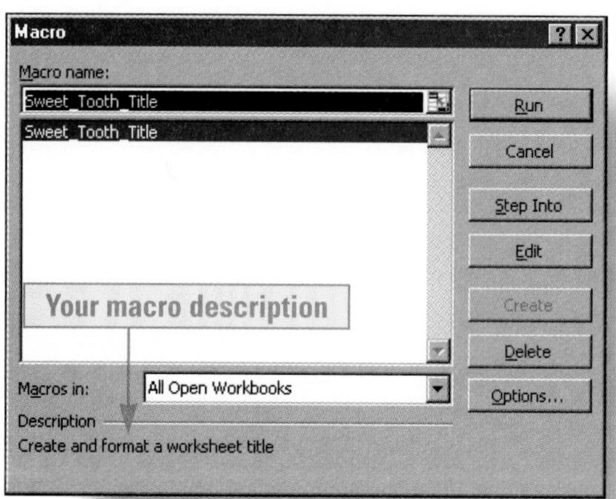

> **QUICK TIP**
>
> You can access the Macro dialog box by pressing the ALT + F8 keys.

Step 6	*Click*	Run

The macro performs the steps that you recorded earlier. Your screen should look similar to Figure 15-4.

FIGURE 15-4
Running the Sweet_Tooth_Title Macro

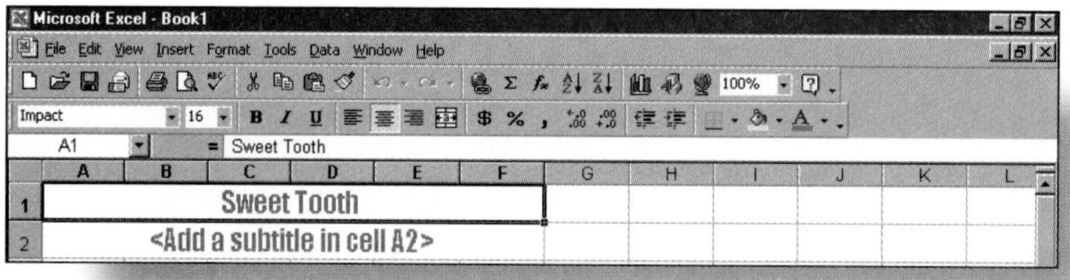

15.c Editing a Macro

> **QUICK TIP**
>
> You can access the Visual Basic Editor by pressing the ALT + F11 keys.

Using the Visual Basic Editor, you can edit macros that you've previously recorded or written. The Visual Basic Editor is a separate program that runs in its own window, outside of Excel, and provides toolbars and menus specifically intended for working with Visual Basic programming code. To edit the Sweet_Tooth_Title macro:

Step 1	*Click*	Tools
Step 2	*Point to*	Macro
Step 3	*Click*	Macros

Step 4	*Select*	the Sweet_Tooth_Title macro
Step 5	*Click*	Edit

The Visual Basic Editor opens, with the selected macro open on the right side, as shown in Figure 15-5. Notice that the Visual Basic Editor program button appears in the taskbar.

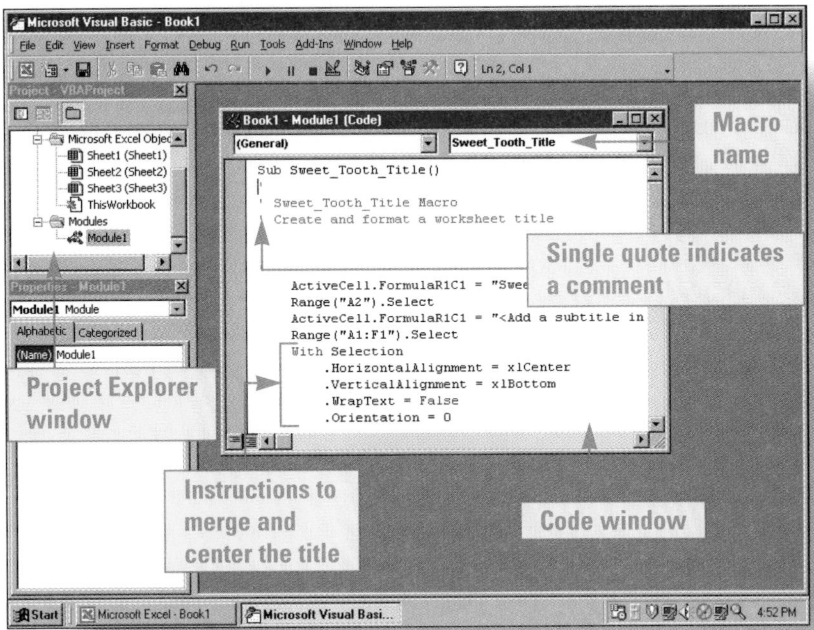

FIGURE 15-5
Visual Basic Editor

QUICK TIP

You can also write new macros, test, debug, and delete macros from the Visual Basic Editor.

On the left side of the Visual Basic Editor window, you see the Project Explorer window. Project Explorer displays a hierarchical list of all open projects and each of the items associated with each particular project. A **project** includes objects in the workbook, including the worksheets, **modules** (where macro code is stored), and **forms** (custom dialog boxes). In addition to these items, projects can contain other items, such as ActiveX controls, class modules, and references to other projects. Visual Basic Help provides information about other items that can be included in a project.

The Code window to the right contains the macro code for the Sweet_Tooth_Title macro.

Step 6	*Scroll*	the Code window to review the code

Table 15-1 explains different sections of the code.

TABLE 15-1
Macro Code Description

Macro Line	Description
Sub Sweet_Tooth_Title()	Sub appears in blue text and defines the beginning of a procedure. The title of the macro appears on the Sub line and appears in black text.
Green text lines	Green text lines are remark, or comment, lines. Everything you enter after an apostrophe or REM (short for REMARK) is considered a remark. You use remarks to explain certain steps in your program. Notice that the description you entered in the Record Macro dialog box appears at the top of your code.
ActiveCell.FormulaR1C1 = "Sweet Tooth"	Enters the text "Sweet Tooth" in the current cell. (Uses R1C1 style cell references; use Office Assistant to learn more about this topic).
Range("A2").Select	Activates cell A2.
All lines starting with Range("A1:F1").Select to Selection.Merge	Merges and centers cells A1:F1.
All lines beginning with Range("A1:F2").Select to End With	Selects cells A1:F2 and sets the font options.
End Sub	Indicates the end of the macro

MOUSE TIP

Click the Maximize button in the Code window to make the Code window fill the space on the right.

Whenever a Sweet Tooth employee uses this macro, the current date should be added in a blue font to cell A3. To modify the code:

Step 1	***Locate***	the line that reads Range ("A1:F1").Select near the end of the macro
Step 2	***Drag***	the I-beam pointer over A1:F1 to select it
Step 3	***Key***	A3
Step 4	***Press***	the END key to move to the end of the line
Step 5	***Press***	the ENTER key
Step 6	***Key***	ActiveCell.FormulaR1C1 = "=TODAY()"

This line enters the TODAY date formula in the current cell, A3.

Step 7	***Press***	the ENTER key
Step 8	***Key***	Selection.Font.ColorIndex = 5

This line sets the font color to 5, which is the color index code for the color blue.

Step 9	***Press***	the ENTER key
Step 10	***Key***	Range("A1").

After you type the period, a list appears displaying a list of valid actions belonging to the Range group of functions.

Step 11	***Scroll***	down the list until you see Select
Step 12	***Double-click***	Select

Your screen should look similar to Figure 15-6.

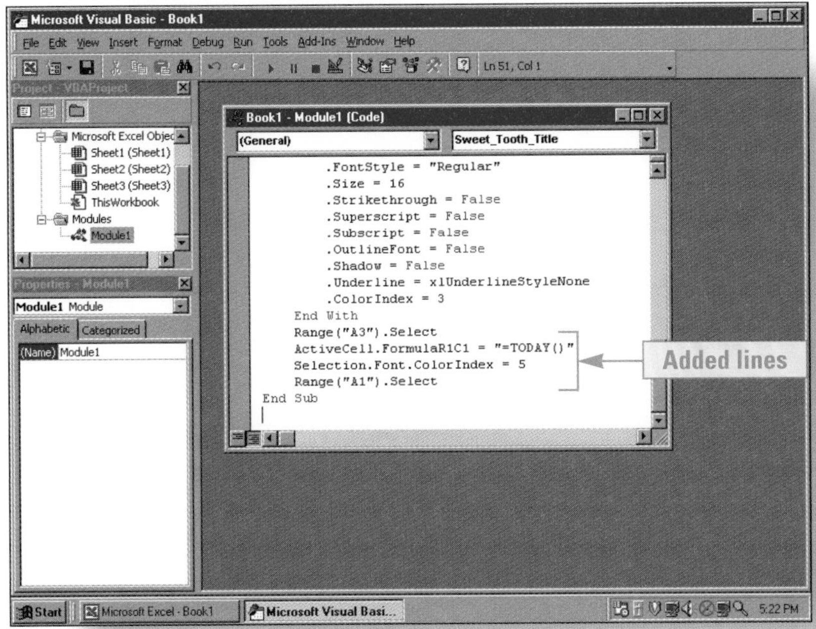

FIGURE 15-6
Editing a Macro

Now you can run your revised macro. To run your revised macro:

Step 1	***Click***	the Excel taskbar button
Step 2	***Click***	the Sheet3 worksheet tab
Step 3	***Click***	Tools
Step 4	***Point to***	Macro

Step 5	*Click*	Macros
Step 6	*Select*	Sweet_Tooth_Title from the list of available macros
Step 7	*Click*	Run

Your screen should look similar to Figure 15-7.

FIGURE 15-7
Results of the Revised Macro

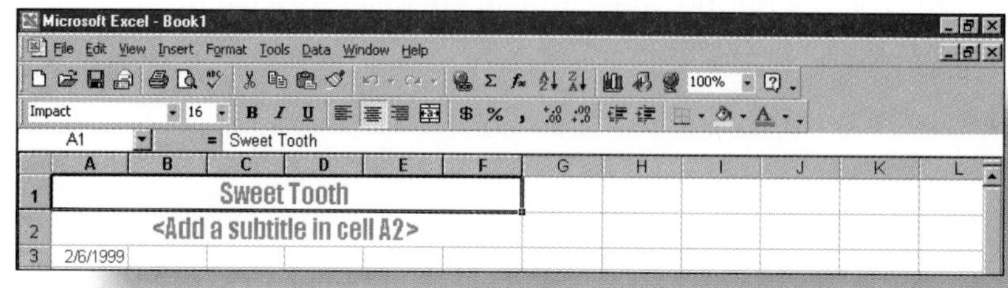

CAUTION TIP

If cell A3 displays TODAY(), click the Visual Basic taskbar button, click before the T in TODAY, and key an equal sign. Switch back to Excel and run the macro again.

To print the macro code and close the Visual Basic Editor:

Step 1	*Click*	the Visual Basic Editor taskbar button
Step 2	*Click*	File
Step 3	*Click*	Print
Step 4	*Click*	OK to print the current module
Step 5	*Click*	File
Step 6	*Click*	Close and Return to Microsoft Excel

The Visual Basic Editor closes, and the Excel window becomes the active window.

Step 7	*Save*	the workbook as *Sweet Tooth Title Macro*

15.d Using Workbooks Containing Macros

When you share workbooks with other users or download files from the Internet, your file(s)—or the downloaded files—could be infected with viruses. Viruses are malicious programs that can destroy files and data. **Macro viruses** are a special class of viruses that embed themselves in macros. When you open a workbook containing a macro virus, the virus can replicate itself to other workbooks, destroy files on your hard drive, and do other types of damage. Because of this threat, Excel prompts you before opening any file containing macros.

Opening a Workbook with Macros

The *Sweet Tooth Header Macro* workbook on your Data Disk contains a macro to automatically set up a header, and you want to edit it. To open a workbook containing a macro:

Step 1	*Open*	the *Sweet Tooth Header Macro* workbook on your Data Disk

Excel displays a warning dialog box, as shown in Figure 15-8.

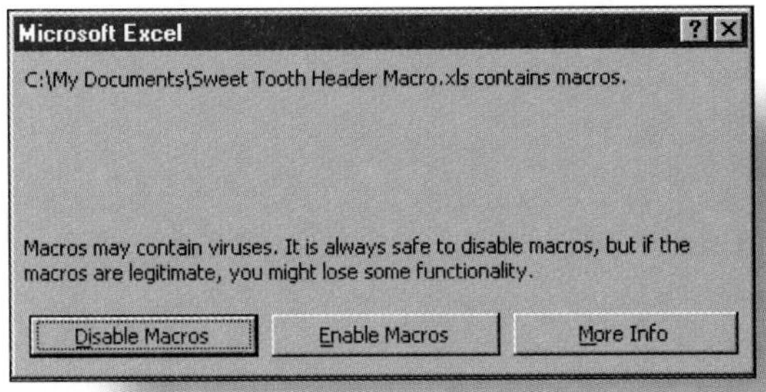

FIGURE 15-8
Macro Virus Warning Dialog Box

> **QUICK TIP**
>
> To scan your files for viruses, you must purchase special antivirus software capable of scanning your files, hard drive(s), and floppy drive(s). Most newer antivirus programs can scan files containing macros for macro viruses. For more information about macro viruses, use the Office Assistant.

Excel cannot determine whether a macro is actually a macro virus. If you are not sure about the origins of the workbook, you would select Disable Macros. The contents of the workbook can still be edited, but any special macros stored in the notebook cannot be executed. If possible, contact the person who created the workbook to find out which macros should appear in the workbook. Because you know that the source of this workbook is safe, you can open the file with macros enabled.

Step 2	*Click*	Enable Macros

Copying Macro Code to Another Workbook

You would like to copy the macro in this workbook to the *Sweet Tooth Title Macro* you created earlier. To copy macro code:

Step 1	*Click*	Tools
Step 2	*Point to*	Macro

Step 3	*Click*	Visual Basic Editor

Visual Basic Editor opens to the Sweet_Tooth_Header macro module.

Step 4	*Press*	the CTRL + A keys to select all of the code
Step 5	*Click*	the Copy button on the Visual Basic Editor Standard toolbar

In the Project Explorer window, you can expand the view for the Sweet Tooth Title project.

Step 6	*Click*	the + icon next to VBAProject (Sweet Tooth Title Macro.xls)

CAUTION TIP

Make sure you are clicking the + icon next to the VBAProject for Sweet Tooth Title Macro.xls, not Sweet Tooth Header Macro.xls.

If a – (minus sign) appears next to VBAProject (Sweet Tooth Title Macro.xls), do not click it.

Step 7	*Scroll*	down the Project Explorer window, if necessary
Step 8	*Right-click*	the Modules folder indented under VBAProject (Sweet Tooth Title Macro.xls)
Step 9	*Point to*	Insert
Step 10	*Click*	Module

A blank macro module opens.

Step 11	*Click*	the Paste button on the Visual Basic Editor Standard toolbar

The macro from *Sweet Tooth Header Macro* is pasted into the *Sweet Tooth Title Macro* workbook.

15.e Adding Visual Basic Functions to a Macro

Of course, macros can do more than modify font and alignment settings for a few cells. They can create charts, set header and footer options, and perform many other tasks. By adding a special Visual

Basic function called an InputBox, you can retrieve information from the user while the macro is running. You decide to add an InputBox to the Sweet_Tooth_Header macro that prompts Sweet Tooth employees to key in a header title. The macro automatically creates a custom header for printing reports from the header that the employee inputs. To add the InputBox function to the macro:

Step 1	*Press*	the CTRL + HOME keys to move to the top of the macro module
Step 2	*Move*	the insertion point in front of the W on the line With ActiveSheet.PageSetup (the first one)
Step 3	*Press*	the ENTER key to insert a new line
Step 4	*Press*	the UP ARROW key
Step 5	*Key*	HeaderText = InputBox("Enter a Header Title")

QUICK TIP

To find out more about Visual Basic functions, use Visual Basic Editor Help.

A **variable** is a placeholder for data; it is replaced by the actual data. By adding this line, you have assigned a variable called *HeaderText* to the result of a Visual Basic function called *InputBox*. This function displays a box with a space in which the user can enter new text. The text between quotes in the line you added appear as a prompt in the InputBox. Your screen should look similar to Figure 15-9.

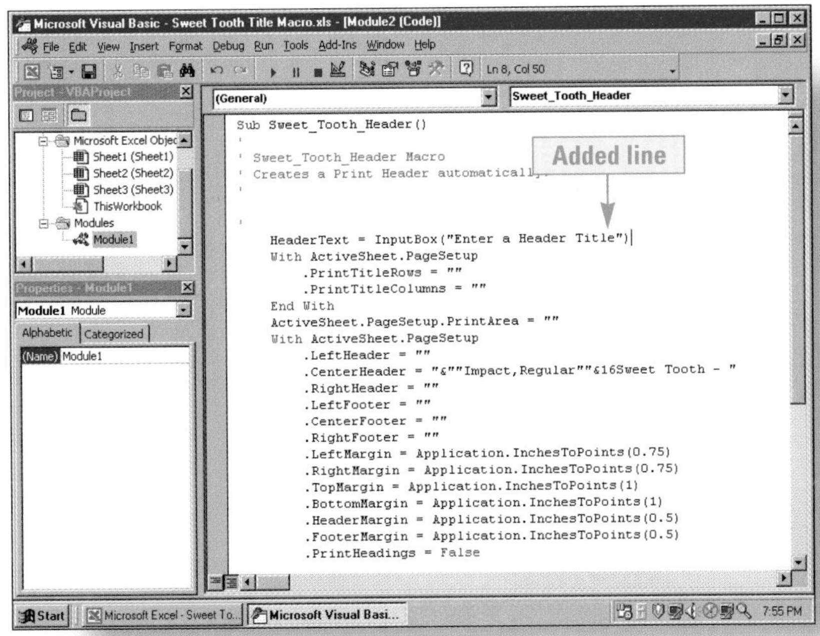

FIGURE 15-9
Adding an InputBox Function to a Macro

Now you need to tell the macro where to use the data held by the variable HeaderText.

Step 6	***Move***	the insertion point down eight lines to the line that reads .CenterHeader = "&""Impact,Regular""&16Sweet Tooth – "
Step 7	***Press***	the END key to move to the end of the line
Step 8	***Press***	the SPACEBAR
Step 9	***Key***	& HeaderText

This line adds the text "Sweet Tooth – " to the data held by the variable HeaderText. Your screen should look similar to Figure 15-10.

FIGURE 15-10
Using a Variable to Replace Values

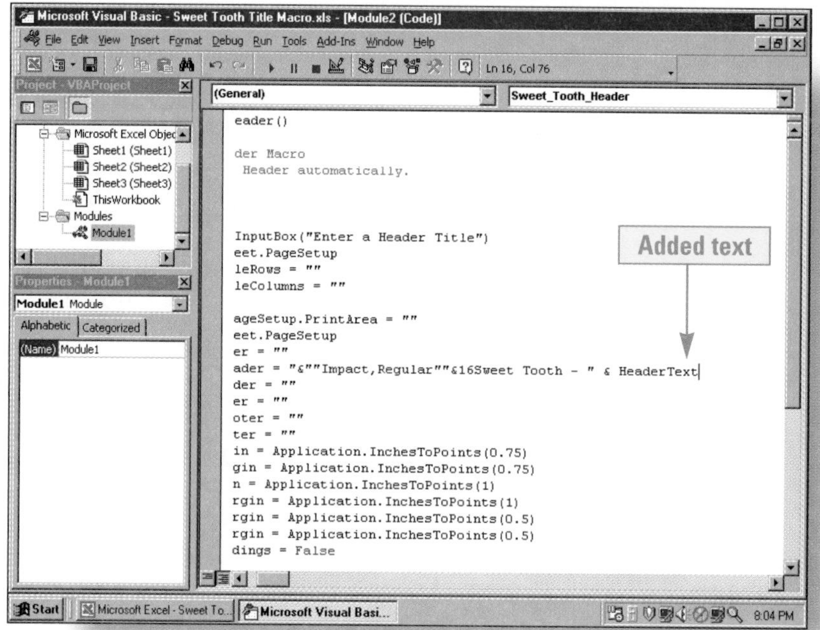

QUICK TIP

You can assign a macro to a toolbar button. Open the Customize dialog box, and click the Commands tab. Right-click a custom button that you've added to a toolbar, then click Assign Macro. Select the desired macro, then click OK.

Now test your macro. To run the macro:

Step 1	***Click***	the Excel taskbar button
Step 2	***Click***	Window
Step 3	***Select***	Sweet Tooth Title Macro from the menu list
Step 4	***Click***	Tools
Step 5	***Point to***	Macro
Step 6	***Click***	Macros
Step 7	***Select***	This workbook from the Macros in: list

Step 8	***Run***	the Sweet_Tooth_Header macro

The macro runs, and you see a dialog box similar to Figure 15-11.

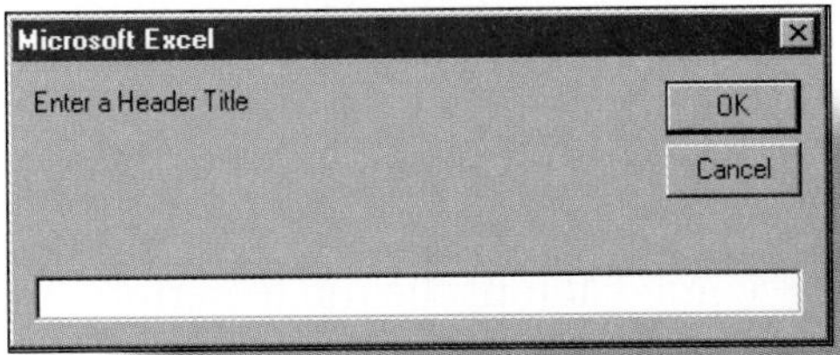

FIGURE 15-11
An InputBox

Step 9	***Key***	Central Region in the box
Step 10	***Click***	OK

After a moment (depending on the speed of your computer), you can edit your worksheet. To view your header:

Step 1	***Click***	the Print Preview button on the Standard toolbar
Step 2	***Print***	the worksheet
Step 3	***Save & Close***	the *Sweet Tooth Title Macro* workbook
Step 4	***Click***	the Visual Basic Editor taskbar button
Step 5	***Click***	File
Step 6	***Click***	Print
Step 7	***Click***	OK
Step 8	***Click***	File
Step 9	***Click***	Close and Return to Microsoft Excel
Step 10	***Close***	the *Sweet Tooth Header Macro* workbook

The macro you created will make it a snap to create new workbooks.

Summary

- A macro is a set of instructions that executes several commands automatically. Macros can be simple recorded steps, or they can be complex programs capable of making decisions based on user input.
- Recording a macro is the simplest way to create a macro. During the recording process, Excel records exactly what you do.
- Once a macro is recorded, it must be run to perform the desired task.
- Edit macros using the Visual Basic Editor. Visual Basic is the programming language used by Excel and other Office 2000 applications. The Visual Basic Editor is a separate application used to create, edit, delete, and test Visual Basic modules or macros.
- Some macros can contain viruses, or programs that can damage file on your computer system. If you are unsure of a workbook's origin, disable macros when you open the workbook. You can still view and edit data in the workbook.
- Copy macro code between Visual Basic projects (other workbooks) using the Cut and Paste commands.
- Use Visual Basic functions, like InputBox, to retrieve information from the user, assign that information to a variable, and then use the variable in other locations throughout your program.

Commands Review

Action	Menu Bar	Shortcut Menu	Toolbar	Keyboard
Record a macro	Tools, Macro, Record New Macro			ALT + T, M, R
Run or edit a macro	Tools, Macro, Macros then Run or Edit button			ALT + T, M, M, then R or E ALT + F8
Open the Visual Basic Editor	Tools, Macro, Visual Basic Editor			ALT + T, M, V ALT + F11

Concepts Review

Circle the correct answer.

1. Macros:
- [a] are much too difficult for the average user to program.
- [b] waste time because they run every time you open a workbook.
- [c] consist of a set of instructions that automatically executes a set of commands.
- [d] can never be modified.

2. Which of the following tasks can be performed by macros?
- [a] printing worksheets
- [b] creating and modifying charts
- [c] sorting lists
- [d] all of the above

3. To make a macro available in all workbooks, you should save it:
- [a] in every workbook you use.
- [b] in the Personal Macro Workbook.
- [c] on a floppy disk.
- [d] to the All Macros folder on your hard drive.

4. You edit macros in the:
- [a] Excel application window.
- [b] Macro dialog box.
- [c] Visual Basic Editor program window.
- [d] Record Macro dialog box.

5. Visual Basic is the programming language used by:
- [a] only Microsoft Excel.
- [b] only Microsoft Word.
- [c] only Microsoft Access.
- [d] all Office 2000 applications.

6. If you see REM, or an apostrophe (') in Visual Basic, what does it signify?
- [a] a shortened version of the REMOVE command
- [b] a blank line follows
- [c] a shortened version of REMARK, preceding a comment section
- [d] a shortened version of REMEMBER, preceding a programmer's reminder section

7. When you record a macro, you:
- [a] must write all the actions you want to perform, then key them in the Visual Basic Editor program window.
- [b] start recording, then Excel automatically records every keystroke.
- [c] must open the Visual Basic Editor first before Excel will record your keystrokes.
- [d] click the Record button after each keystroke so that mistakes are not recorded.

8. If you see a message telling you that a workbook contains macros, you should:

[a] always click Disable Macros because the workbook contains a virus.

[b] always click Enable Macros because the workbook will not display all the data unless you do.

[c] cancel the operation quickly because the macro may contain a virus.

[d] decide whether the workbook comes from a reliable source, then click either Disable or Enable Macros.

Circle **T** if the statement is true or **F** if the statement is false.

T F 1. Macros save a lot of time.

T F 2. It is nearly impossible to add user input to a macro.

T F 3. The Visual Basic Editor is part of the Excel application.

T F 4. You can write macros that work across several Office 2000 applications.

T F 5. Learning the basics of Visual Basic can help you write macros in all of the Office 2000 applications.

T F 6. The easiest way to create a macro is to open the Visual Basic Editor and key in the code by hand.

T F 7. If you make a mistake recording a macro, you have to record a new macro.

T F 8. When you see the macro virus warning when opening an Excel workbook, you should not open the workbook because it contains a macro virus.

T F 9. Macro viruses are usually harmful programs capable of copying themselves to other files and destroying data.

T F 10. A module is the basic storage unit for macros.

Skills Review

SCANS

Exercise 1

1. Open the *Sort List* file on your Data Disk.
2. Click any cell within the list of data on Sheet1.
3. Record a new macro called Sort1 and save it in the current workbook.
4. Sort the list by name in ascending order.
5. Stop recording the macro.
6. Record a second macro called Sort2 and save it in the current workbook.
7. Sort the list by region and then by name in ascending order.
8. Stop recording the macro.
9. Save the workbook as *Sort List with Macros.*

Exercise 2 

1. Open the *Sort List with Macros* workbook that you created in Exercise 1.
2. Display the Drawing toolbar.
3. Insert two bevel shapes from the Basic Shapes palette of the AutoShapes button.
4. Add Text to the first bevel shape that reads “Sort by Name.”
5. Add Text to the second bevel shape that reads “Sort by Region & Name.”
6. Resize the buttons so as to make it possible to read all text, if necessary.
7. Right-click the “Sort by Name” bevel object and select Assign Macro.
8. Select Sort1 from the Macro name: list, and click OK.
9. Repeat steps 7 and 8 to assign the Sort2 macro to the “Sort by Region & Name” bevel object.
10. Make sure that the active cell is within the list, then move your pointer over either of the bevel objects.
11. Click the bevel object to sort the list. Try the other bevel object. (*Hint:* You get a run-time error if the active cell is not within the list when you click one of the bevel objects. Click the End button and return to Excel. Move the active cell within the list and try again.)
12. Save the workbook as *Sort List with Macros 2.*

Exercise 3 

1. Open the *Sort List with Macros 2* workbook that you created in Exercise 2.
2. Record a new macro called Filter_Region, and save it in the current workbook.
3. Activate a cell within the list.
4. Apply AutoFilters.
5. Click the AutoFilter arrow for the Region column and select Central.
6. Open the Page Setup Dialog box (from the File menu), and select Landscape layout on the Page tab.
7. Click the Print button, then click OK to print the report.
8. Click the AutoFilter arrow for the Region column and select (All).
9. Stop recording the macro.
10. Save the workbook as *Sort List with Macros 3.*

Exercise 4 

1. Open the *Sort List with Macros 3* workbook that you created in Exercise 3.
2. Select the Filter_Region macro from beginning to end. (*Hint:* Press the CTRL + A keys in the code window to select all.)
3. Copy the code using the Copy button on the Visual Basic Editor Standard toolbar.
4. Move the insertion point to a new line below End Sub.
5. Paste the code using the Paste button on the Visual Basic Editor Standard toolbar.
6. Change the name of the second macro to Filter_Region2 by modifying the second Sub Filter_Region() line.
7. Edit the Filter_Region2 macro as follows (**bold** identifies added or modified sections):

   ...Leave the remarks section of the macro as is.
   CriteriaName = InputBox("Enter Region Name (Central, Mountain, East Coast, West Coast)")
   Selection.AutoFilter Field:=1, Criteria1:=**CriteriaName**
   With ActiveSheet.PageSetup
   ...Leave the rest of the macro as is.
   This change adds an InputBox that prompts the user for a region to filter and print. The response is assigned to the variable, CriteriaName, which is then used as the filter criteria.
8. Save the changes to your macro, print your macro, and return to Excel.
9. Run the new Filter_Region2 macro from the Macro dialog box.
10. Save the workbook as *Sort List with Macros 4*, then print the worksheet.

Exercise 5 

1. Open the *Central Region Sales 2* workbook on your Data Disk.
2. Record a macro called Chart. Store the macro in This Workbook.
3. Select cells A4:E8, and click the Chart Wizard button on the Standard toolbar.
4. Create a chart with the following characteristics:
   a. Select the Clustered Column with a 3-D visual effect chart subtype.
   b. Enter "Central Region Summary" for the Chart title.
   c. Create the chart as a new sheet.
   d. Name the new sheet "Central Region Summary Chart."
5. When the chart appears, click the Stop Recording button to stop recording the macro.
6. Delete the new chart sheet tab.
7. Run the macro to verify that it works correctly.
8. Save the workbook as *Central Region Sales 2 Chart.*

Exercise 6 

1. Open the *Central Region Sales 2 Chart* workbook that you created in Exercise 5.

2. Open the Macro dialog box, and select the Chart macro for editing.

3. In the Visual Basic Editor, edit the macro code as follows (insert the text in **bold**):

a. Insert **NM = ActiveSheet.Name** before the line Range("A4:E8").Select

b. Use Replace (press the CTRL + H keys) to replace "Central Region Summary" (including the quotation marks) with **NM**

c. Use Replace to replace all occurrences of "Central Region Summary Chart" (including the quotation marks) with **NM & " Summary Chart"** (include a space between the first quotation mark and the letter S).

d. In the line .ChartTitle.Characters.Text = "Central Region Summary Chart" replace "Central Region Summary Chart" with **NM & " Summary Chart"**

These changes find the current worksheet tab name and assign it to the variable NM. The macro then uses this variable to create and automatically give a title to a new chart, on a new chart sheet that it also names automatically.

4. Click the Excel taskbar button.

5. Click the South Division worksheet tab.

6. Run the Chart macro.

7. Create charts for each of the Division pages of your workbook using the Chart macro.

8. Print the charts.

9. Save the workbook as *Central Region Sales 2 Chart Revised.*

Exercise 7 

1. Open the *Central Region Sales 2 Chart Revised* workbook that you created in Exercise 6.

2. Record a new macro called "Set_Footer."

3. Use the Page Setup dialog box to set the following Footing options:

a. In the left section, print the Date.

b. In the center section, print the Tab name.

c. In the right section, print the Time.

4. Click OK to close the Footer and Page Setup dialog boxes.
5. Stop recording the macro.
6. Click the Central Region Summary Chart worksheet tab, and test your macro.
7. Print the macro.
8. Preview and print the chart.
9. Save the workbook as *Central Region Sales 2 Chart Revised 2*.

Exercise 8 

1. Open the *Central Region Sales 2 Chart Revised 2* workbook that you created in Exercise 7.
2. Save the workbook as *Central Region Sales 2 Chart Revised 3*.
3. Open the Macro dialog box, and click the Set_Footer macro.
4. Click Options.
5. Hold down the SHIFT key and press the F key to assign the hotkey CTRL + SHIFT + F to your macro.
6. Close the Macro dialog box.
7. Click the West Division Summary Chart tab.
8. Use the new hotkey to run the macro.
9. Print the worksheet.
10. Create a new toolbar called "Chart Tools."
11. Add two new Custom buttons to the toolbar from the Macro category on the Commands tab of the Customize dialog box.
12. Right-click the first button, and name it &Chart.
13. Click Assign Macro and assign the Chart macro to the button.
14. Right-click the second button and name it &Set Footer.
15. Click Assign Macro and assign the Set_Footer macro to the button.
16. Click the Toolbars tab in the Customize dialog box, then click Assign Macro.
17. Attach the toolbar to the workbook.
18. Save and close the workbook.
19. Open the Customize dialog box and delete the Chart Tools toolbar on the Toolbars tab.

Case Projects

Project 1 

As a busy student who uses Excel for many homework assignments, you find it tedious to constantly add your name, class, and date to your workbooks before you turn them in. In a new workbook, record a macro to insert three rows at the top of your workbook, and insert your name in cell A1, the class name in cell A2, and today's date in cell A3. Name the macro Name_Stamp. Test your macro on Sheet2 of your workbook. Save the workbook as *Name Stamp Macro*. Print your macro code and the worksheet.

Project 2 

Use the Web toolbar to locate your favorite search engine. Search the Internet for information about Visual Basic and Visual Basic for Applications. Focus your search on tutorials, especially those intended for beginners. Print at least two beginner tutorials, and save five links in your browser's Favorites or Bookmarks.

Project 3  

As the manager of a retail music store, you create a chart every week listing the best-selling CDs. Use the Internet to search for the Top 15 Best-Selling CDs for the current week. Create a new workbook containing the album title, artist name, and number of CDs sold. Generate fictitious sales data (for your store) for each CD.

Record a macro to do the following:

1. Sort the list by number of CDs sold, then by album title.
2. Create a chart selecting the top 10 best-selling albums.
3. Create a centered header with your store's name.
4. Create a footer with the date on the left and the time on the right.
5. Change the page layout to landscape orientation.
6. Print the chart.

Randomly change the number of albums sold, then run the macro again. Save the workbook as *Record Sales*. Print your macro code and the worksheet.

Project 4 

As an accountant who deals with a high volume of clients every day, you would like to be able to see the current date and time when you switch between clients. Start a new blank workbook, and save it as *Time Clock*. Using the Drawing tools, draw something resembling a clock face and group the objects. Open the Visual Basic Editor and double-click Module 1 of the Time Clock.xls project in the Project Explorer window. Use Visual Basic Help to create a message box that displays the current date and time. (*Hint:* Search for the MsgBox, Date, and Time functions.) Assign the macro to your clock object. Save the workbook as *Time Clock*. Print your macro code and the worksheet.

Project 5 

As a busy account manager, you are constantly adding new worksheets to existing workbooks. Create a macro to automatically insert a new sheet and prompt the user for a sheet name using an InputBox. Assign the shortcut keys CTRL + SHIFT + N to your macro. (*Hint:* Record the steps to insert and name a worksheet first, then add the InputBox function using the Visual Basic Editor. Just after the Sheets.Add line, insert a new line: NM = ActiveSheet.Name to assign the new sheet name to the variable NM. Next, replace sheet name references with the variable. Your macro will then insert new sheets as often as you want.) Save the workbook as *Insert New Sheet*. Print your macro code and the worksheet.

Project 6

As the newly hired personnel manager, you have located several workbooks on your computer that list employees' first names, but not their last names. Create a new workbook with five first names. Copy this list to Sheet2 in your workbook. Record a macro called Replace_Names to find and replace one of the names on the worksheet with the first and last name of the employee. In the Visual Basic Editor, copy the two lines recorded by the macro four additional times (above the End Sub line). Modify the copied code to search and replace each of the names you listed on Sheet1 with the first and last names of each employee. Go back to Excel, and run your macro on Sheet2. Save the workbook as *Replace Names*. Print your macro code and the worksheets.

Project 7

You are worried about the security of workbooks that you share with other people over the Internet. Search the Internet for information about Excel macro viruses. Print at least one page identifying one existing Excel macro virus, explaining what it does, and describing how you can eliminate it.

Project 8

You would like to find out more about writing macros to automate Excel. Search the Internet for pages that contain macro tutorials or explain how to create macros in Excel. Print at least one page.

Using What-If Analysis

Chapter Overview

Finding solutions to complex business problems is one of the things that Excel does best. Data tables allow you to quickly recalculate a formula by replacing one argument with several values. Goal Seek and Solver help you reach a desired outcome. Scenarios let you save and restore several variables in your worksheets.

Learning Objectives

- Create data tables
- Use Goal Seek and Solver
- Create scenarios

Case profile

To be successful in business, you must know how to analyze information and how to make decisions based on the analysis of that information. This month, Sweet Tooth is looking to expand its fleet of cars and needs to know how much the company can afford to borrow. The warehouse division is also seeking a solution to some scheduling problems. Using a variety of what-if analysis tools, you can resolve all of these problems.

chapter sixteen

16.a Creating Data Tables

One of Excel's key strengths is its ability to help you perform what-if analyses. In a **what-if analysis,** you change data values and then observe the effect on calculations—for example, "What if I change the value in cell A2?" To make this kind of trial-and-error process easier, you can use **data tables** to show the results of a formula by replacing one or two of the variables with several different values. **One-variable data tables** can be created to show the results of changing one variable in several formulas at once. **Two-variable data tables** can show the results of changing two variables in a single formula.

Creating a One-Variable Data Table

You learned about using variables when creating macros. A variable is a placeholder for a value. You can assign different values to a **variable**, then use that variable in a formula or calculation. A **one-variable data table** uses a variable to replace one of the arguments in a given formula and then calculates results using several different values for that one argument.

Sweet Tooth is considering purchasing a fleet of automobiles for some of its sales representatives. The purchase amount of each car is $25,000, with a loan interest rate of 10%. The company wants to find out what the monthly payment will be per car, and how much interest will be paid depending on the term of the loan. In this case, the term argument is the variable.

To set up a one-variable data table:

Step 1	***Open***	the *Interest Calculator* workbook on your Data Disk
Step 2	***Save***	the workbook as *Interest Calculator Revised* in your Data Files folder

QUICK TIP

For more information about these functions, use the Office Assistant.

Recall from Chapter 7, the CUMIPMT function calculates the cumulative interest paid, given a start and end period. The PMT function calculates the monthly payment on a loan. Both of these financial functions share common arguments, including the rate (percentage), nper (number of periods in the life of the loan), and pv (present value of the loan).

In this workbook, the loan information has already been entered. Cell B5 holds the value representing the nper argument used in both the CUMIPMT and the PMT functions. This value will be replaced by the values in cells C5:C8, which are shaded in green. (In this case, the period of time for the nper argument is months.) The payment (PMT) calculation takes place in column D. The cumulative interest (CUMIPMT) is calculated in column E.

Step 3	***Enter***	=PMT(B4/12,B5,B6) in cell D4
Step 4	***Enter***	=CUMIPMT(B4/12,B5,B6,1,B5,1) in cell E4

Your screen should look similar to Figure 16-1.

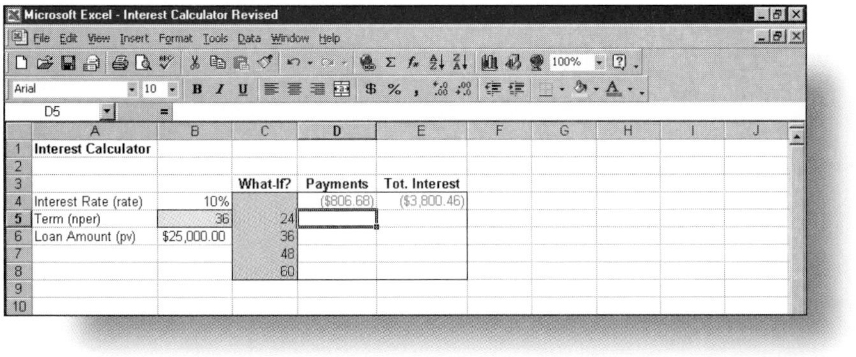

FIGURE 16-1
Setting Up a One-Variable Data Table

Now that the formulas and information are set up, you can see what happens if you change the term of the loan.

To perform a what-if analysis using a one-variable data table:

Step 1	***Select***	cells C4:E8
Step 2	***Click***	Data
Step 3	***Click***	Table

The Table dialog box opens. Because the replacement values you will use are arranged in a column, you use a Column input cell.

Step 4	***Click***	in the Column input cell: box
Step 5	***Click***	cell B5

The data table automatically replaces the value in cell B5 with each of the values in the leftmost column of the data table you've selected.

First, Excel calculates the PMT function using the value 24 (the first value in column C) instead of the current value of cell B5. Then, Excel calculates the PMT function again, using the next value in column C, 36, in place of the current value of cell B5. Excel continues this process until it reaches the end of the table you selected. See Figure 16-2.

FIGURE 16-2
Choosing the Variable in a One-Variable Data Table

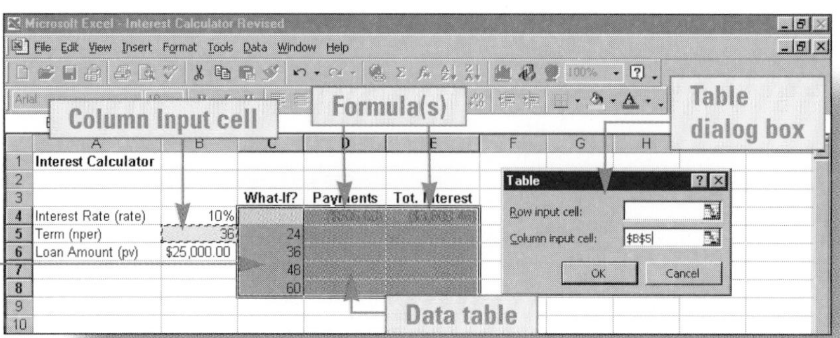

Step 6	*Click*	OK
Step 7	***Click***	**cell A1**

The monthly payment and cumulative interest for each term length are calculated, as shown in Figure 16-3.

FIGURE 16-3
One-Variable Data Table Calculated

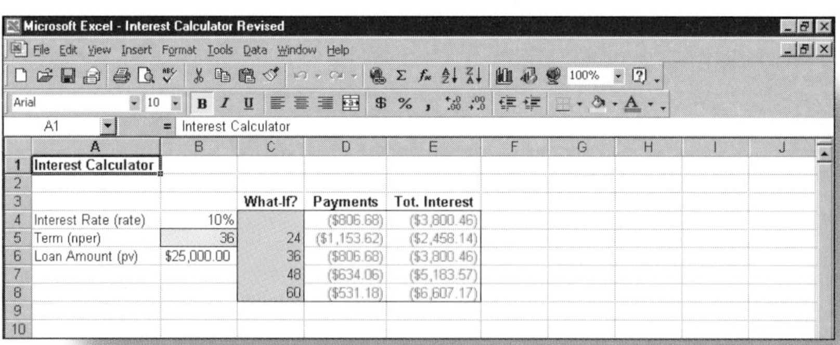

Step 8	*Save*	the workbook

Creating a Two-Variable Data Table

Two-variable data tables allow you to see the results of a formula that uses two variables. You want to calculate the monthly payments on the auto loan for various terms at different interest rates.

To set up a two-variable data table:

Step 1	*Click*	the Two Variable worksheet tab
Step 2	*Enter*	=PMT(B4/12,B5,B6) in cell C4

Two-variable data tables can use only one formula at a time, and this formula must be located in the cell directly above the column of the first replacement values and to the right of the second replacement values. The result of the formula, ($806.68), appears in cell C4, as shown in Figure 16-4.

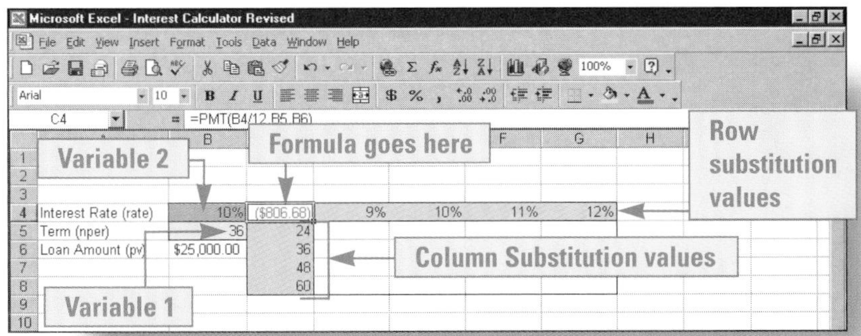

FIGURE 16-4
Preparing a Two-Variable Data Table

Now you can perform the what-if calculations. To perform a what-if analysis using a two-way data table:

Step 1	*Select*	cells C4:G8
Step 2	*Click*	Data
Step 3	*Click*	Table
Step 4	*Click*	cell B4 so that it appears as an absolute reference in the Row input cell: box
Step 5	*Click*	in the Column input cell: box
Step 6	*Click*	cell B5
Step 7	*Click*	OK
Step 8	*Click*	cell A1

Your final data table should look similar to Figure 16-5.

FIGURE 16-5
Two-Variable Data Table

	A	B	C	D	E	F	G
1	**Interest Calculator**						
2							
3							
4	Interest Rate (rate)	10%	($806.68)	9%	10%	11%	12%
5	Term (nper)	36	24	($1,142.12)	($1,153.62)	($1,165.20)	($1,176.84)
6	Loan Amount (pv)	$25,000.00	36	($794.99)	($806.68)	($818.47)	($830.36)
7			48	($622.13)	($634.06)	($646.14)	($658.35)
8			60	($518.96)	($531.18)	($543.56)	($556.11)
9							
10							

Step 9	***Save & Close*** the workbook

16.b Using Goal Seek and Solver

Excel includes several tools to help you solve complex problems. When you know the desired result of a formula but the values currently used in the formula don't produce the correct result, you can use the **Goal Seek** tool to change a variable in the formula and obtain the correct result. Goal Seek can modify only one variable. **Solver** works in much the same way, but it allows you to change the values of several variables; at the same time, it sets constraints on how much you can alter those variables.

Using Goal Seek

Sweet Tooth has decided to purchase 40 new cars for the company, at a total cost of $1,000,000. The company would like to pay off the loan in 36 months, but it has a budget of only $30,000 per month available to make payments. The Board of Directors needs to know how much money Sweet Tooth can borrow at 10%, and how much cash it needs to meet this budget limitation.

To set up the workbook:

Step 1	***Open***	the *Car Purchase* workbook on your Data Disk
Step 2	***Save***	the workbook as *Car Purchase Revised* in your Data Files folder
Step 3	***Enter***	=PMT(B8/12,B9,B10) in cell B13

The monthly payment is calculated at $32,267.19. You need to adjust the loan amount so that the monthly payment fits the budget of $30,000. To use Goal Seek:

Step 1	*Activate*	cell B13
Step 2	*Click*	Tools
Step 3	*Click*	Goal Seek
Step 4	*Click*	in the To value: box
Step 5	*Key*	-30000

The company will be paying this amount out, so you use a negative number to indicate it is an expense.

Step 6	*Press*	the TAB key to move to the By changing cell: box
Step 7	*Click*	cell B10

The completed Goal Seek dialog box is shown in Figure 16-6.

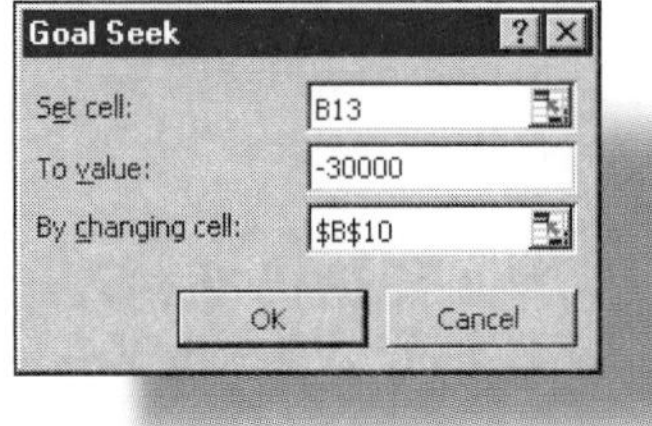

FIGURE 16-6
Goal Seek Dialog Box

Goal Seek finds the solution and displays the Goal Seek Status dialog box. When you click the OK button, Excel changes the value of the variable cell—B10 in this case—so that the formula in cell B13 meets your goal.

Step 8	*Click*	OK

Figure 16-7 shows the results of the Goal Seek operation. To meet the budgeted payment amount of $30,000 per month, Sweet Tooth can borrow a maximum of $929,737.

FIGURE 16-7
Goal Seek Status Dialog Box

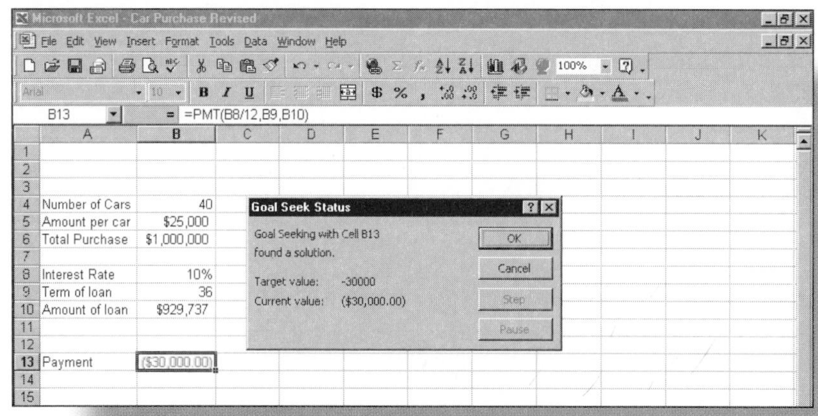

Step 9	***Click*** OK to accept the Goal Seek solution
Step 10	***Save & Close*** the workbook

notes

Solver is an Excel Add-In that must be installed before you can use it. If you do not have a Solver option on the Tools menu, click Tools, then click Add-Ins. Click Solver Add-In, and then click OK to install Solver.

Using Solver

Amy Lee, Sweet Tooth's president, has requested that all divisions of the company study ways to save the company money. Many departments are overstaffed, but some departments are understaffed or are not scheduling employees efficiently. The warehouse has especially serious scheduling problems.

The warehouse division currently employs 64 employees and runs seven days a week. Each employee works a schedule of five days on, two days off. Under the current schedule, approximately 45 employees are scheduled each day, but this system creates problems. More employees are needed during the week, when the warehouse is at its busiest. The goal is to minimize the amount of payroll paid out each week, by reducing the staff required to meet the demand for each day. Sound like a complicated problem? It is, and that's why Solver is so useful.

To open the workbook and save it with a new name:

Step 1	***Open***	the *Warehouse Personnel Scheduling* workbook on your Data Disk
Step 2	***Save***	the workbook as *Warehouse Personnel Scheduling Solution* in your Data Files folder

This worksheet shows the scheduling for employees in the warehouse. The number of employees currently assigned to each shift appears in cells C5:C11, with the total number of employees being displayed in cell C13. Cells D13:J13 calculate the number of employees working each day by multiplying the number of employees on each shift by the on value of 1 or the off value of 2 for each day on the schedule. Cells D15:J15 indicate the actual numbers of employees that the warehouse needs on staff each day. Cells C18 and C19 calculate the payroll total for each week. Each warehouse employee is paid $70 per day.

To use Solver to create the most efficient schedule:

Step 1	***Click***	Tools
Step 2	***Click***	Solver

The Solver Parameters dialog box appears, as shown in Figure 16-8.

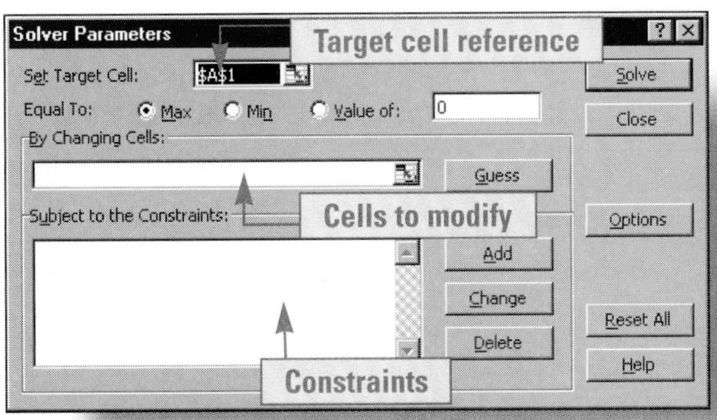

FIGURE 16-8
Solver Parameters Dialog Box

The goal of this activity is to reduce the total payroll, so cell C19 is the target. To set the Solver target:

Step 1	***Click***	cell C19
Step 2	***Click***	the Min option button next to Equal To:

Solver looks for the solution that results in the lowest possible value for the target cell C19. Next, you need to specify which cells can be changed to reach the goal.

To identify which cells can be changed:

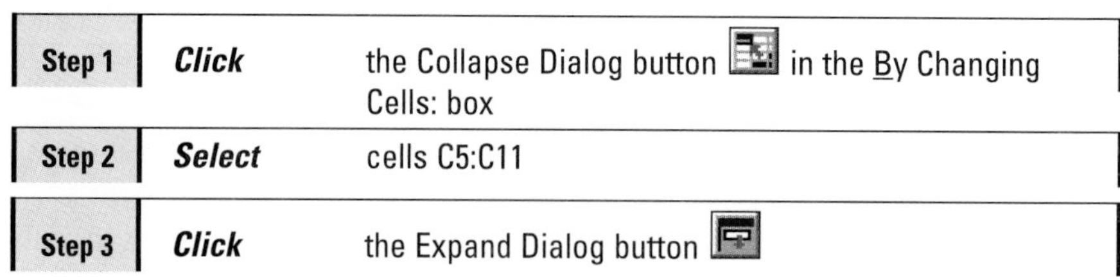

Step 1	***Click***	the Collapse Dialog button in the By Changing Cells: box
Step 2	***Select***	cells C5:C11
Step 3	***Click***	the Expand Dialog button

Solver now changes the number of employees on each shift to best reduce the amount of payroll paid each week. Before Solver eliminates the entire warehouse staff, you should apply some constraints. The first constraint is to make sure that at least one employee serves on each shift. Second, the number of employees on each shift must be greater than or equal to the total demand for each day. Finally, you need to force Excel to use whole numbers—after all, it's difficult to get 0.58 of a worker to appear at work on any given day.

To add constraints:

Step 1	***Click***	Add

The Add Constraint dialog box appears with the insertion point blinking in the Cell Reference box.

Step 2	***Select***	cells D13:J13
Step 3	***Select***	>= in the constraint type list (in the middle of the dialog box)
Step 4	***Key***	1 in the Constraint: box

Your screen should look similar to Figure 16-9.

FIGURE 16-9
Add Constraint Dialog Box

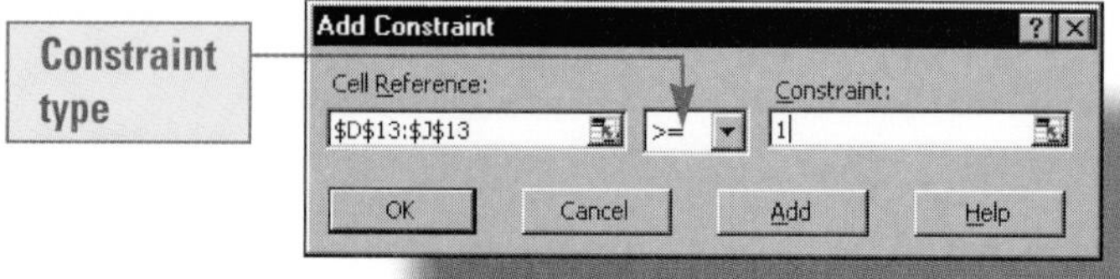

Step 5	*Click*	OK

The constraint is displayed in the Subject to the Constraints list. Next, you add a constraint to ensure that the total demand for employees for each day is met.

To add this constraint:

Step 1	*Click*	Add
Step 2	*Select*	cells D13:J13 in the Cell Reference: box
Step 3	*Select*	>= in the constraint type list
Step 4	*Select*	cells D15:J15 in the Constraint: box

This constraint requires the values in cells D13:J13 to be greater than or equal to the values in cells D15:J15. You need the number of employees on each schedule to be a whole number, so you also apply an integer constraint.

Step 5	*Click*	Add

This adds the constraint, and clears the Add Constraint dialog box for a new entry.

Step 6	*Select*	cells C5:C11
Step 7	*Select*	int in the constraint type list
Step 8	*Click*	OK
Step 9	*Click*	Solve

Depending on the worksheet and the speed of your computer, Solver may take a few seconds to perform its calculations. Solver figures out the solution, displays the results on your worksheet, and opens the Solver Results dialog box.

QUICK TIP

The Options button provides settings to optimize Solver's calculation methods; it also allows you to save and load Solver models for use in other worksheets. If you want to change the way that Solver calculates solutions, open the Solver dialog box, then click Options. Use the What's This? command or the Office Assistant to learn more about the Solver Options dialog box.

Your screen should look similar to Figure 16-10.

FIGURE 16-10
Solver Results Dialog Box

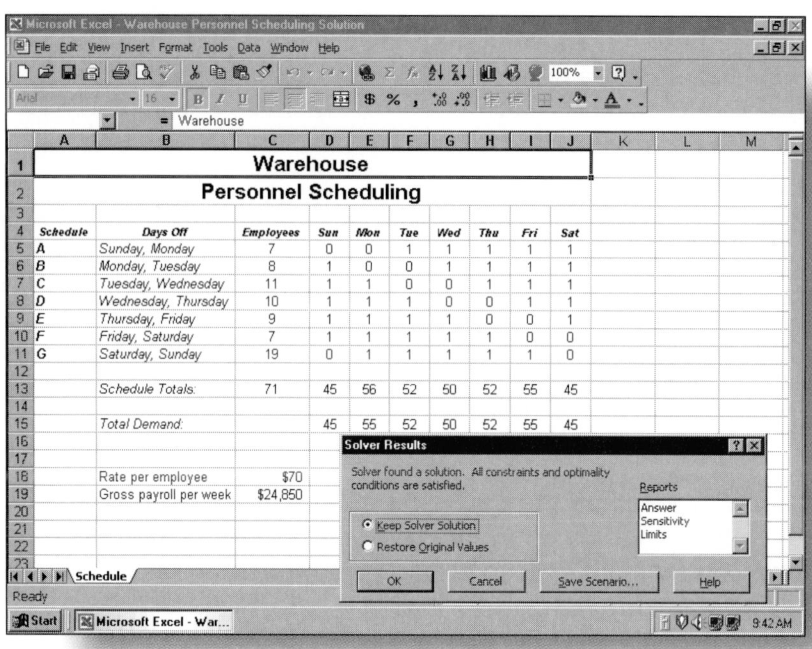

CAUTION TIP

Once you complete the Solver operation, you cannot undo it. Before closing the Solver Results dialog box, you have the option of restoring the original values. Click the Restore Original Values option button, then click OK.

Interestingly, the best solution for the warehouse is to add more employees. By doing so, Solver came up with a scheduling solution that provides the correct number of employees for each day of the week. Only once does the number of employees exceed the required number of employees.

Step 10	*Click*	Answer in the Reports list box
Step 11	*Click*	OK

The Answer Report 1 worksheet tab is added to your workbook.

Step 12	*Click*	the newly created Answer Report 1 worksheet tab

The Answer Report provides information about the calculations and constraints used by Solver to generate the solution. It displays information about the date on which this solution was created, and provides all data used in the solution, including the target cell, adjustable cells, and constraints. Original cell values are shown adjacent to the final cell values after Solver is run. Your screen should look similar to Figure 16-11.

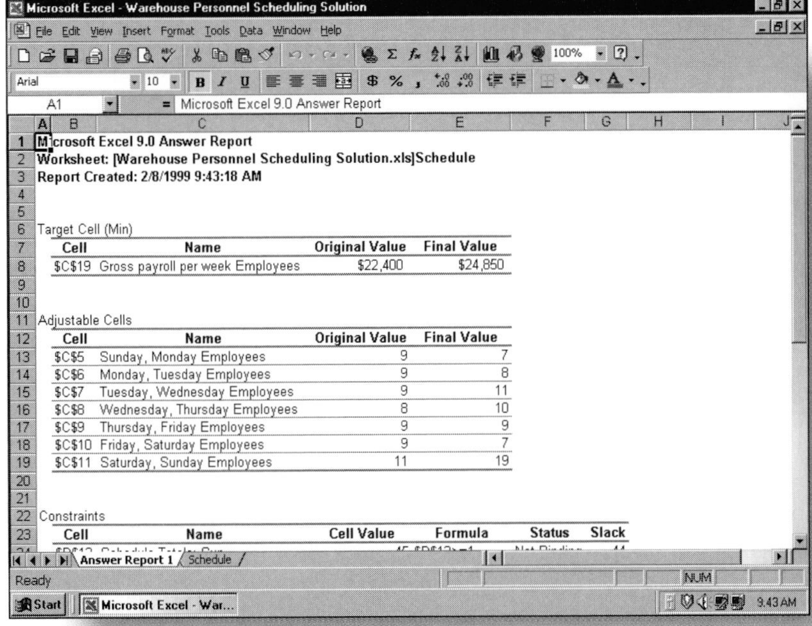

FIGURE 16-11
Solver Answer Report

QUICK TIP

To find out more information about the Limits and Sensitivity reports, use the Office Assistant.

Step 13	*Save*	the workbook

16.c Creating Scenarios

The tools introduced in this chapter—data tables, Goal Seek, and Solver—are designed to allow you maximum flexibility in asking the question, "What if?" Many times, you need to quickly see the results of several "What if?" situations. For example, what if the current level of activity in the warehouse drops off? What if the current level of activity in the warehouse increases, as it always does during the holiday season?

The demand values in cells D15:J15 indicate how many employees are needed on a given day. By using scenarios, you can change the values contained in these cells and run Solver using the new set of values to find a solution that satisfies the constraints of the given scenario.

Creating Scenarios

Scenarios allow you to quickly replace the values in several cells with another set of values, which you can then use in formulas throughout the worksheet. To create scenarios:

Step 1	***Click***	the Schedule worksheet tab
Step 2	***Select***	cells D15:J15
Step 3	***Click***	Tools
Step 4	***Click***	Scenarios

The Scenario Manager dialog box appears, as shown in Figure 16-12.

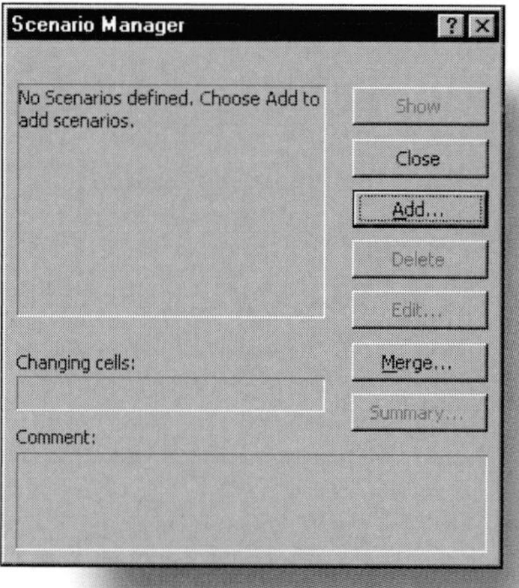

FIGURE 16-12
Scenario Manager Dialog Box

Step 5	***Click***	Add

The Add Scenario dialog box opens. In this dialog box, you can name your scenario, select the cells to be changed under the new scenario, and add descriptive comments about your scenario.

QUICK TIP

Drag the scroll box down to see the rest of the cells you selected.

Step 6	***Enter***	Normal Demand in the Scenario name: box
Step 7	***Verify***	that the Changing cells: box references D15:J15
Step 8	***Click***	at the end of the Created by...on MM/DD/YY comment in the Comment: box
Step 9	***Press***	the ENTER key

Step 10	*Key*	This is normal demand for April-September.
Step 11	*Click*	OK

The Scenario Values dialog box appears, allowing you to enter different values for each of the changing cells. See Figure 16-13. Because the values currently in those cells are the Normal Demand values, you can leave them alone.

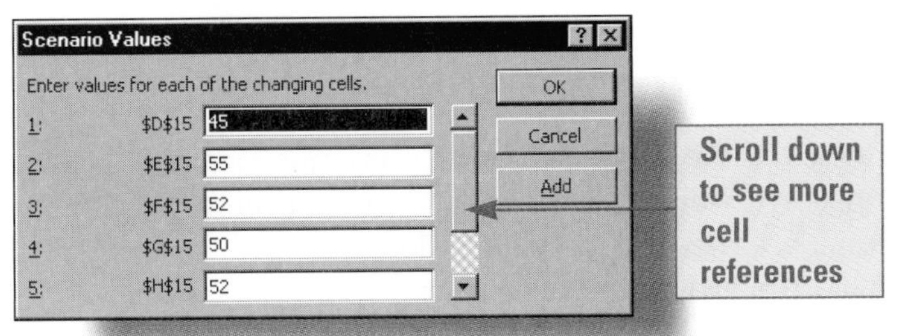

FIGURE 16-13
Scenario Values Dialog Box

QUICK TIP

Press the TAB key to move from box to box in the Scenarios Values dialog box.

Step 12	*Click*	OK to return to the Scenario Manager dialog box
Step 13	*Click*	Add and create another scenario named Low Demand that covers January-March
Step 14	*Click*	OK in the Add Scenario dialog box
Step 15	*Key*	20 in the 1: box next to D15
Step 16	*Press*	the TAB key
Step 17	*Continue*	replacing the current values in Table 16-1

TABLE 16-1
Low Demand

Changing Cell	New Value
D15	20
E15	45
F15	45
G15	40
H15	45
I15	50
J15	20

Step 18	*Click*	OK
Step 19	*Create*	a scenario named High Demand that covers October-December and uses the values in Table 16-2

TABLE 16-2
High Demand

Changing Cell	New Value
D15	40
E15	60
F15	60
G15	60
H15	60
I15	65
J15	40

QUICK TIP

To show your scenario as a PivotTable, select the Scenario PivotTable option button. You must also select Result cells that perform calculations on the cells saved in your scenario(s).

Displaying Scenarios

Once you've created different scenarios, you can display each one and replace the values in row 15, then run Solver to calculate the number of employees needed for each period.

To display different scenarios:

Step 1	*Select*	Low Demand in the Scenarios: list in the Scenario Manager dialog box
Step 2	*Click*	Show
Step 3	*Click*	Close

The values in cells D15:J15 have changed to display the scenario values you created.

Step 4	*Click*	Tools
Step 5	*Click*	Scenario
Step 6	*Show*	the High Demand scenario
Step 7	*Click*	Close

You can create a scenario report to display the values contained in each scenario. To create a scenario report:

Step 1	*Open*	the Scenario Manager dialog box
Step 2	*Click*	Summary
Step 3	*Verify*	that the Scenario summary option button is selected
Step 4	*Click*	OK

A scenario summary is created and inserted on a new worksheet named Scenario Summary, which automatically becomes the active worksheet. Your summary should look similar to Figure 16-14.

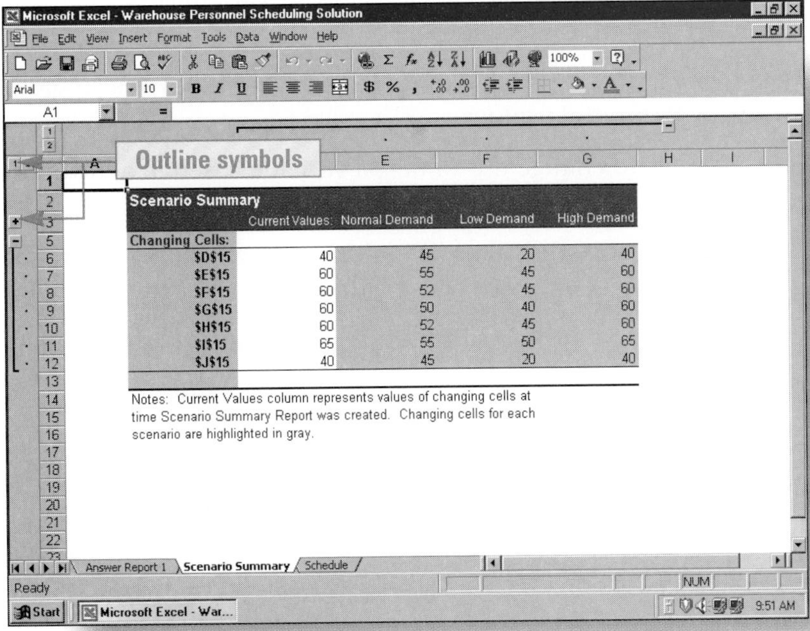

FIGURE 16-14
Scenario Summary

This scenario summary lists the current values of the changing cells as well as the values for each of the defined scenarios.

Step 5	***Print***	the workbook
Step 6	***Save***	the workbook
Step 7	***Close***	the workbook

Using these different scenarios, you can run Solver to find the best solution for each period of the year.

MOUSE TIP

Click the Outline symbols on the left to expand the outline and view the comments for each scenario.

QUICK TIP

C Report Manager is a useful add-in that helps you create and organize a **report**, a combination of a worksheet, a custom view, and a scenario. Using Report Manager you can create multiple reports for each workbook, making it easy to print several different areas of your workbook at once. Once installed and activated in the Add-Ins dialog box, you can find the Report Manager command on the View menu. For more information about creating reports with Report Manager, use the Office Assistant.

Summary

- Use a one-variable data table to replace one variable of a formula(s) with multiple values.
- Use a two-variable data table to replace two variables of a single formula with multiple values.
- Use Goal Seek to change the values of variables used in a formula to obtain a certain result.
- Use Solver to change the values of multiple cells and apply constraints to limit the changes of those cells so as to obtain a certain result.
- Create a solution report to summarize the changes made by Solver.
- Use scenarios to store cell values for different situations.
- Create a scenario report to see the information saved in Scenario Manager.

Commands Review

Action	Menu Bar	Shortcut Menu	Toolbar	Keyboard
Create a data table	Data, Table			ALT + D, T
Use Goal Seek	Tools, Goal Seek			ALT + T, G
Use Solver	Tools, Solver			ALT + T, V
Create scenarios	Tools, Scenarios			ALT + T, E

Concepts Review

Circle the correct answer.

1. If you want to see how different interest rates and different terms affect the payment of a loan, which of the following tools would you use?
[a] one-variable data table
[b] two-variable data table
[c] Solver
[d] Goal Seek

2. Solving complex business problems often requires you to:
[a] look at a problem several ways.
[b] know the expected outcome of a formula.
[c] perform a what-if analysis.
[d] all of the above.

3. Which of the following is not a Solver report?
[a] Answer
[b] Sensitivity
[c] Limits
[d] Scenario

4. Which of the following is not a setting used by Solver?
[a] Target
[b] Changing cells
[c] Constraints
[d] Summary

5. Goal Seek is useful when you:
[a] know the outcome and have to change only one variable.
[b] know the outcome and have to change multiple variables.
[c] don't know the outcome, but know one of the variables.
[d] don't know the outcome, but know two of the variables.

6. Constraints:
[a] cannot be modified.
[b] set limits regarding how much a cell's value can be changed.
[c] help Solver run faster.
[d] set limits regarding the speed at which Solver runs.

7. A what-if analysis can show you:
[a] how changing data affects various calculations.
[b] how to set up one-variable data tables if you don't know the value of any of the variables.
[c] which feature is the better choice to solve your problem—Goal Seek or Solver.
[d] which calculations change if you change a variable.

8. In a two-variable data table you can replace:
- [a] two variables in more than one formula.
- [b] two variables in a single formula.
- [c] one variable in two formulas.
- [d] one variable in one formula.

9. The Scenario Manager allows you to:
- [a] add a new scenario.
- [b] delete a scenario.
- [c] generate a Scenario Summary Report.
- [d] all of the above.

10. If you know the outcome you want for a given formula and can change multiple values, which tool should you use?
- [a] scenarios
- [b] Solver
- [c] one-variable data table
- [d] Goal Seek

Circle **T** if the statement is true or **F** if the statement is false.

T F 1. You can use more than one formula in a one-variable data table.

T F 2. You can use more than one formula in a two-variable data table.

T F 3. You can create a what-if analysis by manually changing the values of cells referenced in a formula.

T F 4. Goal Seek can create a report when it finds a solution.

T F 5. Solver is the best tool to use whenever you're trying to do a what-if analysis.

T F 6. Solver can create three different reports when it has found a solution.

T F 7. You can save a scenario from Solver.

T F 8. The formula for a two-variable data table must appear immediately above the column variables and immediately to the right of row variables.

T F 9. Once you run Solver, you cannot get back your original data.

T F 10. A Scenario Summary Report and the Solver Answer Report are the same thing.

Skills Review

Exercise 1

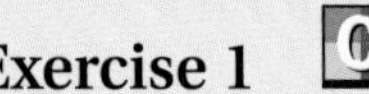

1. Open the *Warehouse Personnel Scheduling 2* file on your Data Disk.

2. Set up constraints in the Solver Parameters dialog box to accomplish the following:

a. The goal is to reduce the value of cell C19 to a minimum.

b. The values in cells C5:C11 can change, but must be integers and must be greater than or equal to 1.

c. The values in cells D13:J13 must meet the total demand in cells D15:J15.

3. Solve the workbook and create an Answer Report.
4. Print the schedule and the Answer Report.
5. Save the workbook as *Warehouse Personnel Scheduling Solution 1.*

Exercise 2 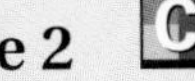

1. Open the *Warehouse Personnel Scheduling Solution 1* workbook that you created in Exercise 1.
2. Create four scenarios called 1st Quarter, 2nd Quarter, 3rd Quarter, and 4th Quarter by changing cells D15:J15 on the Schedule tab. Values for each scenario are listed below:
   a. 1st Quarter—use values as currently set
   b. 2nd Quarter—D15=37, E15=54, F15=56, G15=56, H15=60, I15=52, J15=40
   c. 3rd Quarter—D15=35, E15=52, F15=52, G15=50, H15=55, I15=48, J15=37
   d. 4th Quarter—D15 = 45, E15 = 55, F15 = 55, G15 = 55, H15 = 60, I15 = 55, J15 = 45
3. Create and print the Answer Report.
4. Save the workbook as *Warehouse Personnel Scheduling Scenarios.*

Exercise 3 

1. Open the *Warehouse Personnel Scheduling Scenarios* workbook that you created in Exercise 2.
2. Rename the Answer Report 1 tab to 1st Quarter Answer.
3. Show the 2nd Quarter scenario.
4. Run Solver and create an Answer Report.
5. Rename the tab 2nd Quarter Answer.
6. Repeat steps 3–5 to show the 3rd and 4th Quarter scenarios, run Solver and generate an Answer Report, and rename the Answer Report tab.
7. Print the Answer Report tabs.
8. Save the workbook as *Warehouse Personnel Scheduling Scenarios 2.*

Exercise 4 

1. Open the *Warehouse Personnel Scheduling Scenarios 2* workbook that you created in Exercise 3.
2. Click the Schedule tab.
3. Generate a Scenario summary.
4. Print the Scenario summary.
5. Save the workbook as *Warehouse Personnel Scheduling Scenarios 3.*

Exercise 5

1. Open the *Home Purchase* workbook on your Data Disk.
2. Use Goal Seek to find the maximum amount of loan given the following:
   a. Use B8 as the goal, with a value of 650.
   b. Change the value in cell B5.
3. Save the workbook as *Home Purchase Loan* and print the workbook.

Exercise 6

1. Open the *System Purchase* file on your Data Disk.
2. Use Solver to find the optimum purchasing solution given the following parameters:
   a. Seek the minimum total purchase price in cell D7.
   b. Change cells C4:C7.
   c. Use the following constraints:
   C4:C7 must be integers.
   You need to buy at least 65 new computers.
   At least 15 computers need to be PII-450s.
   At least 20 computers need to be PII-333s.
   The total number of K6-2 333s cannot exceed 20.
3. Generate an Answer Report.
4. Print your solution and the Answer Report.
5. Save the workbook as *System Purchase Solution.*

Exercise 7 

1. Open the *Manufacturing Production* workbook on your Data Disk.
2. Use Solver to find a solution to maximize total profit (cell G8). Use the following constraints.
   a. The number of cases to be produced can be changed with the constraints.
   b. Number of cases must be an integer.
   c. Number of cases of each product must be at least 1.
   d. Minimum number of A-123 to produce is 100.
   e. Maximum number of A-128 to produce is 25.

f. Minimum number of A-128 to produce is 10.

g. The total storage space must not exceed 25,000.

h. The maximum production hours is 80.

3. Create an Answer Report.

4. Print the Answer Report and the solution.

5. Create a scenario using the constraint values in cells B11:B15. Name it "Normal Production Schedule."

6. Save the workbook as *Manufacturing Production Solution*.

Exercise 8 

1. Open the *Manufacturing Production Solution* workbook that you created in Exercise 7.

2. Create a new scenario, called Low Production Schedule, using the following constraint values:

a. Warehouse storage available=15000

b. Minimum A-123=75

c. Maximum A-128=20

d. Minimum A-128=10

e. Total Production Hours=60

3. Create and print a solution for maximum profit.

4. Create another scenario called High Production Schedule using the following constraint values:

a. Warehouse storage available=40000

b. Minimum A-123=200

c. Maximum A-128=50

d. Minimum A-128=40

e. Total production hours = 120

5. Create a solution for each of the above scenarios.

6. Create and print a solution for maximum profit.

7. Save the workbook as *Manufacturing Production Solution 2,* and close the workbook.

Case Projects

Project 1

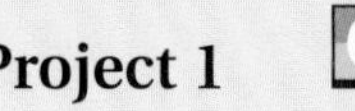

You want to buy a new house. To buy the house you want, you need a loan of $100,000. You've been shopping for loans and found one offering an interest rate of 9.5% with a 15-year term, 8.5% with a 20-year term, 7.5% with a 25-year term, and 7% with a 20-year term. Use a data table(s) to calculate your monthly payments for each interest rate, and what your total interest would be for each loan. Save the workbook as *Home Loan Calculator.*

Project 2

Use the Web toolbar to search the Internet for Excel Solver tutorials. Locate at least one tutorial and print the Web page(s) containing the tutorial.

Project 3

You want to buy a car for $18,500. The car dealer has offered to finance your purchase at 8.5% for 48 months. You can afford to make payments of $250.00 per month. Use Goal Seek to find the maximum amount you can borrow at this interest rate. Save the workbook as *Car Loan* and print the solution.

Project 4

Use the Office Assistant to look up guidelines for designing a model to use with Solver. Write a two-paragraph summary describing what you learned. Save this document as *Creating Workbooks for Solver.doc.*

Project 5

Set up a budget for a sales company with an estimated gross sales income of $25,000 per month. Figure an amount for rent of $5,000, utilities and overhead of $5,000, payroll of $8,500, and advertising costs of $2,500. Set up a workbook to calculate the net profit or loss using these figures. Save the gross sales income, payroll, and advertising costs as a scenario called Best Case. Create a second scenario called Worst Case, with the following amounts: income = $17,500, payroll = $5,000, advertising = $1,000. Save the workbook as *Best and Worst Case Sales.*

Project 6

You are deciding between two jobs located in two different cities. Job offer #1 provides a salary of $35,000 per year. Job offer #2 includes a salary of $40,000 per year. Create a workbook to calculate a budget based on each scenario. In your budget, you estimate that 30% of your salary can be spent on house payments, 10% can be spent on car payments, 30% on living expenses, and 10% for savings. Also include a formula to sum the total budgeted expenses, then subtract this amount from the salary. Save the workbook as *Job Offers.*

Project 7

You would like to reduce the length of time needed to pay off your car loan. Instead of paying off the $10,000 loan (at 8%) in 48 months, you would like to see what your monthly payments would be if you paid off the loan in 42, 36, and 30 months. Create a one-variable table to calculate these payments, and save the workbook as *Quick Payoff.*

Project 8

You are applying for a student loan for college. You want to find out how much you can borrow at 5% interest, paid back over 120 payments (10 years) with a maximum payment of $150.00. Use Goal Seek to help you find the solution. Save the workbook as *Student Loan.*

Working with Windows 98

Appendix Overview

The Windows 98 operating system creates a workspace on your computer screen, called the desktop. The desktop is a graphical environment that contains icons you click with the mouse pointer to access your computer system resources or to perform a task such as opening a software application. This appendix introduces you to the Windows 98 desktop by describing the default desktop icons and showing how to access your computer resources, use menu commands and toolbar buttons to perform a task, and select dialog box options.

Learning Objectives

- Review the Windows 98 desktop
- Access your computer system resources
- Use menu commands and toolbar buttons
- Use the Start menu
- Review dialog box options
- Use Windows 98 shortcuts
- Understand the Recycle Bin
- Shut down Windows 98

A

appendix

A.a Reviewing the Windows 98 Desktop

Whenever you start your computer, the Windows 98 operating system automatically starts and the Windows 98 desktop appears on your screen. To view the Windows 98 desktop:

Step 1	*Turn on*	your computer and monitor
Step 2	*Observe*	the Windows 98 desktop, as shown in Figure A-1

FIGURE A-1
Windows 98 Desktop

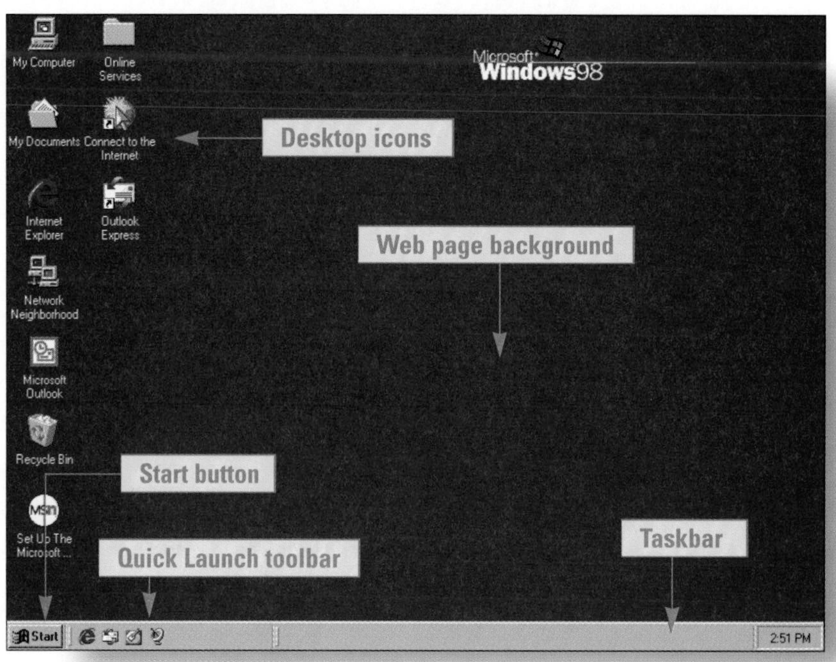

QUICK TIP

Internet **channels** are Web pages you subscribe to that automatically send updated information to your computer. An **active desktop** contains live Web content. You can create an active desktop by adding windows to the desktop that contain automatically updated Web pages. To add Web pages to your desktop, right-click the desktop, point to Active Desktop, click Customize my Desktop, and click the Web tab in the Display Properties dialog box. For more information on Active Desktop features, see online Help.

The Windows 98 desktop contains three elements: icons, background, and taskbar. The icons represent Windows objects and shortcuts to opening software applications or performing tasks. Table A-1 describes some of the default icons. By default, the background is Web-page style. The taskbar, at the bottom of the window, contains the Start button and the Quick Launch toolbar. The icon types and arrangement, desktop background, or Quick Launch toolbar on your screen might be different.

The Start button displays the Start menu, which you can use to perform tasks. By default, the taskbar also contains the **Quick Launch toolbar**, which has shortcuts to open Internet Explorer Web browser, Outlook Express e-mail software, and Internet channels, as well as to switch between the desktop and open application windows. You can customize the Quick Launch toolbar to include other toolbars.

TABLE A-1
Common Desktop Icons

Icon	Name	Description
	My Computer	Provides access to computer system resources
	My Documents	Stores Office 2000 documents (by default)
	Internet Explorer	Opens Internet Explorer Web browser
	Microsoft Outlook	Opens Outlook 2000 information manager software
	Recycle Bin	Temporarily stores folders and files deleted from the hard drive
	Network Neighborhood	Provides access to computers and printers networked in your workgroup

A.b Accessing Your Computer System Resources

The My Computer window provides access to your computer system resources. To open the My Computer window:

Step 1	***Point to***	the My Computer icon on the desktop
Step 2	***Observe***	a brief description of the icon in the ScreenTip
Step 3	***Double-click***	the My Computer icon to open the My Computer window shown in Figure A-2

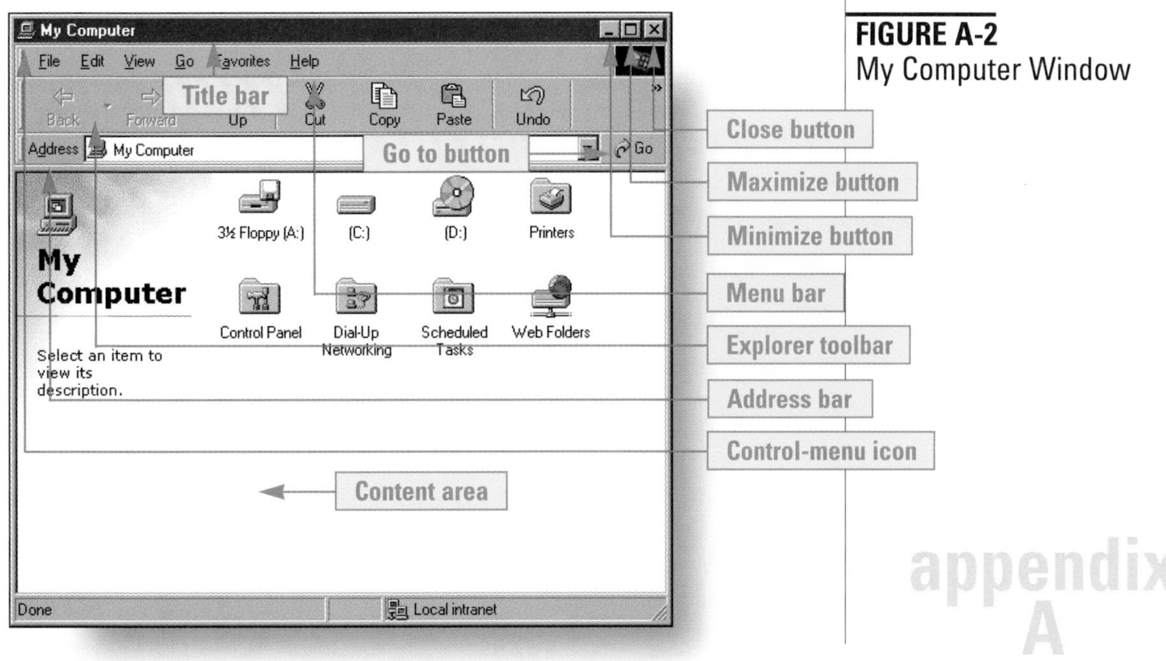

FIGURE A-2
My Computer Window

appendix A

MOUSE TIP

Point means to place the mouse pointer on the command or item. **Click** means to press the left mouse button and release it. **Right-click** means to press the right mouse button and release it. **Double-click** means to press the left mouse button twice very rapidly. **Drag** means to hold down the left mouse button as you move the mouse pointer. **Right-drag** means to hold down the right mouse button as you move the mouse pointer. **Scroll** means to use the application scroll bar features or the IntelliMouse scrolling wheel.

A window is a rectangular area on your screen in which you view operating system options or a software application, such as Internet Explorer. Windows 98 has some common window elements. The **title bar**, at the top of the window, includes the window's Control-menu icon, the window name, and the Minimize, Restore (or Maximize), and Close buttons. The **Control-menu icon**, in the upper-left corner of the window, accesses the Control menu that contains commands for moving, restoring, sizing, minimizing, maximizing, and closing the window. The **Minimize** button, near the upper-right corner of the window, reduces the window to a taskbar button. The **Maximize** button, to the right of the Minimize button, enlarges the window to fill the entire screen viewing area above the taskbar. If the window is already maximized, the Restore button appears in its place. The **Restore** button reduces the window size. The **Close** button, in the upper-right corner, closes the window. To maximize the My Computer window:

Step 1	***Click***	the Maximize button on the My Computer window title bar
Step 2	***Observe***	that the My Computer window completely covers the desktop

When you want to leave a window open, but do not want to see it on the desktop, you can minimize it. To minimize the My Computer window:

Step 1	***Click***	the Minimize button on the My Computer window title bar
Step 2	***Observe***	the My Computer button added to the taskbar

The minimized window is still open but not occupying space on the desktop. To view the My Computer window and then restore it to a smaller size:

Step 1	***Click***	the My Computer button on the taskbar to view the window
Step 2	***Click***	the Restore button on the My Computer title bar
Step 3	***Observe***	that the My Computer window is reduced to a smaller window on the desktop

You can move and size a window with the mouse pointer. To move the My Computer window:

Step 1	***Position***	the mouse pointer on the My Computer title bar

Step 2	*Drag*	the window down and to the right approximately ½ inch
Step 3	*Drag*	the window back to the center of the screen

Several Windows 98 windows—My Computer, My Documents, and Windows Explorer—have the same menu bar and toolbar features. These windows are sometimes called **Explorer-style windows**. When you size an Explorer-style window too small to view all its icons, a vertical or horizontal scroll bar may appear. A scroll bar includes scroll arrows and a scroll box for viewing different parts of the window contents.

To size the My Computer window:

Step 1	*Position*	the mouse pointer on the lower-right corner of the window
Step 2	*Observe*	that the mouse pointer becomes a black, double-headed sizing pointer
Step 3	*Drag*	the lower-right corner boundary diagonally up approximately ½ inch and release the mouse button
Step 4	*Click*	the right scroll arrow on the horizontal scroll bar to view hidden icons
Step 5	*Size*	the window twice as large to remove the horizontal scroll bar

You can open the window associated with any icon in the My Computer window by double-clicking it. Explorer-style windows open in the same window, not separate windows. To open the Control Panel Explorer-style window:

Step 1	*Double-click*	the Control Panel icon
Step 2	*Observe*	that the Address bar displays the Control Panel icon and name, and the content area displays the Control Panel icons for accessing computer system resources

A.c Using Menu Commands and Toolbar Buttons

You can click a menu command or toolbar button to perform specific tasks in a window. The **menu bar** is a special toolbar located below the window title bar that contains the File, Edit, View, Go, Favorites, and Help menus. The **toolbar**, located below the menu bar, contains shortcut "buttons" you click with the mouse pointer to execute a variety of commands. You can use the Back and Forward

QUICK TIP

The Explorer-style windows and the Internet Explorer Web browser are really one Explorer feature integrated into Windows 98 that you can use to find information on your hard drive, network, company intranet, or the Web. Explorer-style windows have a Web-browser look and features. You can use Internet Explorer to access local information by keying the path in the Address bar or clicking an item on the Favorites list.

MOUSE TIP

You can display four taskbar toolbars: Quick Launch, Address, Links, and Desktop. The Quick Launch toolbar appears on the taskbar by default. You can also create additional toolbars from other folders or subfolders and you can add folder or file shortcuts to an existing taskbar toolbar. To view other taskbar toolbars, right-click the taskbar, point to Toolbars, and then click the desired toolbar name.

QUICK TIP

You can use Start menu commands to create or open Office 2000 documents, connect to the Microsoft Web site to download operating system updates, open software applications, open a favorite folder or file, or open one of the last fifteen documents you worked on. You can also change the Windows 98 settings, search for files, folders, and resources on the Internet, get online Help, run software applications, log off a network, and shut down Windows 98.

buttons on the Explorer toolbar or the Back or Forward commands on the Go menu to switch between My Computer and the Control Panel. To view My Computer:

Step 1	*Click*	the Back button on the Explorer toolbar to view My Computer
Step 2	*Click*	the Forward button on the Explorer toolbar to view the Control Panel
Step 3	*Click*	Go on the menu bar
Step 4	*Click*	the My Computer command to view My Computer
Step 5	*Click*	the Close button on the My Computer window title bar

A.d Using the Start Menu

The **Start button** on the taskbar opens the Start menu. You use this menu to access several Windows 98 features and to open software applications, such as Word or Excel. To open the Start menu:

Step 1	*Click*	the Start button on the taskbar to open the Start menu (see Figure A-3)

FIGURE A-3
Start Menu

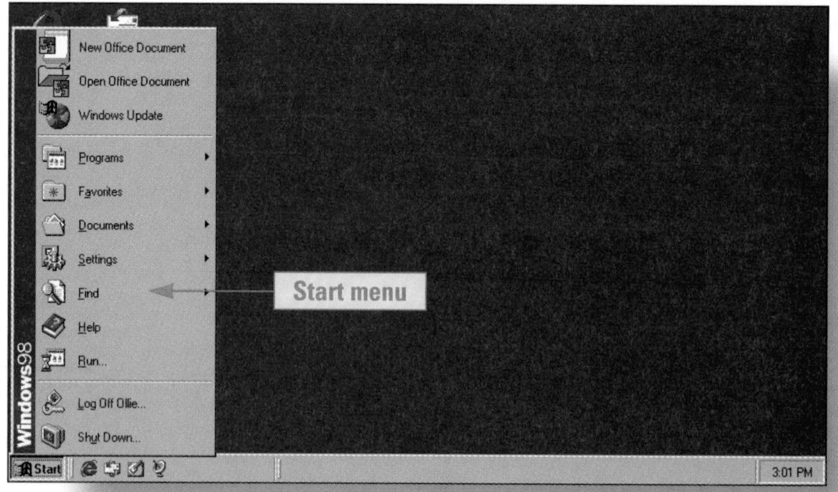

Step 2	*Point to*	Programs to view the software applications installed on your computer
Step 3	*Click*	the desktop outside the Start menu and Programs menu to close them

A.e Reviewing Dialog Box Options

A **dialog box** is a window that contains options you can select, turn on, or turn off to perform a task. To view a dialog box:

Step 1	*Click*	the Start button [Start] on the taskbar
Step 2	*Point to*	Settings
Step 3	*Point to*	Active Desktop
Step 4	*Click*	Customize my Desktop to open the Display Properties dialog box
Step 5	*Click*	the Effects tab (see Figure A-4)

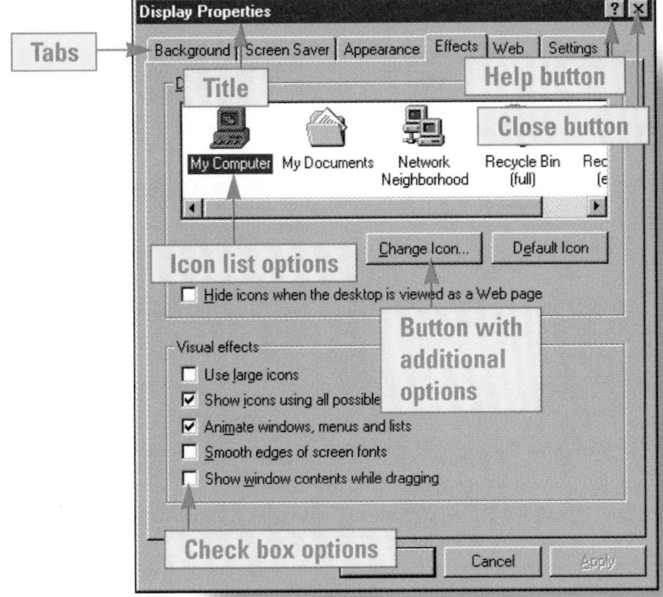

FIGURE A-4
Effects Tab in the Display Properties Dialog Box

Step 6	*Click*	each tab and observe the different options available *(do not change any options unless directed by your instructor)*
Step 7	*Right-click*	each option on each tab and then click What's This? to view its ScreenTip
Step 8	*Click*	Cancel to close the dialog box without changing any options

QUICK TIP

Many dialog boxes contain sets of options on different pages organized on **tabs** you click. Options include drop-down lists you view by clicking an arrow, text boxes in which you key information, check boxes and option buttons you click to turn on or off an option, and buttons that access additional options.

QUICK TIP

Many of the Windows 98 shortcuts are also available in Windows 95 and NT 4.0 if you have Internet Explorer 4.0 or later and Windows Desktop Update installed.

MOUSE TIP

One way to speed up tasks is to single-click (rather than double-click) a desktop icon just like you single-click a Web page hyperlink. You can create a Web-style, single-click environment by opening the Folder Options dialog box from the View menu in any Windows 98 Explorer-style window or from the Settings command on the Start menu. The Web Style option adds an underline to icon titles, similar to a hyperlink.

A.f Using Windows 98 Shortcuts

You can use the drag-and-drop method to reposition or remove Start menu commands. You can also right-drag a Start menu command to the desktop to create a desktop shortcut. To reposition the Windows Update item on the Start menu:

Step 1	*Click*	the Start button Start on the taskbar
Step 2	*Point to*	the Windows Update item
Step 3	*Drag*	the Windows Update item to the top of the Start menu

To remove the Windows Update shortcut from the Start menu and create a desktop shortcut:

Step 1	*Drag*	the Windows Update item to the desktop
Step 2	*Observe*	that the desktop shortcut appears after a few seconds
Step 3	*Verify*	that the Windows Update item no longer appears on the Start menu

To add a Windows Update shortcut back to the Start menu and delete the desktop shortcut:

Step 1	*Drag*	the Windows Update shortcut to the Start button Start on the taskbar and then back to its original position when the Start menu appears
Step 2	*Close*	the Start menu
Step 3	*Drag*	the Windows Update shortcut on the desktop to the Recycle Bin
Step 4	*Click*	Yes

You can close multiple application windows at one time from the taskbar using the CTRL key and a shortcut menu. To open two applications and then use the taskbar to close them:

Step 1	*Open*	the Word and Excel applications (in this order) from the Programs menu on the Start menu

Step 2	*Observe*	the Word and Excel buttons on the taskbar (Excel is the selected, active button)
Step 3	*Press & Hold*	the CTRL key
Step 4	*Click*	the Word application taskbar button (the Excel application taskbar button is already selected)
Step 5	*Release*	the CTRL key
Step 6	*Right-click*	the Word or Excel taskbar button
Step 7	*Click*	Close to close both applications

You can use the drag-and-drop method to add a shortcut to the Quick Launch toolbar for folders and documents you have created. To create a new subfolder in the My Documents folder.

Step 1	*Click*	the My Documents icon on the desktop to open the window
Step 2	*Right-click*	the contents area (but not a file or folder)
Step 3	*Point to*	New
Step 4	*Click*	Folder
Step 5	*Key*	Example
Step 6	*Press*	the ENTER key to name the folder
Step 7	*Drag*	the Example folder to the end of the Quick Launch toolbar (a black vertical line indicates the drop position)
Step 8	*Observe*	the new icon on the toolbar
Step 9	*Close*	the My Documents window
Step 10	*Position*	the mouse pointer on the Example folder shortcut on the Quick Launch toolbar and observe the ScreenTip

You remove a shortcut from the Quick Launch toolbar by dragging it to the desktop and deleting it, or dragging it directly to the Recycle Bin. To remove the Example folder shortcut and delete the folder:

Step 1	*Drag*	the Example folder icon to the Recycle Bin
Step 2	*Click*	Yes
Step 3	*Open*	the My Documents window
Step 4	*Delete*	the Example folder icon using the shortcut menu
Step 5	*Close*	the My Documents window

CAUTION TIP

Selecting items in a single-click environment requires some practice. To **select** (or highlight) one item, simply point to the item. *Be careful not to click the item; clicking the item opens it.*

You can use the SHIFT + Click and CTRL + Click commands in the single-click environment. Simply *point to* the first item. Then press and hold the SHIFT or CTRL key and *point to* the last item or the next item to be selected.

MENU TIP

In the Windows environment, clicking the right mouse button displays a **shortcut menu** of the most commonly used commands for the item you right-clicked. For example, you can use a shortcut menu to open applications from the Programs submenu. You can right-drag to move, copy, or create desktop shortcuts from Start menu commands.

MENU TIP

You can open the Recycle Bin by right-clicking the Recycle Bin icon on the desktop and clicking Open. To restore an item to your hard drive after opening the Recycle Bin, click the item to select it and then click the Restore command on the File menu. You can also restore an item by opening the Recycle Bin, right-clicking an item, and clicking Restore.

To empty the Recycle Bin, right-click the Recycle Bin icon and click Empty Recycle Bin.

A.g Understanding the Recycle Bin

The **Recycle Bin** is an object that temporarily stores folders, files, and shortcuts you delete from your hard drive. If you accidentally delete an item, you can restore it to its original location on your hard drive if it is still in the Recycle Bin. Because the Recycle Bin takes up disk space you should review and empty it regularly. When you empty the Recycle Bin, its contents are removed from your hard drive and can no longer be restored.

A.h Shutting Down Windows 98

It is very important that you follow the proper procedures for shutting down the Windows 98 operating system when you are finished, to allow the operating system to complete its internal "housekeeping" properly. To shut down Windows 98 correctly:

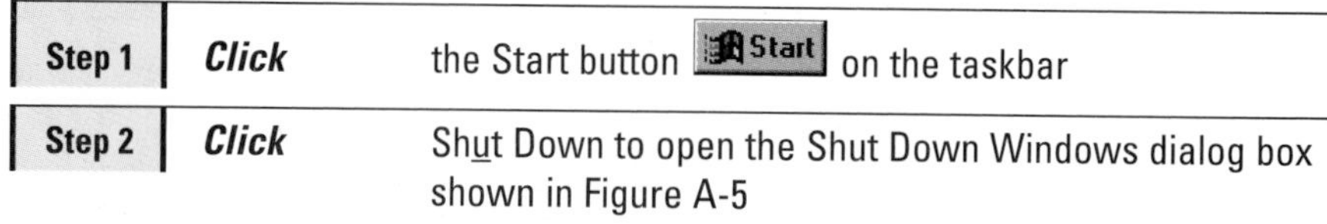

Step 1	*Click*	the Start button [Start] on the taskbar
Step 2	*Click*	Shut Down to open the Shut Down Windows dialog box shown in Figure A-5

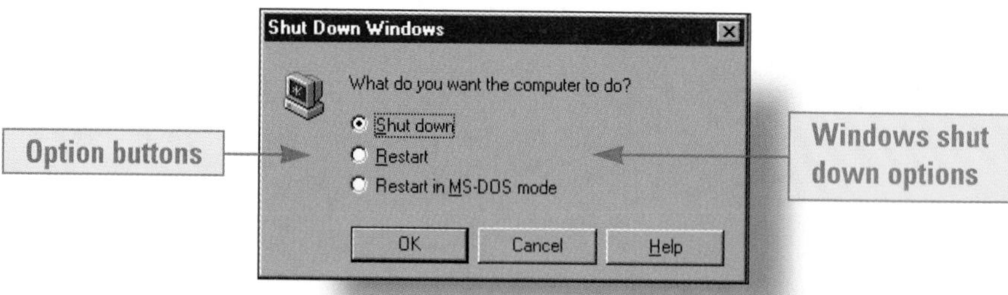

FIGURE A-5
Shut Down Windows Dialog Box

You can shut down completely, restart, and restart in MS-DOS mode from this dialog box. You want to shut down completely.

Step 3	*Click*	the Shut down option button to select it, if necessary
Step 4	*Click*	OK

Managing Your Folders and Files Using Windows Explorer

Appendix Overview

Windows Explorer provides tools for managing your folders and files. This appendix introduces the Windows Explorer options of expanding and collapsing the folder view, creating new folders, renaming folders and files, deleting folders and files, and creating desktop shortcuts.

Learning Objectives

- Open Windows Explorer
- Review Windows Explorer options
- Create a new folder
- Move and copy folders and files
- Rename folders and files
- Create desktop shortcuts
- Delete folders and files

notes

The default Windows 98 Custom folder options are used in the hands-on activities and figures. If you are using the Windows 95 operating system, your instructor will modify the hands-on activities and your screen will look different.

B.a Opening Windows Explorer

You can open Windows Explorer from the Programs command on the Start menu or from a shortcut menu. To open Windows Explorer using a shortcut menu:

Step 1	***Right-Click***	the Start button Start on the taskbar
Step 2	***Click***	Explore
Step 3	***Maximize***	the Windows Explorer window, if necessary (see Figure B-1)

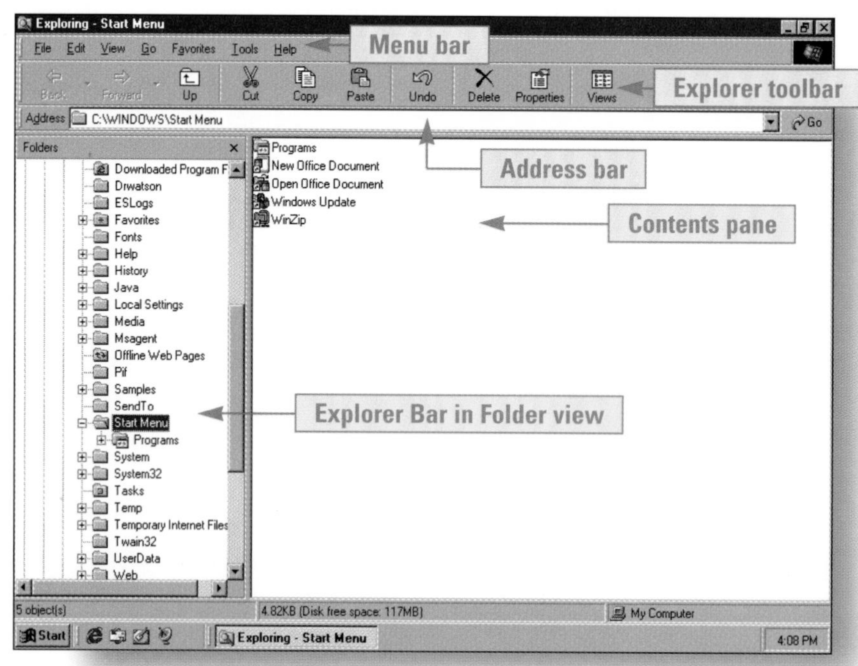

FIGURE B-1
Windows Explorer Window

QUICK TIP

You can also use the My Computer Explorer-style window to manage your files and folders. If you are using Windows 95, the list of disk drives and folders is called the **Tree pane**.

The window below the menu bar, toolbar, and Address bar is divided into two panes: The **Explorer Bar** on the left shows the computer's organizational structure, including all desktop objects, My Computer objects, and the disk drive folders. The **Contents pane** on the right shows all subfolders and files for the folder selected in the Explorer Bar. The panes are divided by a **separator bar** that you drag left or right to resize the panes.

B.b Reviewing Windows Explorer Options

You can view disk drive icons, folders, and files (called **objects**) for your computer by selecting an item from the Address bar list or by clicking an object in the Explorer Bar. To view all your computer's disk drives and system folders:

Step 1	***Click***	the Address bar list arrow
Step 2	***Click***	My Computer to view a list of disk drives and system folders in the Contents pane
Step 3	***Click***	the (C:) disk drive object in the Explorer Bar to view a list of folders (stored on the C:\ drive) in the Contents pane

You can expand or collapse the view of folders and other objects in the Explorer Bar. To collapse the view of the C:\ drive in the Explorer Bar:

Step 1	***Click***	the minus sign (–) to the left of the (C:) disk drive object in the Explorer Bar
Step 2	***Observe***	that the C:\ drive folders list is hidden and the minus sign becomes a plus sign (+)
Step 3	***Click***	the plus sign (+) to the left of the (C:) disk drive object in the Explorer Bar
Step 4	***Observe***	that the list of folders stored on the C:\ drive is again visible

You can view a folder's contents by clicking the folder in the Explorer Bar or double-clicking the folder in the Contents pane. To view the contents of the folder that contains the Data Files:

Step 1	***Click***	the disk drive in the Explorer Bar where the Data Files are stored

MOUSE TIP

Point means to place the mouse pointer on the command or item. **Click** means to press the left mouse button and release it. **Right-click** means to press the right mouse button and release it. **Double-click** means to press the left mouse button twice very rapidly. **Drag** means to hold down the left mouse button and then move the mouse pointer. **Right-drag** means to hold down the right mouse button and then move the mouse pointer. **Scroll** means to use the application scroll bar features or the IntelliMouse scrolling wheel.

MENU TIP

By default, the Explorer Bar shows your local and network folders. This is the Explorer Bar Folder view option. You can view Internet resources and a list of favorites by clicking View, pointing to Explorer Bar, and clicking Search, Favorites, or History.

Step 2	*Double-click*	the Data Files folder in the Contents pane (scroll, if necessary) to view a list of Data Files and folders

You can resize and reposition folders and files in the Contents pane and add more details about the file size, type, and date modified. To change the size and position of the Data Files and folders:

Step 1	*Click*	the Views button list arrow on the Explorer toolbar
Step 2	*Click*	Large Icons to view horizontal rows of larger folder and file icons in the Contents pane
Step 3	*Click*	Small Icons on the Views button list to view horizontal rows of smaller folder and file icons in the Contents pane
Step 4	*Click*	Details on the Views button list to view a vertical list of folders and files names, sizes, types, and dates modified
Step 5	*Click*	List on the Views button list to view a simple list of the files and folders

QUICK TIP

The minus sign (–) indicates all the items stored in that object are displayed, or expanded, below the icon. The plus sign (+) indicates these items are hidden, or collapsed.

You can sort the list of files and folders by name, size, type, and date modified in ascending or descending order by clicking the Name, Size, Type, or Modified buttons above the list in the Contents pane.

B.c Creating a New Folder

You can create a new folder for an object in the Explorer Bar or the Contents pane. To add a folder to the My Documents folder in the C:\ drive folder list:

Step 1	*Click*	the My Documents folder in the Explorer Bar to select it (scroll, if necessary)
Step 2	*Click*	File
Step 3	*Point to*	New
Step 4	*Click*	Folder
Step 5	*Observe*	the newly created folder object in the Contents pane with the selected temporary name New Folder

CAUTION TIP

After you move or copy files or folders or add or remove files or folders, you may need to refresh the view of the folder list in the Explorer Bar and the Contents pane to see the changes. Click the Refresh command on the View menu.

To name the folder and refresh the Explorer Bar view:

Step 1	*Key*	Practice Folder
Step 2	*Press*	the ENTER key
Step 3	*Observe*	the new folder name in the Contents pane
Step 4	*Click*	View

Step 5	*Click*	Refresh
Step 6	*Observe*	that the My Documents folder has a plus sign, indicating that the folder list can be expanded

B.d Moving and Copying Folders and Files

You select folders and files by clicking them. You can then copy or move them with the Cut, Copy and Paste commands on the Edit menu or shortcut menu, the Copy and Paste buttons on the Explorer toolbar, or with the drag-and-drop or right-drag mouse methods. To copy a file from the Data Files folder to the Practice Folder using the right-drag method:

Step 1	*View*	the list of Data Files in the Contents pane
Step 2	*Right-drag*	any file to the My Documents folder in the Explorer Bar and pause until the My Documents folder expands to show the subfolders
Step 3	*Continue*	to right-drag the file to the Practice Folder subfolder under the My Documents folder in the Explorer Bar
Step 4	*Click*	Copy Here on the shortcut menu
Step 5	*Click*	the Practice Folder in the Explorer Bar to view the copied file's icon and filename in the Contents pane

MOUSE TIP

You can use the SHIFT + Click method to select adjacent multiple folders and files in the Contents pane by clicking the first item to select it, holding down the SHIFT key, and then clicking the last item. You can use the CTRL + Click method to select nonadjacent files and folders in the Contents pane by clicking the first item, holding down the CTRL key, and then clicking each additional item.

B.e Renaming Folders and Files

Sometimes you want to change an existing file or folder name to a more descriptive name. To rename the copied file in the Practice Folder:

Step 1	*Verify*	the icon and filename for the copied file appears in the Contents pane
Step 2	*Right-click*	the copied file in the Contents pane
Step 3	*Click*	Rename
Step 4	*Key*	Renamed File
Step 5	*Click*	the Contents area (not the filename) to accept the new filename

MENU TIP

You can quickly copy a file to a disk from a hard disk or network drive, create a desktop shortcut, or send the file as an attachment to an e-mail message by right-clicking the file, pointing to Send To, and clicking the appropriate command.

QUICK TIP

To erase all the files stored on a disk, you can reformat it. Insert a used disk in drive A, right-click the drive A icon in the Explorer Bar, and click Format. Specify the disk's capacity. Select the Full option to erase all files and check the disk for bad sectors. Click the Start button.

B.f Creating Desktop Shortcuts

You can add a shortcut for folders and files to the Windows desktop by restoring the Windows Explorer window to a smaller window and right-dragging a folder or file icon to the desktop. You can also right-drag a folder or file icon to the Desktop icon in the Explorer Bar inside the Windows Explorer window. To create a desktop shortcut to the Practice Folder using the Desktop icon:

Step 1	*Expand*	the My Documents folder in the Explorer Bar, if necessary, to view the Practice Folder subfolder
Step 2	*Right-drag*	the Practice Folder to the Desktop icon at the top of the Explorer Bar
Step 3	*Click*	Create Shortcut(s) Here
Step 4	*Minimize*	the Windows Explorer window to view the new shortcut on the desktop
Step 5	*Drag*	the Shortcut to Practice Folder desktop shortcut to the Recycle Bin to delete it
Step 6	*Click*	Yes
Step 7	*Click*	the Exploring-Practice Folder taskbar button to maximize the Windows Explorer window

MOUSE TIP

You can delete a file or folder by dragging or right-dragging it to the Recycle Bin object on the desktop or the Recycle Bin object in the Explorer Bar. If you hold down the SHIFT key while dragging the file or folder to the Recycle Bin, Windows deletes the file or folder without placing it in the Recycle Bin.

B.g Deleting Folders and Files

When necessary, you can delete a folder and its contents or a file by selecting it and then clicking the Delete command on the File menu or shortcut menu, or pressing the DELETE key. You can also delete multiple selected folders and files at one time. To delete the Practice Folder and its contents:

Step 1	*Click*	the Practice Folder in the Explorer Bar to select it, if necessary
Step 2	*Press*	the DELETE key
Step 3	*Click*	Yes to send the folder and its contents to the Recycle Bin

Formatting Tips for Business Documents

Appendix Overview

Most organizations follow specific formatting guidelines when preparing letters, envelopes, memorandums, and other documents to ensure the documents present a professional appearance. In this appendix you learn how to format different size letters, interoffice memos, envelopes, and formal outlines. You also review a list of style guides and learn how to use proofreader's marks.

LEARNING OBJECTIVES

- Format letters
- Insert mailing notations
- Format envelopes
- Format interoffice memorandums
- Format formal outlines
- Use proofreader's marks
- Use style guides

C.a Formatting Letters

The quality and professionalism of a company's business correspondence can affect how customers, clients, and others view a company. That correspondence represents the company to those outside it. To ensure a positive and appropriate image, many companies set special standards for margins, typeface, and font size for their business correspondence. These special standards are based on the common letter styles illustrated in this section.

Most companies use special letter paper with the company name and address (and sometimes a company logo or picture) preprinted on the paper. The preprinted portion is called a **letterhead** and the paper is called **letterhead paper**. When you create a letter, the margins vary depending on the style of your letterhead and the length of your letter. Most letterheads use between 1 inch and 2 inches of the page from the top of the sheet. There are two basic business correspondence formats: block format and modified block format. When you create a letter in **block format**, all the text is placed flush against the left margin. This includes the date, the letter address information, the salutation, the body, the complimentary closing, and the signature information. The body of the letter is single spaced with a blank line between paragraphs.[1] Figure C-1 shows a short letter in the block format with standard punctuation.

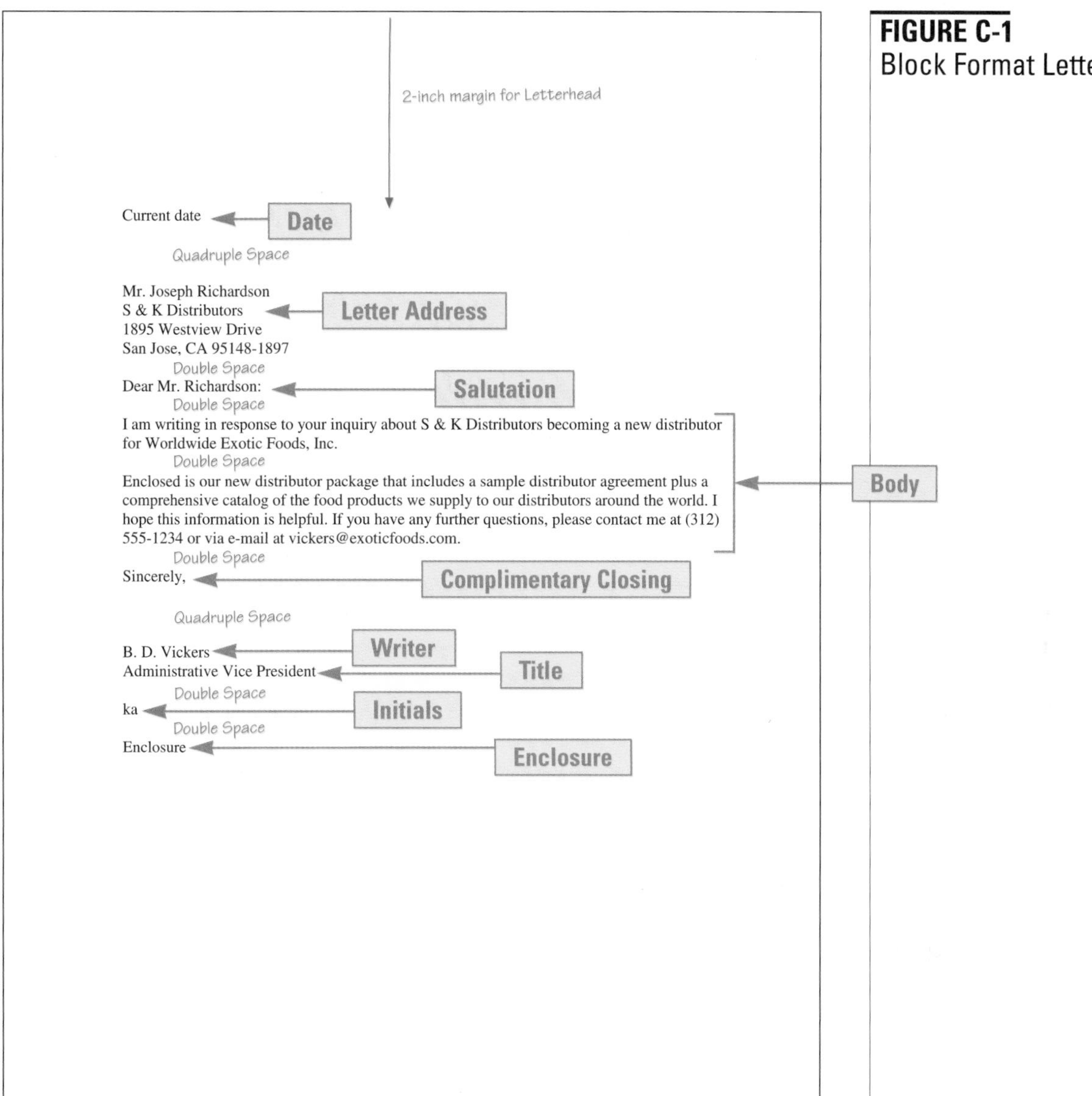
Current date

Mr. Joseph Richardson
S & K Distributors
1895 Westview Drive
San Jose, CA 95148-1897

Dear Mr. Richardson:

I am writing in response to your inquiry about S & K Distributors becoming a new distributor for Worldwide Exotic Foods, Inc.

Enclosed is our new distributor package that includes a sample distributor agreement plus a comprehensive catalog of the food products we supply to our distributors around the world. I hope this information is helpful. If you have any further questions, please contact me at (312) 555-1234 or via e-mail at vickers@exoticfoods.com.

Sincerely,

B. D. Vickers
Administrative Vice President

ka

Enclosure

FIGURE C-1
Block Format Letter

QUICK TIP

When you key a letter on plain paper in the modified block format, the return address usually appears near the right margin and above the date, with one blank line between the return address and the date.

In the **modified block format**, the date begins near the center of the page or near the right margin. The closing starts near the center or right margin. Paragraphs can be either flush against the left margin or indented. Figure C-2 shows a short letter in the modified block format with standard punctuation.

Both the block and modified block styles use the same spacing for the non-body portions. Three blank lines separate the date from the addressee information, one blank line separates the addressee information from the salutation, one blank line separates the salutation from the body of the letter, and one blank line separates the body of the letter from the complimentary closing. There are three blank lines between the complimentary closing and the writer's name. If a typist's initials appear below the name, a blank line separates the writer's name from the initials. If an enclosure is noted, the word "Enclosure" appears below the typist's initials with a blank line separating them. Finally, when typing the return address or addressee information, one space separates the state and the postal code (ZIP+4).

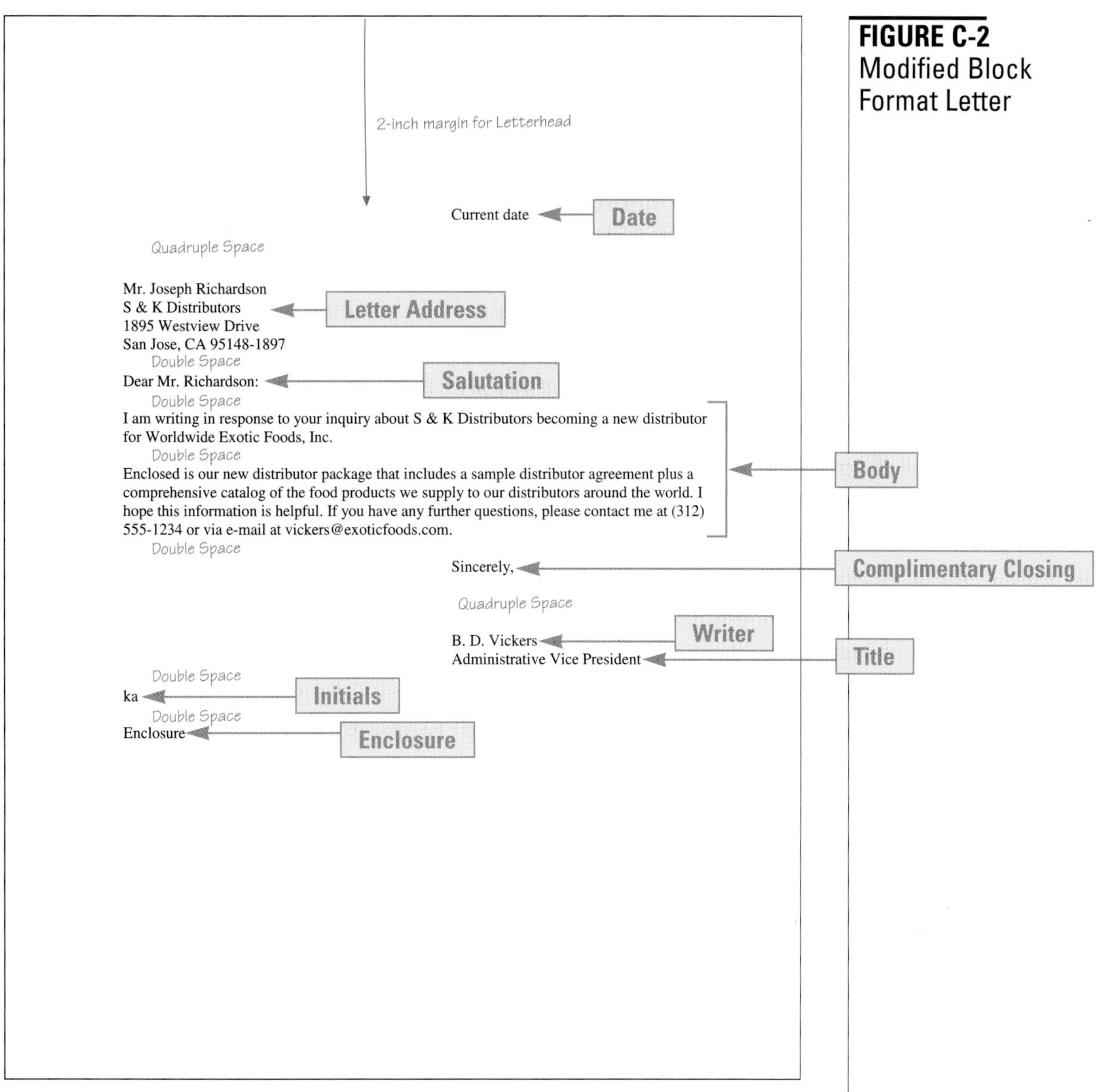
2-inch margin for Letterhead

Current date

Quadruple Space

Mr. Joseph Richardson
S & K Distributors
1895 Westview Drive
San Jose, CA 95148-1897

Double Space

Dear Mr. Richardson:

Double Space

I am writing in response to your inquiry about S & K Distributors becoming a new distributor for Worldwide Exotic Foods, Inc.

Double Space

Enclosed is our new distributor package that includes a sample distributor agreement plus a comprehensive catalog of the food products we supply to our distributors around the world. I hope this information is helpful. If you have any further questions, please contact me at (312) 555-1234 or via e-mail at vickers@exoticfoods.com.

Double Space

Sincerely,

Quadruple Space

B. D. Vickers
Administrative Vice President

Double Space

ka

Double Space

Enclosure

FIGURE C-2
Modified Block Format Letter

C.b Inserting Mailing Notations

Mailing notations add information to a business letter. For example, the mailing notations CERTIFIED MAIL or SPECIAL DELIVERY indicate how a business letter was sent. The mailing notations CONFIDENTIAL or PERSONAL indicate how the person receiving the letter should handle the letter contents. Mailing notations should be keyed in uppercase characters at the left margin two lines below the date.[2] Figure C-3 shows a mailing notation added to a block format business letter.

Current date
Double Space
CERTIFIED MAIL ← Mailing Notation
Double Space
Mr. Joseph Richardson
S & K Distributors
1895 Westview Drive
San Jose, CA 95148-1897

Dear Mr. Richardson:

I am writing in response to your inquiry about S & K Distributors becoming a new distributor for Worldwide Exotic Foods, Inc.

Enclosed is our new distributor package that includes a sample distributor agreement plus a comprehensive catalog of the food products we supply to our distributors around the world. I hope this information is helpful. If you have any further questions, please contact me at (312) 555-1234 or via e-mail at vickers@exoticfoods.com.

Sincerely,

B. D. Vickers
Administrative Vice President

ka

Enclosure

FIGURE C-3
Mailing Notation on Letter

C.c Formatting Envelopes

Two U. S. Postal Service publications, *The Right Way* (Publication 221), and *Postal Addressing Standards* (Publication 28) available from the U. S. Post Office, provide standards for addressing letter envelopes. The U. S. Postal Service uses optical character readers (OCRs) and barcode sorters (BCSs) to increase the speed, efficiency, and accuracy in processing mail. To get a letter delivered more quickly, envelopes should be addressed to take advantage of this automation process.

Table C-1 lists the minimum and maximum size for letters. The post office cannot process letters smaller than the minimum size. Letters larger than the maximum size cannot take advantage of automated processing and must be processed manually.

TABLE C-1
Minimum and Maximum Letter Dimensions

Dimension	Minimum	Maximum
Height	3½ inches	6⅛ inches
Length	5 inches	11½ inches
Thickness	.007 inch	¼ inch

The delivery address should be placed inside a rectangular area on the envelope that is approximately ⅝ inch from the top and bottom edge of the envelope and ½ inch from the left and right edge of the envelope. This is called the **OCR read area**. All the lines of the delivery address must fit within this area and no lines of the return address should extend into this area. To assure the delivery address is placed in the OCR read area, begin the address approximately ½ inch left of center and on approximately line 14.[3]

The lines of the delivery address should be in this order:

1. any optional nonaddress data, such as advertising or company logos, must be placed above the delivery address
2. any information or attention line
3. the name of the recipient
4. the street address
5. the city, state, and postal code (ZIP+4)

The delivery address should be complete, including apartment or suite numbers and delivery designations, such as RD (road), ST (street), or NW (northwest). Leave the area below and on both sides of the delivery address blank. Use uppercase characters and a sans serif font (such as Arial) for the delivery address. Omit all punctuation except the hyphen in the ZIP+4 code.

Figure C-4 shows a properly formatted business letter envelope.

QUICK TIP

Foreign addresses should include the country name in uppercase characters as the last line of the delivery address. The postal code, if any, should appear on the same line as the city.

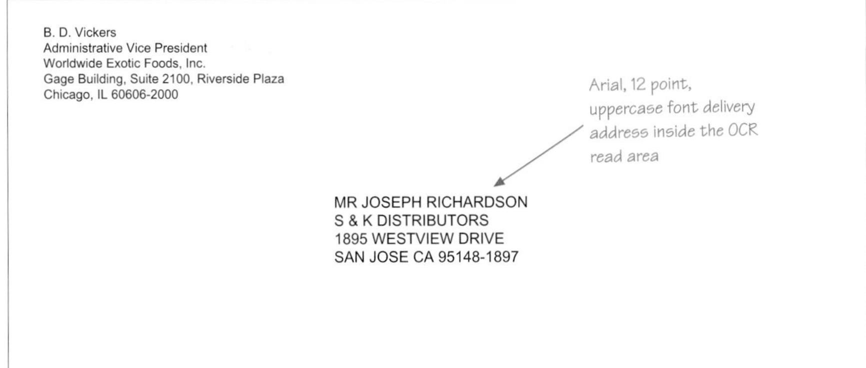

FIGURE C-4
Business Letter Envelope

appendix C

C.d Formatting Interoffice Memorandums

Business correspondence that is sent within a company is usually prepared as an **interoffice memorandum**, also called a **memo**, rather than a letter. There are many different interoffice memo styles used in offices today, and word processing applications usually provide several memo templates based on different memo styles. Also, just as with business letters that are sent outside the company, many companies set special standards for margins, typeface, and font size for their interoffice memos.

A basic interoffice memo should include lines for “TO:”, “FROM:”, “DATE:”, and “SUBJECT:” followed by the body text. Memos can be prepared on blank paper or on paper that includes a company name and even a logo. The word MEMORANDUM is often included. Figure C-5 shows a basic interoffice memorandum.

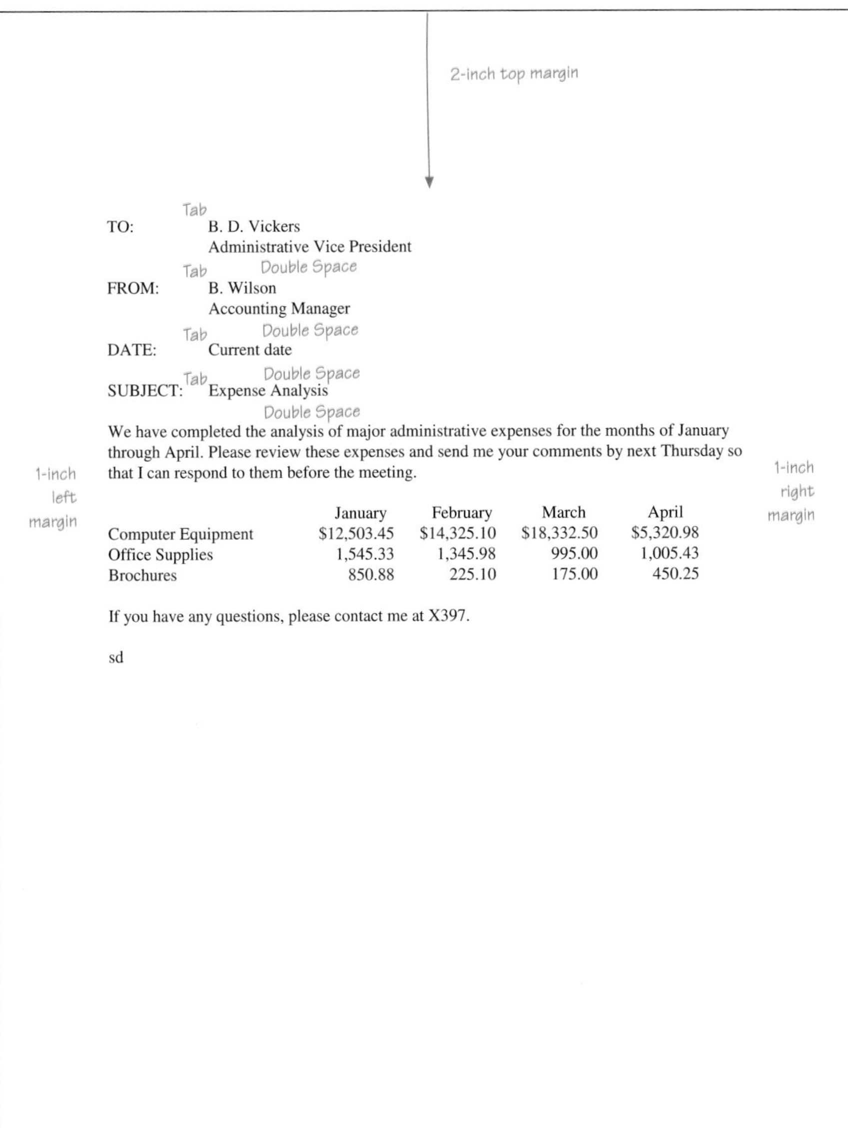

2-inch top margin
Tab
TO: B. D. Vickers
Administrative Vice President
Tab Double Space
FROM: B. Wilson
Accounting Manager
Tab Double Space
DATE: Current date
Tab Double Space
SUBJECT: Expense Analysis
Double Space
We have completed the analysis of major administrative expenses for the months of January through April. Please review these expenses and send me your comments by next Thursday so that I can respond to them before the meeting.
1-inch left margin
1-inch right margin
January February March April
Computer Equipment $12,503.45 $14,325.10 $18,332.50 $5,320.98
Office Supplies 1,545.33 1,345.98 995.00 1,005.43
Brochures 850.88 225.10 175.00 450.25
If you have any questions, please contact me at X397.
sd

FIGURE C-5
Interoffice Memorandum

appendix C

C.e Formatting Formal Outlines

Companies use outlines to organize data for a variety of purposes, such as reports, meeting agenda, and presentations. Word processing applications usually offer special features to help you create an outline. If you want to follow a formal outline format, you may need to add formatting to outlines created with these special features.

Margins for a short outline of two or three topics should be set at 1½ inches for the top margin and 2 inches for the left and right margins. For a longer outline, use a 2-inch top margin and 1-inch left and right margins.

The outline level-one text should be in uppercase characters. Second-level text should be treated like a title, with the first letter of the main words capitalized. Capitalize only the first letter of the first word at the third level. Double space before and after level one and single space the remaining levels.

Include at least two parts at each level. For example, you must have two level-one entries in an outline (at least I. and II.). If there is a second level following a level-one entry, it must contain at least two entries (at least A. and B.). All numbers must be aligned at the period and all subsequent levels must begin under the text of the preceding level, not under the number.[4]

Figure C-6 shows a formal outline prepared using the Word Outline Numbered list feature with additional formatting to follow a formal outline.

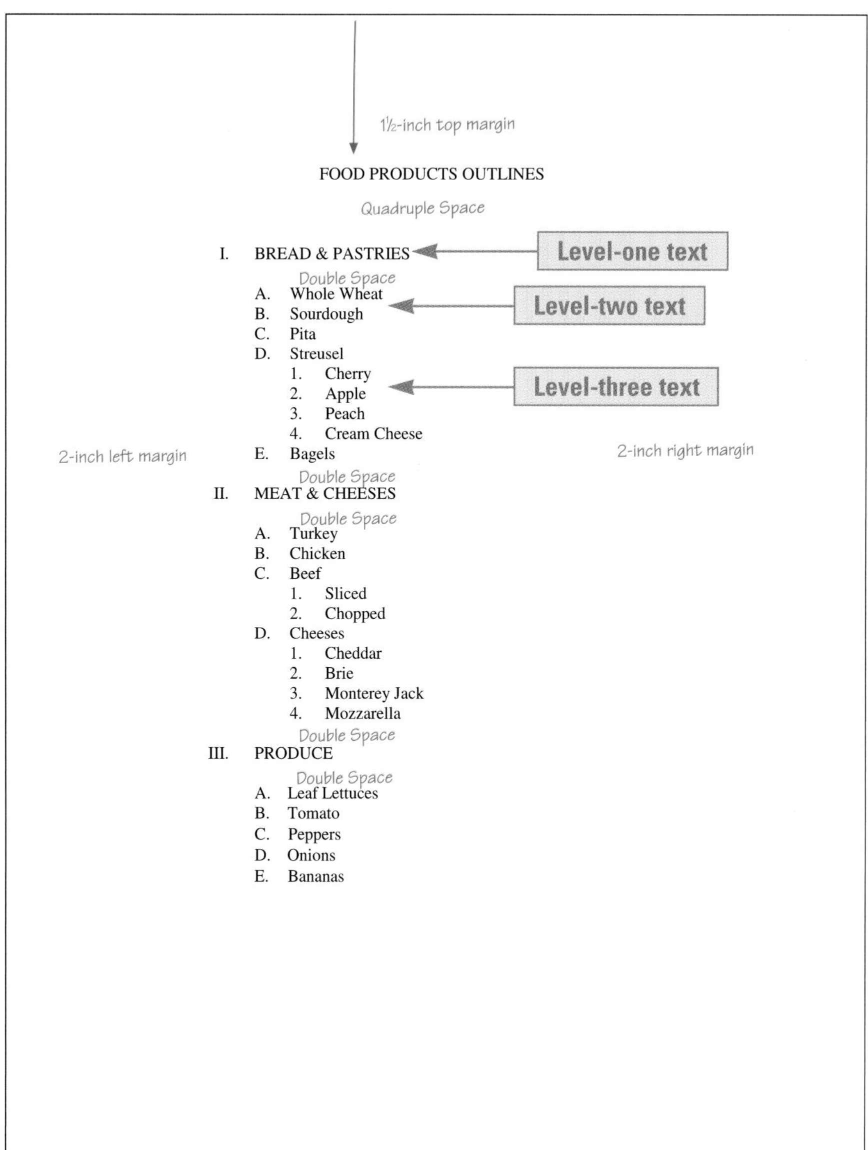

FIGURE C-6
Formal Outline

C.f Using Proofreader's Marks

Standard proofreader's marks enable an editor or proofreader to make corrections or change notations in a document that can be recognized by anyone familiar with the marks. The following list illustrates standard proofreader's marks.

Defined		Examples
Paragraph	¶	¶ Begin a new paragraph at this
Insert a character	^	point. Insrt a letter here.
Delete	ℯ	Delete these words. Disregard
Do not change	stet or . . .	the previous correction. To
Transpose	tr	transpose is to around turn.
Move to the left	[	Move this copy to the left.
Move to the right	]	Move this copy to the right.
No paragraph	No ¶	No ¶ Do not begin a new paragraph
Delete and close up		here. Delete the hyphen from
		pre-empt and close up the space.
Set in caps	Caps or ≡	a sentence begins with a capital
Set in lower case	lc or /	letter. This Word should not
Insert a period	⊙	be capitalized. Insert a period
Quotation marks	" "	Quotation marks and a comma
Comma	^	should be placed here he said.
Insert space	#	Space between thesewords. An
Apostrophe	'	apostrophe is whats needed here.
Hyphen	=	Add a hyphen to Kilowatthour. Close
Close up	⁀	up the extra spa ce.
Use superior figure	∨	Footnote this sentence. Set
Set in italic	Ital. or ——	the words, sine qua non, in italics.
Move up	⌐¬	This word is too low. That word is
Move down	└┘	too high.

C.g Using Style Guides

A **style guide** provides a set of rules for punctuating and formatting text. There are a number of style guides used by writers, editors, business document proofreaders, and publishers. You can purchase style guides at a commercial bookstore, an online bookstore, or a college bookstore. Your local library likely has copies of different style guides and your instructor may have copies of several style guides for reference. Some popular style guides are *The Chicago Manual of Style* (The University of Chicago Press), *The Professional Secretary's Handbook* (Barron's), *The Holt Handbook* (Harcourt Brace College Publishers), and the *MLA Style Manual and Guide to Scholarly Publishing* (The Modern Language Association of America).

Endnotes

[1] Jerry W. Robinson et al., *Keyboarding and Information Processing* (Cincinnati: South-Western Educational Publishing, 1997).

[2] Ibid.

[3] Ibid.

[4] Ibid.

Index

Special Characters

A

D

E

F

G

H

I

K

L

M

P

Q

R

S

T

U

V

W

X

Y

Z